A MAN OF MODERN LETTERS

Hemingway and the Rise of Modern Literature

Volume 2

WYLIE GRAHAM McLALLEN

OXFORD SOUTHERN

an imprint of Sunbury Press, Inc.
Mechanicsburg, PA USA

OXFORD SOUTHERN

an imprint of Sunbury Press, Inc.
Mechanicsburg, PA USA

For information about special discounts for bulk purchases, please contact Sunbury Press Orders Dept. at (855) 338-8359 or orders@sunburypress.com.

To request one of our authors for speaking engagements or book signings, please contact Sunbury Press Publicity Dept. at publicity@sunburypress.com.

FIRST OXFORD SOUTHERN EDITION: March 2022

Set in Adobe Garamond | Interior design by Crystal Devine | Cover by Lawrence Knorr | Edited by Jennifer Cappello.

Publisher's Cataloging-in-Publication Data
Names: McLallen, Wylie Graham, author.
Title: A man of modern letters / Wylie Graham McLallen.
Description: First trade paperback edition. | Mechanicsburg, PA : Oxford Southern, 2021.
Summary: The early years of Ernest Hemingway's career are covered, including his travels to Europe, in this second part of a two volume set.
Identifiers: ISBN : 978-1-62006-528-0 (softcover).
Subjects: BIOGRAPHY & AUTOBIOGRAPHY / Literary Figures | BIOGRAPHY & AUTO-BIOGRAPHY / Adventurers & Explorers | BIOGRAPHY & AUTOBIOGRAPHY / Rich & Famous.

Product of the United States of America
0 1 1 2 3 5 8 13 21 34 55

Continue the Enlightenment!

To our children,
Lyda Bayne and Elisha Whitman

CONTENTS

ACKNOWLEDGMENTS

NO ONE really does anything by themselves; there are always other people involved in many ways. I would like to give thanks to the staff at the main branch of the Vancouver Public Library; they were always courteous and helpful, often searching for and finding obscure books in the stacks. I would like to thank Angela Hemingway, the widow of Jack Hemingway, who quickly and graciously granted me access to copyrighted material in the Hemingway Collection at the JFK Library in Boston, and also express my gratitude to Maryrose Grossman, an archivist of the Hemingway Collection at the JFK Library in Boston, who was courteous and interested and always quick to respond to my requests when we spoke on the phone. I give special thanks to Valerie Hemingway, who during the time I was conceiving this project, not yet even sure if I would do it, generously responded in detail to many emails I sent that were full of questions about Ernest Hemingway and the people he knew in Paris: in his last years, Valerie was a close assistant to Hemingway, an unforgettable man by all accounts. Don Stewart of McLeod's Books in downtown Vancouver was always helpful and encouraging, setting aside books crucial to my research and even providing for purchase an authentic copy of the *Transatlantic Review*, which published Hemingway's first stories. My older brother Lyman, a teacher whose love of literature is perhaps even keener than mine, also made contributions in his own special way. I thank Bill Ellis, an English professor at Simon Fraser University in Vancouver (and a true modern despite his love of nineteenth-century literature), who provided outstanding editing advice from time to time and whose friendship was always encouraging. There's the creative team at Sunbury Press: Terry Kennedy, Joe Walters, Crystal Devine, and Senior Editor Jennifer Cappello (who put many hours into the project)—who care about their authors and help bring their books to life. And, lastly, but not least, to my family, for their understanding and all the undisturbed hours of concentration.

PURGATORY

THE HEMINGWAYS returned to North America late in the summer of 1923 to have their baby born in the best hospitals, much better than those in Paris, in the healthy environment of Canada, and for Ernest to work as a full-time reporter with an excellent salary for the *Toronto Star*. They planned to live in Toronto for at least a year and face the future with strong aspirations of one day returning to the creative life of Paris, a day that would come much sooner than they thought. For neither Ernest nor Hadley could really leave Paris and the people they knew there behind—especially not since the extraordinary literary achievement, if as yet only barely noticed, that the city had sparked in Ernest. There were no bullfights in Ontario as there were in Spain or wonderful chatty cafes like those on the boulevard of Montparnasse. In Paris, Ernest derogatorily called Toronto "the City of churches"[1]; he would call it much worse while he lived there during this fall. The strange and different people who were an accepted part of the charm of Paris were mostly shunted aside in Toronto, which in spirit was an extension of the Great Midwest of America they had left two years before, fleeing from the dearth of new ideas and freedom of thought smothered in the pursuit of money that was as much a religion as that in the churches; from the self-righteousness of Prohibition; and Warren G. Harding's return to "Normalcy," ignoring the Great War. Though there was no Prohibition in Canada, which supplied the booze to the bootleggers in America, a paucity of new ideas was in place, and in addition, there was a

---

1. EH to Isabelle Simmons, June 24, 1923, *The Letters of Ernest Hemingway, Vol. 2.*

new assistant managing editor of the *Star*, who hated Ernest Hemingway before he even saw him.

When they landed in Quebec, debarking from the Cunard liner *Andania*, there were notes from John Bone and Greg Clark exuberantly welcoming them to "the land of trouts and deers and spaces."[2] Greg Clark and his wife, Helen, were eager to meet Hadley. "The paper needs you," wrote Greg, "and you will be in a position to tear into things and write your name on the skies." Greg greeted them in Toronto with warmth and, as the feature editor of the *Star Weekly* attuned to the literary world, was impressed by the way Ernest spoke easily and familiarly and without bravado of Gertrude Stein and Ezra Pound and James Joyce. Hemingway returned as a veteran newsman with some stature; most of the staff was new and had read all of his European dispatches. Herbert Cranston, his editor at the *Star Weekly*, was pleased with his success but had reservations about his temperamental capacity to adjust to the demands of a daily paper. It was a good job at one hundred and twenty-five dollars a week (almost twice what Hadley's trust funds paid, though the dollar went a lot further in Paris than Toronto), and it was assumed that he would be assigned to interviewing local and visiting celebrities. Hemingway would be working under John Bone for the *Daily Star*, where his immediate supervisor, the assistant managing editor, was a man named Harry Hindmarsh.

Harry Comfort Hindmarsh was married to the publisher's daughter, and he was a force to be reckoned with in Canadian journalism. A large man with close-cropped hair, he wanted to boost circulation and at the same time rid the paper of the raffish young men who made wide circulation possible. He automatically concluded that Hemingway, fresh from the undisciplined routine of overseas work, was of that type and decided to break him down. When Hemingway reported for work on Monday, September 10, despite his lavish salary, Hindmarsh immediately put him on the most drudging mundane assignments he could give a reporter, and would work him hard, early and late, and not give him his share of

---

2. Carlos Baker, *Hemingway: A Life*, 150.

by-lines. A young college intern named Morley Callaghan remembered checking the assignment book one morning and seeing that Hemingway's "were all piddling . . . just junk assignments;"[3] at that moment, Hemingway walked over, looked at the book and muttered, "Jesus Christ." Hindmarsh treated most of his reporters in a similar manner to establish his authority, but with Hemingway it was a mistake. Motivated by good pay, Hemingway played the game as well as he could, but his days were filled with trivia, and he found no time to even write letters.

On his first day, Hindmarsh sent him on a Pullman sleeper to Kingston, Ontario, to report on a prisoner's escape from the penitentiary. Upon his return, he was immediately put to work researching and investigating a dubious businessman who put together bogus mining companies. Hemingway worked hard on the story, interviewing people in the company's Toronto office, and all but exposed it as a fraudulent operation. Hindmarsh didn't bother to read his report, sending him instead to Sudbury where the actual mine was located. Ernest went up there and tramped the fields, looked at mining samples an engineer said was not commercial coal, and turned in an excellent piece of reporting that should have earned him a few days' rest, but was almost immediately put back to work. He covered concerts at Massey Hall, and once, after working late into the night, was summoned from bed at four in the morning to cover a one-alarm fire. Hadley thought Hindmarsh's treatment "an ugly case of mean jealousy,"[4] and complained to Ernest's parents, "So many trips, no sleep and countless unimportant assignments."[5]

Ernest became tired and frustrated. "I have understood for the first time how men can commit suicide simply because of too many things in business piling up ahead of them that they can't get through,"[6] he wrote to Gertrude and Alice, and confessing to Pound, "I am now undertaking the show on a day by day basis. Get through today. Then get through tomorrow tomorrow. Like 1918." He read *Ulysses* to cheer himself up and took pride in knowing that, as a favor to Sylvia, he had successfully

---

3. Charles Fenton, *The Apprenticeship of Ernest Hemingway*, 246.
4. James R. Mellow, *Hemingway: A Life Without Consequences*, 241.
5. Hadley Mowrer to CEH & GHH, Sept. 27, 1923, Hemingway Collection, JFK Library.
6. EH to Stein & Toklas, Oct. 11, 1923, *Letters of Ernest Hemingway, Vol. 2*.

smuggled several copies for distribution to American bookstores, assuring Pound, "Someday someone will live here and be able to appreciate the feeling with which I launched *Ulysses* on the states (not a copy lost) from this city."[7]

At the end of September, they moved from a rented room in a red brick mansion on Sherbourne Street into a new building at 1599 Bathurst Street on the south end of a ravine about half a mile north of the Connables' mansion. Ernest was on an assignment, so Hadley, in her ninth month of pregnancy, relied on friends and an elderly janitor to move furniture and luggage sent from Chicago and St. Louis. Their apartment was a fourth-floor railroad flat with a small bedroom between the living room and kitchen. A piano was leased for Hadley to play, and on the walls they hung their paintings by Andre Masson and Dorothy Pound. Hadley's spirits were lifted when a trunk arrived from Chicago packed by Dr. Hemingway containing clothes and china and crystal along with Hadley's diploma from the Mary Institute and two pairs of her reading glasses. There was a nice view of the autumn trees changing colors in open country beyond the ravine. Hadley had difficulty walking up the creaking stairs, and as cold weather came, they had to stuff blankets under the doors and windowsills to keep out the snow and wind. The baby wasn't due until the end of October, but when the birth actually came, Hemingway was away on yet another assignment.

Despite Ernest's plea that his wife would almost certainly be delivering their baby, Hindmarsh sent him to New York City to cover the arrival of Lloyd George in America. Ernest was "furious and left practically in tears because he sensed that the birth was going to happen while he was away,"[8] recalled Hadley. A feature on Britain's prime minister's visit to North America would produce multiple stories and require at least two reporters to hustle the material, but the *Star* sent only Ernest, and six days of reports and interviews and speeches made for early mornings and late nights. He was able to buy a copy of the spring issue of the *Little Review* with his six vignettes of "in our time" and his poem "They All

---

7. EH to Ezra Pound, Oct. 13, 1923, *Letters of Ernest Hemingway, Vol. 2.*
8. Hadley Mowrer, Alice Sokoloff tapes, Hemingway Collection, JFK Library.

Made Peace," and read an enigmatic sketch by Gertrude Stein called "A Valentine to Sherwood Anderson" that made Hemingway miss Paris and the afternoons at rue de Fleurus. He wrote to Gertrude and Alice that Lloyd George was "a cantankerous, mean temperamental and vicious man."[9]

Losing sleep, patience, and enthusiasm for his work, he wanted to be with Hadley, who was at the Connables' when her contractions began on Tuesday evening, October 9. She checked into Wellesley Hospital where, very early the next morning, a healthy baby boy was born; Ernest was en route in the press car of Lloyd George's train. Ten miles outside of Toronto, he was awakened with the news of the birth of his boy, the message saying nothing about the mother's condition. Giving his copy to someone else to deliver, he went directly from the station to the hospital where he broke down from the strain and fatigue of the trip but pulled himself together and became kind and sweet. Ernest and Hadley blamed Hindmarsh for him missing the birth, but the birth had gone smoothly and wonderfully, and the mother was in fine health. They named their child John Hadley Nicanor Hemingway.

At the paper the next day, an explosion happened between Hindmarsh and Hemingway. Facing each other in his office, Hindmarsh bawled out Hemingway for not filing his copy before visiting the hospital. Consequently, Ernest wrote to Ezra, "[I] came in intending to kill city editor, Hindmarsh, compromised by telling him would never forgive him of course and that all work done by me from now on would be with the most utter contempt and hatred for him and all his bunch of masturbating mouthed associates. Also offered knockdown if editor's trap opened."[10] Whatever was actually said, the words could not be taken back, and it was the death knell for Hemingway in Toronto. Within days he transferred to the *Weekly Star* under Cranston but was never free from Hindmarsh's presence and was frustrated that he couldn't work on his fiction. "It is impossible for me to do any writing of my own," he wrote to Sylvia Beach. "The paper wanta all day and all night. Much longer and

---

9. EH to Stein & Toklas, Oct. 11, 1923, *Letters of Ernest Hemingway Vol. 2.*
10. EH to Ezra Pound, Oct. 13, 1923, *Letters of Ernest Hemingway, Vol. 2.*

I would never be able to write anymore."[11] Pound wrote him that Ford Madox Ford was starting a new journal that would be the best one yet and wanted Ernest to write something and send it in, but he could not find the time. Hadley soon wrote to Isabelle Simmons, "I think we are going to leave here as soon as I am safely strong again. It is too horrible to describe or linger over and it will kill or scar my tiny if we stay too long."[12]

The trees along the ravine outside their apartment were bright with fall colors, and the baby gained weight steadily on feedings spaced four hours apart. Through the coolness of the fall in Toronto, the Hemingways retained the feel of Left Bank bohemians in their appearance: Ernest in worn sports shirts and Hadley with short hair, simple clothes, and no makeup. They were treated special around the newspaper office, almost like celebrities, and were good additions to parties with Hadley playing the piano and Ernest using his Italian officer's cape to demonstrate matador techniques. Morley Callaghan noted that Hemingway was proud of Hadley and talked about her a lot. They had not told Ernest's parents about the baby until a few weeks before his birth because, Hadley wrote, they didn't want them worrying; but the more likely reason was that Ernest didn't want them involved as he had no place for them in his life as a writer and Paris bohemian.

Congratulatory telegrams and gifts arrived from the Hemingways in Oak Park and the Ushers in St. Louis and from friends in the US and Paris. Ernest's parents sent his lace christening gown and baby spoons and a check for $150 to cover hospital expenses. The young Hemingways truly did love their son, whom they were calling Bumby "because of the round, solid feel of him"[13] in their arms. They hired a strong old woman to help to help clean and cook, and there was a cat Ernest had brought back from Sudbury. At a month, the baby laughed at his parents: the father wrote to Gertrude Stein, "I am getting very fond of him."[14]

---

11. EH to Sylvia Beach, Nov. 6, 1923, *Letters of Ernest Hemingway, Vol. 2.*
12. Hadley Mowrer to Isabelle Simmons, Oct. 12, 1923, Hemingway Collection, JFK Library.
13. Gloria Diliberto, *Hadley*, 161.
14. EH to Stein & Toklas, Nov. 9, 1923, *Letters of Ernest Hemingway, Vol. 2.*

Ernest's newspaper work had become potboilers for the *Star Weekly*: writing feature stories on Lloyd George's brief meeting with eighty-year-old Robert Todd Lincoln, the water level of the Great Lakes, iodine treatment for goiter, and the Nobel Prize award to William Butler Yeats. They were interesting features written with keen and interesting observations, but he was only doing it for the paycheck. He read about the Munich Beer Hall putsch by the most fanatical of the right-wing German leaders, Adolf Hitler, and thought it more amusing than grim, writing to Gertrude Stein, "It sounds very funny. The early dispatches so far."[15] He felt bored around the office and was just kind of biding his time, but some of the other reporters saw him differently. "He made me feel that he was eagerly and deeply involved in everything," wrote Callaghan. "Then we began to talk about literature. All his judgments seem to come out of intense and fierce convictions, but he offered them to you as if he were letting you in on something. 'James Joyce is the greatest writer in the world,' he said . . . always appearing to be sharing a secret yet watching me intently."[16] Greg Clark said his manner was intense: "He was an articulate guy. Tried three or four ways to say everything he had to say."[17] When Ernest got the proof sheets of *in our time* from Bill Bird, he brought them around to the office saying, "I've discovered a new form [of writing]." Morley Callaghan admired the sketches, and when he asked what people in Paris thought, Ernest calmly answered, "Ezra Pound thinks it is the best prose he has read in forty years." Behind the calm, Morley sensed "that he was willing to be ruthless with himself or with anything or anybody that got in the way of the perfection of his work."[18]

Ernest's spirits lifted early in November when a letter arrived from Edward O'Brien asking permission to dedicate *The Best Short Stories of 1923* to "Ernest Hemenway."[19] Not bothered by the misspelling of his name, Hemingway, who had sent a copy of *Three Stories & Ten Poems* to O'Brien to show that his story had been published, replied, "Your letter

15. EH to Stein & Toklas, Nov. 9, 1923, *Letters of Ernest Hemingway, Vol. 2.*
16. Carlos Baker, *Hemingway: A Life*, 155-6.
17. Baker, 156.
18. Baker, 157.
19. Baker, 154.

couldn't have had any greater effect if it had been to inform me that I'd just been given a million dollars" or "the news that I'd been elected to the Academie to replace Anatole France. Yes, you may dedicate the book to me." O'Brien also asked if he had enough stories for a book for Boni & Liveright. Ernest confessed that he had been feeling "pretty low and discouraged" in Toronto and working so hard for the newspaper that he was "too tired at night to think let alone write," and then "in the morning a story starts in your head on the streetcar and have to choke it off because it was coming so perfectly and easily and clear and right and you know that if you let it go on it will be finished and gone."[20]

He did take time to write Edmund Wilson, the finest young critic of their generation, sending along a copy of *Three Stories & Ten Poems*, of which, he informed Wilson, Gertrude Stein had written a review. Wilson, who had shown Burton Rascoe copies of Hemingway's sketches in the *Little Review,* which Rascoe mentioned in his column in the *New York Tribune,* liked the book and offered a notice in the small review section of the *Dial.* Hemingway asked him to wait until *in our time* comes out in a month and do a joint review; and, knowing the importance of influential reviewers, he told Wilson that "yours is the only critical opinion in the States I have any respect for," and informed him of Edward O'Brien's dedication and wrote of his friendship with Gertrude Stein, "had been at a very fine lunch at Gertrude Steins and talked there all afternoon and read a lot of her new stuff."[21] Unable to write new fiction in Toronto, at least he was garnering some of the critical notice he needed so badly.

Gertrude sent a copy of her review of his first book in which she wrote: "Three stories and ten poems is very pleasantly said. So far so good, further than that and as far as that, I may say of Ernest Hemingway that as he sticks to poetry and intelligence it is both poetry and intelligence . . . I should say that Hemingway should stick to poetry and intelligence and eschew the hotter emotions and more turgid vision."[22] Miss Stein gave words her own private meanings and whatever she found

---

20. EH to Edward O'Brien, Nov. 18, 1923, *Letters of Ernest Hemingway, Vol. 2.*
21. EH to Edmund Wilson, Nov. 25, 1923, *Letters of Ernest Hemingway, Vol. 2.*
22. Michael Reynolds, *Hemingway: The Paris Years*, 152-3.

turgid in the stories and poems is hard to decipher, but anything written by Gertrude Stein, however cryptic, brought favorable notice to a writer. Other news from Paris made Hemingway miss his life in Europe: Bill Bird wrote that the puppy had died, that *in our time* would soon be at the bindery, and that Ezra Pound had appropriated the Birds' apartment for music practice for the violinist Olga Rudge and a young composer named George Antheil, who were creating music to some of Ezra's compositions. John Bone must have sensed that Ernest missed Europe because nearly all his articles were about bullfights in Pamplona, Paris gargoyles, and skiing in Switzerland. Ezra, himself, had told Ernest in a letter that he had made a mistake by returning to Canada. It was true. One night he came home dejected, saying, "I just can't take it, Hash. If I have to stay with [Hindmarsh] I'll go crazy," and Hadley replied, "Well, let's leave." Years later she remembered, "Ernest was the most sensitive person I ever knew, at times ridiculously so, but it was real."[23]

In December, the Hemingways booked three passages for two hundred and ninety dollars, the cheapest they could find, on the Cunard liner *Antonia* scheduled to leave New York for Cherbourg on January 19, 1924. Ernest's youngest sister Carol pleaded for his return to Oak Park for Christmas; Dr. Hemingway even offered to reimburse the cost for round-trip train tickets. A week before Christmas, Ernest regretfully wrote his father: "It is quite impossible for us all to come. When we are shortly to leave on a long trip on which it is absolutely necessary that both Hadley and the baby be in the best of shape it is impossible to jeopardize their condition by a flying trip of over six hundred miles as a preliminary."[24] Ernest made the trip to Oak Park alone, taking a night train that arrived in Chicago on Sunday morning, December 24. His father was very emotional, and his mother cried sentimental tears to find him so mature and caring; "a thoroughbred,"[25] she called him. Marcelline and her new husband, Sterling Stanford, had come down from Detroit. Pictures were taken on the lawn of the family side-by-side bundled in

---

23. Mowrer, Sokoloff tapes, Hemingway Collection, JFK Library.
24. EH to parents, Dec. 18, 1923, *Letters of Ernest Hemingway, Vol. 2*.
25. Carlos Baker, *Hemingway: A Life*, 158.

overcoats. Though they wouldn't have known it, it was the last time they would all be together alive.

In the evening, before the fire in the living room, Ernest gave Marcelline a copy of *Three Stories & Ten Poems*. He had asked her "to keep this from reaching relatives due to the first story which is a whangleberry but would simply shock and give them that familiar 'I'd rather see you dead and buried in your grave than—' feeling."[26] (When Marcelline read the story, "Up in Michigan," on a Pullman berth returning to Detroit, she was filled with revulsion.) Ernest's visit lasted less than a day. That same evening, standing at the Chicago station on Christmas Eve night with a sack of presents for Hadley and the baby, his father shook his hand long and hard. Ernest was back with Hadley on Christmas morning, and they had dinner with the Connables on Christmas night. Before the New Year, he composed two letters to John Bone, regretfully tendering his resignation "to take effect January 1st, 1924, if convenient to you."[27] Since they were jumping their lease, they conspired with friends to help empty the apartment until they were almost gone. On the morning of January 10, they boarded the train to New York, leaving behind conventionality forever in search of further adventure.

Free from structured employment and an oppressive boss, Hemingway felt a restoration of creative energy. While waiting to sail from New York, he took Jane Heap and Margaret Anderson to a prize fight at Madison Square Garden, giving a running commentary that people in seats nearby strained to hear, and keeping it up afterward, round by round, blow by blow, as they walked the streets. "No one ever talked more excitingly about sports,"[28] said Miss Anderson. At the pier on the day of departure, he dressed outlandishly with gold tweed pants, beret, and gnarled walking stick. It was a rough crossing, and when they reached France a lonely woman from California followed them off the boat. Hadley described her as "a dreadful, fat, leechy sort of person who was going to Paris to be independent, but was afraid to leave us for a moment."[29]

26. EH to MHS, Oct. 14, 1923, *The Letters of Ernest Hemingway, Vol. 2.*
27. EH to John Bone, December 1923, *The Letters of Ernest Hemingway, Vol. 2.*
28. Carlos Baker, *Hemingway: A Life,* 159.
29. Hadley to GHH & CEH, Feb. 20, 1924, Hemingway Collection, JFK Library.

Though Ernest cared about people and could perform great kindness, this woman became a target for his venom as he wrote in a sketch that because she couldn't find a suitable man to sleep with she stayed in her room listening to the couple next door making love. This worried Hadley "because it was so unfair,"[30] but she recognized that his unseemly rage against people and the world was something that also fired his talent. Apparently, the stories he had choked off on the tram in Toronto he was now allowing to coalesce in his mind because he soon wrote to Ezra Pound in Rapallo, "I have about 7 stories to write."[31]

30. Mowrer, Sokoloff tapes, Hemingway Collection, JFK Library.
31. EH to Ezra Pound, Feb. 10, 1924, *The Letters of Ernest Hemingway, Vol. 2.*

David Lloyd George

Edmund Wilson

Harry Hindmarsh

The Hemingways on Christmas Eve, 1923

Toronto Star building

THE CARPENTER'S LOFT

THE WEATHER in Paris was cold and damp; the family had coughs and colds. There were many Americans and English in town, and apartments were harder to find. "The town seems, when you can distinguish faces through the rain and snow, to be full of an enormous number of shits,"[1] wrote Ernest to Ezra. Prices had risen, too, but early in February they leased a cold-water flat with no electricity in a white stucco building at 113 rue de Notre-Dame-des-Champs about two blocks from Ezra's studio along the narrow curving street with high shuttered houses directly behind boulevard Montparnasse. The rent was cheap, though not as cheap as Cardinal Lemoine, but this time there was indoor plumbing and at night they read by gas lamps. "We have the whole second story," Hadley wrote her mother-in-law, "tiny kitchen, small dining room, toilet, small bedroom, medium size sitting room with stove, dining room where John Hadley sleeps and the linen and his and our bath things and a very comfortable bedroom." There was a sawmill in the courtyard behind the house: "you're conscious all the time from 7 A.M. to 5 P.M. of a very gentle buzzing noise. They make door and window frames and picture frames. The yard is full of dogs and workmen."[2] Their friend, the poet Archibald MacLeish, would call it "a carpenter's loft,"[3] perhaps in regard to the fictional planes Ernest would precisely create while living here. The neighborhood was prettier and better than before. They were only a short walk from a metro station and the Luxembourg

---

1. EH to Ezra Pound, Feb. 10, 1924, *The Letters of Ernest Hemingway, Vol. 2.*
2. Michael Reynolds, *Hemingway: The Paris Years*, 162.
3. Gloria Diliberto, *Hadley*, 166.

Gardens, Gertrude and Alice were nearby on rue de Fleurus, and all the fashionable cafes on Montparnasse where their American friends gathered to drink and gossip were a few steps away.

The sawmill was owned by a couple named Chautard, the landlords who lived on the first floor. They were not nice people. Grumpy Madame Chautard, her ample frame wrapped in a purple bathrobe, walked the yard in stiletto heels. The Hemingways did not like her, though they relied on her for occasional babysitting. "She was very jealous of me because I had this lovely baby, and she didn't have any children," remembered Hadley. On the evening of George Antheil's Paris debut, they returned home to find Bumby's crib empty, Madame Chautard nowhere to be seen. They ran downstairs to find the Frenchwoman bouncing him in her arms, "showing off to all these very ordinary French people," recalled Hadley. "Everyone was laughing and talking but Bumby, who was screaming. I wasn't very nice about it."[4] At that, Hadley re-hired Marie Rohrbach to help with Bumby and do the housework. The baby's presence assuaged the loneliness Hadley had previously felt in Paris. The proud parents took him around to show him off to friends like Sylvia and Gertrude.

At Shakespeare and Company, *Three Stories & Ten Poems* was still on the shelves, but its sales were slow and disappointing; at rue de Fleurus, Alice was not so happy about the Hemingway baby, but Gertrude spoke to Bumby in a deep, velvety voice and was pleased when she and Alice were asked to stand at the christening as the boy's godparents. Ernest had also convinced Ford Madox Ford to publish *The Making of Americans* in his new periodical the *Transatlantic Review*. "He is delighted with the stuff and is going to call on you," he wrote Gertrude soon after their meeting. "He is going to publish the first installment in the April no. . . . He wondered if you will accept 30 francs a page . . . I made it clear it was a remarkable scoop for his magazine obtained only through my obtaining genius."[5] He was also trying to settle into his new quarters to write. He had written no new fiction in five months, and between Bumby's crying and the noise of the sawmill he found it difficult to begin. The city

---

4. Mowrer, Sokoloff tapes, Hemingway Collection, JFK Library.
5. EH to Gertrude Stein, Feb. 17, 1924, *The Letters of Ernest Hemingway, Vol. 2*.

was changing as change always comes, and despite the bitter February weather, the Hemingways fully reentered Left Bank life and were ready for the change. Obscure and inauspicious, as most great changes are in their beginnings, they did not know that Ernest was about to change the world in a profound and lasting manner.

Two years before, when Ezra Pound and Gertrude Stein broke down his words and gave him a new vision of meaning and thought, he had worked in his room with his new knowledge in the down-at-the-heels neighborhood by rue Mouffetard. At first, the words kept jumping back at him and he had to smooth the recalcitrant syntax into simple, clear sentences that precisely conveyed the meanings he wanted to give as if they had a life of their own. When Ford Madox Ford first read his writing, he would say "Hemingway's words strike you, each one, as if they were pebbles fetched fresh from a brook."[6] It was hard work requiring singular concentration that was often interrupted by journalism that took him away at length from Paris but expanded his outlook by travel and association with older, more knowledgeable men of the world and gave him experience he would use in his fiction.

After the interruptions, he'd set back to work in the mountains of Switzerland and found his writing still had a life of its own as his clear smooth sentences expanded into paragraphs; and he worked on these paragraphs, crafting them into exact vignettes that were modern and different, already impressing the right people, and so precise and clear that they began to allow him to truly realize his theory of omission that something didn't have to be mentioned for a reader to know that it was present. Then, he was interrupted because Hadley was pregnant with Bumby, and they returned to Toronto to have the baby while he worked full-time for the *Toronto Star*. Though in Toronto he was unable to work at the writing that meant the most to him, the fiction had not ceased in his mind but continued to grow. When he returned to Paris and sat down to write in his room above the sawmill, he found that his range had expanded again, this time from paragraphs into

---

6. Ford Madox Ford, Preface to *The Hemingway Reader*.

clear, precise stories exploding off the pages in a natural embodiment of Modernism, adhering to the minds of readers and shaping generations of writers to come.

Soon after settling into the apartment on rue Notre-Dame-des-Champs, Ernest began writing in the smaller bedroom off the hall. Hadley wrote to his parents that while the sawmill "makes the saw dust fly down below . . . Ernest keeps the keys on his Corona flying on the floor just above . . . Ernest has written two dandy stories this week and is at his third."[7]

It wasn't always easy to write in that small room. The whine of the saw, the chuff of the donkey engine, the hollow boom of newly sawn planks smacked onto piles, and the clatter of camions toting them away made for more noise during the working hours of the day than Ernest could stand, and he often picked up his material and crossed the street to write unhindered at a table at the Closerie des Lilas. There was also the baby's crying. In good weather, when Ernest was trying to write, Hadley took Bumby to Luxembourg Gardens in a carriage borrowed from the Straters. One morning, before the baby began crying and the sawmill started its grind, Ernest began working on a story that he let develop slowly, not wanting it to finish.

This story was about a young boy named Nick Adams, who accompanies his doctor father to deliver a Caesarian birth at an Indian camp on a lake in northern Michigan. Ernest had begun the story in his head in Toronto, and now in Paris it was coming out smooth and clear and real on the paper. They set off in rowboats from the shore. There are the sounds of oars in the water, the screams of a woman in childbirth, and the underlying fear the boy has of dying. Hemingway had learned a lot from reading Joyce about beginning and ending a story to make the focus sharp and clear, and as he wrote in Paris the story told itself. Across the lake they follow an Indian with a lantern to a shanty where a woman in labor lay on a wooden bunk. Nick wants his father to make the woman stop screaming: "'No. I haven't any anesthetics,' his father

---

7. Diliberto, *Hadley*, 166-7.

said, 'but her screams are not important. I don't hear them because they are not important.'"

An actual baby began to scream; his own, not the one in the story. And so, he gathered his notebooks and pencils and walked across the street to the Closerie des Lilas. Sipping a cream coffee at a table in the back by the stove, remembering his own fears when Hadley had given birth in the Toronto hospital and he had not been there, he got the story moving again and was back in the shanty with the father and the pregnant woman and the Indian father in the upper bunk lying too quietly after the birth. Dr. Adams discovers the father had slit his throat and died. He tells his son he is sorry he had brought him there. Nick asks his father about dying: "Is dying hard, Daddy?" His father replies, "No, I think it's pretty easy, Nick. It all depends." They get into the boat and re-cross the lake. "A bass jumped, making a circle in the water."[8] The boy feels certain he will never die.

Ernest finished the story by the end of February and called it "Indian Camp." Over the next three months, Hemingway would write eight of the best stories he would ever write, and they all went just like that: one story after another bounding out of his head smooth and clear onto the paper, needing little revision; a mystical experience, as if someone else were doing the writing. The stories so spare and tense that they would outlast the generation for which they were written, and all the critics and publishers, too. "Have written a few stories in cafes and one place and another," he wrote to Ezra in March. "I ain't been writing badly." He knew Joyce sometimes labored a whole day on one sentence to get it right, and the ease with which these stories wrote themselves troubled him. "I am writing some damn good stories," he continued in the letter to Pound. "I wish you were here to tell me so, so I would believe it or else what is the matter with them."[9]

But, as everyone would come to know, the stories were great. After five years dedicated to writing—years of rejection, false starts, clichéd plots, and reading and listening and absorbing the lessons from the great

8. Ernest Hemingway, "Indian Camp," *Short Stories of Ernest Hemingway*, 91.
9. EH to EP, Mar. 17, 1924, *The Letters of Ernest Hemingway, Vol. 2.*

moderns Stein and Pound and Joyce—it all came together for Hemingway upon his return to Paris in the winter and spring of 1924. He was not in rebellion against the fundamentalist mood of the American middle class from which he sprang, but he had discarded its values and was riding the wave of the Modern Movement with its frank literary treatment of the human condition, holding his own judgment, and finding his style and form: a style, form, and subject matter that on the pages of his new stories were his own.

The baby, John Hadley Nicanor Hemingway, glowing with good health and a sunny disposition, was christened on March 16 in the small nearby chapel of St. Luke's Episcopal Church on rue de la Grande Chaumiere with Chink Dorman-Smith and Gertrude Stein and Alice Toklas standing as godparents. Bumby wore his father's christening dress, which Hadley had freshened with blue satin ribbon and lace. After the service the party returned along the narrow cobblestone streets to the "carpenter's loft" above the sawmill to celebrate in traditional French style with champagne and sugared almonds. Ernest had been working as an editor for Ford Madox Ford's new literary review, and on the very afternoon of his son's christening, he remarked at a tea party in the magazine's office that it took years for a man to get his name known. Ford replied, "Nonsense, you will have a great name in no time at all." Ford admired his twenty-four-year-old subeditor: "I did not read more than six words of his," he remembered, "before I decided to publish everything he sent me."[10] The first of his stories that Ford would publish was "Indian Camp."

Ford Madox Ford at fifty was tall, fat, pink and blonde, and wore suits seldom sent to the cleaners. His mouth was habitually ajar, his moustache was stained, and he spoke in a low explosive mumble that was difficult to hear as he copiously and carelessly shared his memories of the many famous men of letters he had known, which included Henry James and Joseph Conrad. He had written dozens of novels, some of which, like *The Good Soldier*, were very good, and made accurate judgments about

---

10. Carlos Baker, *Hemingway: A Life*, 163-4.

the work of other writers. He had moved to Paris to edit the new literary magazine he called the *Transatlantic Review*, named for the literary link between Paris and New York, whose office was in the rear of Bill Bird's Three Mountains Press on Quai d'Anjou where rickety steps led to a raised gallery where Ford had his desk. He had first met Hemingway in Ezra's studio. As Ernest shadow boxed, Pound told Ford, "He's the finest prose stylist in the world."[11] Ford asked him to read manuscripts, and on sunny afternoons, wearing tennis shoes and a patched jacket, Ernest would take a batch of manuscripts and sit outside on the Quai and read and sometimes rewrite them. He was not paid to do this, but the experience and notice gave him a huge leg up and associated him with older men like James Joyce and John Quinn. Gossiped about in the literary scene, McAlmon's wife, Bryher, once heard Adrienne Monnier proclaim in French that "Hemingway will be the best known of you all. He cares for his craft."[12] Ford had launched the review with the promise to make it an outlet for young writers, and he kept that promise with Hemingway, publishing not only "Indian Camp," but also "The Doctor and the Doctor's Wife" and "Cross-Country Snow" in coming issues.

For a brief while, Hemingway was fascinated by Ford and his talk of Conrad and Henry James; it was probably from Ford that he heard the story about Henry James getting black and yellow bruises trying to learn to ride a bike in the resort town of Torquay in Devonshire nearly thirty years before; but the man was so personally unattractive to him that his initial fondness soon dissipated. He wrote to Ezra that Ford was "So goddam involved in being the dregs of an English country gentleman that you can get no good out of him."[13] Finding so little of interest in the first issues of *Transatlantic,* he thought Ford was looking backward, "like some guy in search of a good money maker digging up Jim Jeffries at the present time as a possible heavyweight contender,"[14] and compared the review to conservative American magazines. Ernest wasn't the only one to feel this way about Ford Madox Ford. Robert McAlmon wrote in his

11. Kenneth Lynn, *Hemingway*, 230.
12. Mary Dearborn, *Ernest Hemingway*, 155.
13. EH to EP, Mar. 17, 1924, *The Letters of Ernest Hemingway, Vol. 2.*
14. EH to EP, May 2, 1924, *The Letters of Ernest Hemingway, Vol. 2.*

autobiography, "He wheezed and talked . . . often in a secretive manner, so that I had difficulty understanding him . . . [and] assured me that he was a genius . . . one of the 'masters' who likes to believe that all of the young come sit at his feet."[15]

Officious and pompous and ungainly in appearance, Ford still managed to keep a string of young and lovely mistresses—something Hemingway would have distrusted then since his marriage was still vital and monogamous—and even McAlmon admitted he "had many likeable and admirable traits . . . [and] gave some very amusing parties."[16] In fact, Ford wanted to provide continuity between the pre-war gentlemen of literature, who he sorely missed, and the postwar iconoclasts so eager to abandon their heritage. He did think that the rising young Turks should pay him deference; "It was quite impossible to talk of a place or a person without Ford topping your story,"[17] remembered McAlmon—which was something he would never get from Hemingway, who was determined to do what he wanted.

Ernest conceived the idea of publishing Gertrude's *The Making of Americans* in the *Transatlantic*. Ford did not know it was a thousand pages; he thought it was a novella. Stein was thrilled. She considered the book proof of her rightful place in the vanguard of the Modern Movement, the precursor of Proust and Joyce: "for the first time a piece of the monumental work which was the beginning, really the beginning of modern writing, was printed,"[18] she wrote in *The Autobiography of Alice B. Toklas*. Hemingway and Alice copied the part for publication from the sewn and bound manuscript that had been languishing on her shelves for more than a dozen years. Stein was convinced that Ernest's true reward for his efforts was the benefit, from copying and proofreading, to closely study her style. This is probably true because there is much of Gertrude Stein's rhythmic use of repetition in Ernest Hemingway's writing. "I think it is wonderful stuff," he wrote to Edward O'Brien, "but to get it, really, you have to read it as hard and concentrated as tho [sic] you were

---

15. Robert McAlmon, *Being Geniuses Together*, 116.
16. McAlmon, 116-7.
17. McAlmon, 116.
18. Gertrude Stein, *The Autobiography of Alice B. Toklas*, 203.

reading a proof on it."[19] The first installment was printed in the April issue along with prose by Joyce and early reviews of Hemingway's first two books. Ford's secretary, Marjorie Reed, described the sketches of *in our time* as "moments when life is condensed and clean-cut and significant," and presented "in minute narratives that eliminate every useless word."[20] The issue also contained "Indian Camp," his sensitive tale of childhood. Before the story was published, Ernest lopped off a section that told of the boy being afraid of the dark and firing a rifle to bring his father and uncle back to camp from jacklight fishing on the lake. Doing this, he may have been trying out his theory that something omitted can still affect the reader as if it were there.

Creativity thrives on chaos, and the inefficiency of Ford as editor, plus the inexperience of the subeditors, made the monthly task of putting out the magazine an accomplishment steeped in creative confusion. Though every issue was completed, anything that could go wrong regarding paper, printing, packing, forwarding, and distribution would infallibly do so. The turmoil was further increased by the tea parties Ford held in the office every Thursday. "The noise, lung-power, crashing in, and denunciation," remembered Ford. "[Guests] sat on forms—school benches—cramped round Bird's great hand press."[21] When the teas got out of hand with too many people, Ford shut them down and held weekly dances at the Bal Musette beneath the Hemingways' old apartment on rue de Cardinal Lemoine. When those got too big, he enlarged the candlelight soirees held in the barn-like apartment he shared with his mistress, Stella Bowen, on Boulevard Arago. No matter how many guests he assembled, Ford remained the star of the show. As Samuel Putnam recalled, it gave young Americans like himself the chance to "listen to the onetime collaborator of Conrad and the discoverer of D. H. Lawrence as he reminisced of his yesterdays."[22] Ernest, his hair growing longer and his clothes shabbier, speaking hesitantly and gently, pausing between words

19. EH to Edward O'Brien, Sept. 12, 1924, *The Letters of Ernest Hemingway, Vol. 2.*
20. *The Transatlantic Review, Vol I*, April 1924, 246-8.
21. Lynn, *Hemingway*, 230.
22. Samuel Putman, *Paris Was Our Mistress*, 71.

with great decision (even in conversation behaving more like an artist), would appear at Ford's parties when he felt like it.

Hemingway filled his days with work and play. Getting up early before Hadley awoke and the sawmill started, he sat down to write in the dining room while the streets were still quiet. But he was only domesticated when he wrote in the mornings; the rest of the day he took to the streets as his personal prerogative and roamed throughout Paris as widely as he wanted. Sometimes he sparred in a gym down by the river on rue de Pontoise; he sometimes helped a waiter he befriended at the Closerie des Lilas weed a small vegetable garden near the Porte D'Orleans on the south end of the city; and sometimes he played tennis with a new friend named Harold Loeb, who he met at Ford's tea parties. Harold was a wealthy, athletic Jewish man from New York City, a scion of the wealthy Guggenheim and Loeb families. Eight years older than Ernest and a graduate of Princeton, he had recently made a small splash in the literary world as a founder and editor of the modernist review *Broom* and had written a novel to be published with Boni & Liveright of New York City called *Doodab*. His literary and publishing connections would have been interesting to Ernest, and, in turn, the more Harold saw of Ernest the better he liked him. Loeb thought Ernest was unaffected and observed that after the days of Oscar Wilde and the decadence and aestheticism of the 1890s, which were still close in years to the Modern Movement, men like Hemingway removed the taint of femininity, homosexuality, and decadence, disassociating the male writer from perceived unmanliness.

On the red clay tennis courts on the Boulevard Arago, near the prison where the guillotine was kept, Loeb and Hemingway played regularly. "Ernest's game was not good," remembered Loeb, because of his bad eye and trick knee, "but he tried so hard and got such pleasure out of a successful shot that it was good fun notwithstanding."[23] Sometimes they were joined for sets of doubles by two of Loeb's friends, Paul Fisher and Bill Bullitt. Fisher was a socially prominent architect with athletic good looks. Bullitt was a diplomat from Philadelphia who had

---

23. Harold Loeb, *The Way It Was*, 194.

married John Reed's widow, Louise Bryant, and would later become the US Ambassador to France and Russia. Hemingway also boxed with Loeb and Fisher, once reputedly beating Fisher unmercifully during a match for no reason other than he felt "like blasting hell out of him."[24] Maybe he did so because of the man's wealth. At a time when he and Hadley were strapped for money ("I'm about broke,"[25] he wrote to Edward O'Brien), Hemingway was surrounded by many wealthy people.

Harold and his tall, good-looking girlfriend, Kitty Cannell, Ezra's old friend now separated from the poet Skipworth Cannell, invited the Hemingways to dinner at the Negre de Toulouse and soon called at their apartment above the sawmill. Kitty did not like Hemingway: "I instantly felt that Ernest was undependable and unpredictable,"[26] but she thought Hadley was a very nice girl and resented that Ernest made her live what she thought was a poverty-stricken life in worn clothes and a dingy flat. Hadley's confidence in her looks was at a low. She had not yet lost the weight gained during pregnancy, and she walked around the Quarter in an old shapeless wool skirt and moth-eaten sweaters. Her coat was so worn that "it looked like an old bathroom rug."[27] Though she was tired, often ill, and preoccupied with Bumby's nursing schedule, she loved being a mother. Kitty Cannell, troubled by the shabbiness of Hadley's wardrobe, would gift Hadley clothes and costume jewelry. She did this to please her friend, and also because she knew Ernest would resent it. She felt he had a more sensitive side that he tried to hide by acting the part of a ruthless (which he most certainly was), hairy-chested (and he was this too), unintellectual he-man, and disliking the intense focus he had on his career, she took pleasure in setting a bad example to a submissive wife. Ernest came to dislike Kitty as much as she disliked him, but on the surface, they continued to appear as friends and when Kitty gave the Hemingways a cat, which they named Mr. Feather Puss, Ernest was very pleased.

---

24. Loeb, *The Way It Was*, 216.
25. EH to EO, May 2, 1924, *The Letters of Ernest Hemingway, Vol. 2*.
26. Leslie Blume, *Everybody Behaves Badly*, 9.
27. Mowrer, Sokoloff Tapes, Hemingway Collection, JFK Library.

The Hemingways were not actually very poor, and they kept themselves square with prudence, but their financial problems were real. There was no longer Ernest's income from the *Star,* Hadley's trust funds had dwindled due to the bad judgment of George Breaker, to whom she had entrusted the investment of her money, and with the new baby, their expenses were greater than before. At their request, George Breaker in St. Louis had sold the railroad bonds that Hadley owned, but nearly all the money from the sale was missing. Ernest drafted letters on Hadley's behalf to the Mercantile Trust Bank in St. Louis to track the missing funds, and he wired and wrote to Breaker demanding accountability over the bonds, "you had bought them. Where are they? Or where is the money?"[28] But the money had been embezzled. They were able to recover some of it the following year, but most they never saw again and their income from the trust funds dropped to about $2200 a year. George Breaker, married to one of Hadley's oldest friends, Helen, who had served as one of her bridesmaids, turned out to be an untrustworthy man and would flee to South America never to be heard from again. Helen divorced him and with their two sons moved to Paris where Ernest helped her establish a career as a photographer specializing in book jacket portraits of authors.

The commercial magazines in America that paid so well continued to reject Ernest's stories; but with the Three Mountains Press edition of *in our time* prominently displayed in the windows of Shakespeare and Company, and his exposure in the *Transatlantic Review,* his reputation grew and their social circle expanded. "Almost every American writer in Paris sought Ernest out," Hadley recalled. "We always had a lot of company in the sawmill."[29] While Hadley sat in an armchair nursing Bumby, Ernest would pour drinks. Janet Flanner, *The New Yorker*'s Paris correspondent, remembered, "There was something magnificent about the Hemingways' hospitality. They usually had an egg at lunch, so if you were invited to lunch you had an egg, too. There was always a glass of wine, usually some boiled potatoes."[30] When family or friends from Chicago and St. Louis

---

28. EH to George and Helen Breaker, Aug. 27, 1924, *The Letters of Ernest Hemingway, Vol. 2.*
29. Mowrer, Sokoloff tapes, Hemingway Collection, JFK Library.
30. Diliberto, *Hadley*, 168.

showed up in Paris, the Hemingways showed them the Paris that they knew, not just the tourist sites, by taking them around to Sylvia Beach's bookstore, the office of the *Transatlantic*, to the Closerie des Lilas where they met their literary friends, and then to the Dome or the Dingo Bar.

They also took them to Ford's dances at the Bal Musette. Ford's common-law wife, the artist Stella Bowen, became a good friend of Hadley's. Their child, Julie, was about the same age as Bumby, and the families regularly spent time together. To their friends, the Hemingways seemed an ideal couple devoted to each other and growing more in love all the time. Stella Bowen recalled how they "would brighten up to each other"[31] and that their lack of money mattered little to them. Ernest even arranged for Hadley's use of an upright piano he discovered in a bakery across the street on boulevard Montparnasse. Hadley, a conventional and devoted mother and wife surrounded by hedonistic women who flaunted promiscuity and joked about abortions and venereal disease, was different from most Left Bank women of the time. Though they were surrounded by cheating couples, Harold Loeb remembered Ernest as conspicuously faithful to his wife: "Even at parties he seemed uninterested in other women."[32]

Through the spring the stories continued to flow; for almost seven weeks he suspended his correspondence, writing only his fiction. Later he would write, "The only writing that was any good was what you made up, what you imagined. That made everything [in the story] come true."[33] Nothing deterred him, not Bumby's crying, not the buzzsaw in the lumber yard, nor intrusive friends bothering him at his back table in the Closerie des Lilas. The stories were almost writing themselves. In March he wrote "The Doctor and the Doctor's Wife," a story about a father's confrontation with a large aggressive Indian hired to work on his lake property. The father backs off from the fight and retreats to the cabin in frustration where his wife won't try to understand what happened. As Hemingway was drawn to the primitive violence of the bull and boxing

---

31. Diliberto, *Hadley*, 170.
32. Bertram Sarason, *Hemingway and the Sun Set*, 123.
33. Reynolds, *Hemingway: The Paris Years*, 189.

rings, the fiction he wrote in Paris frequently confronts a man with violent possibilities. He admired boxers who took beatings and still performed well, and bullfighters braving the sharp horns passing very close. His fictional Dr. Adams failed this test. He did not know what to do because his capacity for violence was too diluted by civilizing forces. The story is a classic tale where nothing happens on the surface, violence is deferred, but beneath the surface is the study of a man in anguish over his public failure witnessed by his wife. Over the following three weeks, he finished the first drafts of "Cross-Country Snow," "Soldier's Home," and "Mr. and Mrs. Smith." In the story "Soldier's Home" a veteran returning home from combat finds himself alienated from the family and society he grew up with as the gulf between his parents' patriotic beliefs and the fear he had experienced in the trenches is too large to breach. His parents try to motivate him into a normalcy he has no feeling for, and the vet can neither explain nor compromise his feelings.

Far beneath the surface of "Soldier's Home" is also the author's anticipation of his parents' inability to accept his fiction. They read his journalism with pride, subscribing to the *Toronto Star* just for that purpose, and they wanted to tell their neighbors of their son's achievements. But Hemingway was writing stories that he knew his parents could not read without feeling deeply hurt. He was not ashamed of his stories, he was proud of them, but when "Indian Camp" appeared in the *Transatlantic*, he did not send a copy home. Deep inside, he needed their approval and support, but the favorable reviews he began to get and the high regard in which he was held by Pound, McAlmon, and O'Brien were in stark contrast to the response from his family in Oak Park. Grace and Ed had each ordered five copies of *in our time*. When Marcelline visited her parents after the books had arrived, she found her father grim. They were "shocked and horrified at some of the contents,"[34] she wrote. The vignette based on his broken relationship with Agnes seemed to disturb them the most, especially the last line about contracting gonorrhea from a salesgirl while riding in a cab through Lincoln Park. Grace wanted him to

---

34. Marcelline Hemingway Sanford, *At the Hemingways*, 219.

keep one copy, but Clarence "would not tolerate such filth in his home." Marcelline reported that her father wrote to Ernest "that no gentleman spoke of venereal disease outside a doctor's office," who was deeply hurt when he heard they had returned five copies to the publisher. "I wonder what was the matter," he wrote to his family in Oak Park, "whether the pictures were too accurate and the attitude toward life not sufficiently sentimentally distorted to please whoever bought the books or what."[35] The parents had ordered ten books, so five copies remained in Oak Park, but Ernest may not have known that, nor would it have soothed his hurt. Like nearly all children, he didn't understand his parents, whose intolerance was not as strong as he imagined. He never realized how much pride his father took in his accomplishments, but it was Grace's approval that meant the most.

All the while Ernest was becoming an ever more prominent fixture in the expatriate life of Paris. As April moved on, the weather warmed, tables appeared in front of the Closerie des Lilas, and a faint odor from its lilac bush hung in the air. More than the Dome or the Rotonde, a few blocks west on Montparnasse, this was Hemingway's café. Marshall Ney stood in bronze several feet away exhorting invisible troops to their Napoleonic duty on the battlefield. Sitting at his favorite table, Hemingway read through a satiric piece he was calling "Mr. and Mrs. Smith," invented from Left Bank gossip about a man named Chard Powers Smith, a twenty-nine-year-old Yale graduate and Harvard lawyer-turned-poet. The story's first sentences adroitly reflect the repetitious style of Gertrude Stein in *The Making of Americans*:

> Mr. and Mrs. Smith tried very hard to have a baby. They tried as often as Mrs. Smith could stand it. They tried in Boston after they were married and they tried coming over on the boat. They did not try very often on the boat because Mrs. Smith was quite sick. She was sick and when she was sick she was sick as Southern women are sick.[36]

---

35. EH to family in Oak Park, May 7, 1924, *The Letters of Ernest Hemingway, Vol. 2*.
36. Reynolds, *Hemingway: The Paris Years*, 192.

Smith was the type of Left Bank intellectual that Hemingway despised. In addition to his Ivy League degrees, nice clothes, and genteel background, and along with his literary pretentions, at least as perceived by Hemingway, he had a substantial income that allowed him to rent a chateau. Hemingway satirized the rich in his early years when he had no wealth, and that spring when Hadley's income had diminished, he especially resented someone like Smith. Like most people, Ernest had grown up in awe of money. Money was something he desired, but his desire was a secret he kept even from himself. Satire was often Hemingway's initial response to pretention, but people who knew Smith thought it was a malicious story. However, the malice did not run deep, nor was it particularly personal, and he drew on more sources than Smith's personal life for his characterization. It was really an inspired and creative story containing truth, if not personal truth, about an impotent couple who moved from Paris to a chateau away from Paris and veered toward homosexuality with the wife sleeping with a female friend as the husband happily wrote long poems. Whatever Hemingway knew about Chard Smith and his wife was limited to a brief acquaintance. As the story was forming in his head, he did not know that Mrs. Smith was pregnant and entering a hospital in Naples where she died in childbirth. And as he wrote the story it was as much about himself and Hadley; they, too, had triad friendships and had left Paris soon after their first arrival; and like the couple in the story, Ernest was twenty-four and his wife was much older. Hemingway placed no great value on his models; in time they would disappear leaving only his art.

Late in April, Ernest took a trip down to the Rhone Valley to be alone for the first time in a long while without wife, baby, or cat. He had been moping around the apartment talking about bullfights and how long it was until Pamplona and that they might not have the money to go there anyway. After two months on a continuously creative binge that produced seven new stories, he was sky high, emotionally tense, and ready to explode. Hadley was beginning to recognize the erratic cycles of elation and depression that changed her husband into someone she didn't know and sent him to Provence on a pilgrimage. It was inexpensive, and he relaxed and contemplated nature and art. "I wish to hell I could paint," he wrote to Ezra. "What cypress trees . . . I made a pilgrimage to Van Gogh's whorehouse in Arles and other shrines. A six day trip on 250 francs including railway fares and a seat on the corrida in Nimes."[37] Sitting in cafes in Arles, he imagined how Van Gogh saw it when he was there painting less than forty years before, and he observed people and made notes about them for no one else to see: "There is a girl selling stockings under a canvas shelter in the square."[38] He studied the girl, but would not talk to her, and began a story about how she felt about her hair that went no farther than a beginning. He knew that women's hair fascinated him but did not understand why and no one else would understand either.

When he returned to Paris the weather was fine and Hadley was waiting. She showed him the April twenty-eighth *Tribune* with the scandal about Kenley and Doodles Smith. At Arles he had read the French wire service story in a Marseilles paper but missed the details. On April 24, a young lawyer named Wanda Stopa, who had been having an affair with Y. K. Smith, took a taxi to the Smiths' house in Palos Park, pushed her way past the old caretaker, and entered the house looking for Y. K. Finding Doodles in their bedroom lying ill, she fired a gun at Doodles but missed as Doodles leapt out of the window. Hearing shots, the caretaker rushed into the room where Stopa shot him in the head, killing him, and screamed "I'm going to get Y.K." Instead of going after Y. K., who was at his office, she fled to a hotel in Detroit and killed herself. Among her possessions was a love letter from Y. K. Ernest's parents sent accounts in the Chicago papers, as did his friend Howie Jenkins. He read and listened closely. He and Hadley may have had a laugh about the sordid affair, but any satisfaction would have been self-righteous in that he was right all along about the immorality of Y. K.'s marriage. The breakup with Y. K. remained bitter. Kenley's younger siblings, Bill and Katy, had once been Ernest's closest friends. Ernest missed Bill and Katy very much, especially in the summer. He sometimes worried about his

---

37. EH to EP, May 2, 1924, *The Letters of Ernest Hemingway, Vol. 2*.
38. Reynolds, *Hemingway: The Paris Years*, 196.

own situation, too, telling friends he might have to take up journalism again to make ends meet.

Yet, despite having less money, a baby, and a wife turning matronly, Hemingway found Paris with its artists and cafes and athletic events like bike racing, horse tracks, and boxing more exciting than ever. He was sensitive to his wife's feelings and wrote a story about a couple confined by heavy rain to their hotel room in Rapallo where outside the window the wife sees a cat in the rain and wants it and expresses this and other desires to her husband who lies uninterested on the bed reading a book. Ernest's career was foremost, as Hadley had promised, but she was learning to be herself and take freedoms too. Though their friends were shocked that they lived without heat or electricity, they were happy in their hovel. It was so inexpensive (about $30 a month) that they could lightly indulge in café life, attend boxing matches and the six-day bike races—a new enthusiasm for Ernest—and even occasionally eat at nice restaurants.

Ernest exaggerated their financial problems, creating tales about trapping pigeons for dinner in Luxembourg Gardens and sparring with professional fighters for extra dough, but Harold Loeb said he denied himself little else beyond new clothes, which may not have mattered much to him anyway. When Kitty Cannell saw him in the street in the sweatshirt and ragged pants that became his standard wear, complaining about poverty in a half-sneering, half-joking way, she thought he was self-indulgent. Even with the lost income, they could still put aside money for another trip to Pamplona in July. It was good to be on the streets of Paris that spring. He had his first payment for "Indian Camp," for which he received ten dollars, and in the same issue of the *Transatlantic* was Marjorie Reed's fine review of *in our time*, the little book of vignettes dedicated to Robert McAlmon, Bill Bird, and Chink Dorman-Smith, and though the limited printing of one hundred and seventy copies sold very slowly and there was no profit, it was still a good start in the literary game he was already learning to play very well.

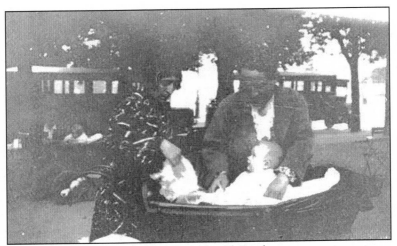

Alice and Gertrude with Bumby

Hemingways with baby inside carpenter's loft

Ford, Joyce, Pound, and John Quinn

Man of Modern Letters

Kitty Cannell

Harold Loeb

Notre-Dame-des-champs

Y. K. Smith in court

La Closerie des Lilas

in our time, Paris edition, 1924

THE TRANSATLANTIC REVIEW, PAMPLONA, AND WRITING

THE *TRANSATLANTIC Review* appeared monthly throughout 1924 with Ernest contributing a series of "notes" in each issue, writing about the boxing matches of Eugene Crique and the presence in the Latin Quarter of American Djuna Barnes, who had a story in the April issue. He published a play by Ring Lardner satirizing Dadaism. Out of print, he griped about Ford, mostly to Pound, because Ford wouldn't publish some of his work because of its sexual content. "Goddamn it he hasn't any advertisers to offend or any subscribers to discontinue why not shoot the moon?"[1] However, as much as he disliked Ford's pompous monologues and British manner, he learned from him. Ford was always promoting himself by keeping his work before the public in his weekly column in the Paris *Tribune*, serializing his own novel in the *Transatlantic*, and writing well about it, too, under a pseudonym. He reminded his readers in his editor's column of his connections with the literary past, often mentioning Henry James, the old master from whom Ford, the master apparent, had listened and learned—even if it wasn't all true.

Literary controversies, Hemingway saw and understood, created free publicity and were a crucial part of the game he felt he needed to play. When Ford asked him to write an editorial column for the May issue of the *Transatlantic*, he did his best to create an uproar by insulting two well-known Left Bank artists, Tristan Tzara and Djuna Barnes—"Dada is

---

1. EH to EP, May 2, 1924, *The Letters of Ernest Hemingway, Vol. 2.*

dead although Tzara still cuddles its emaciated little corpse to his breast and croons a Rumanian folk-song . . . Djuna Barnes, who according to her publishers is that legendary personality that has dominated the intellectual night-life of Europe for a century is in town. I have never met her, nor read her books"[2]—both well-liked by Ford, and he also disparaged the efforts of contemporary writers. It was a three-page column that told the readers more on Hemingway as a clever man who knew his way around the Paris literary world than about the writers on whom he wrote.

"There are lots of nice people in town now,"[3] wrote Ernest to his family as he steadily enlarged his circle of acquaintances in the cafes and soirees. At Sylvia Beach's bookshop, where he appeared in the afternoon to read or borrow books, he renewed a nascent friendship with satirist Donald Ogden Stewart, a Yale graduate he had met the preceding spring, who wrote the *Parody Outline of History* and *Aunt Polly's Story of Mankind*. He also befriended John Dos Passos, who was in and out of Paris frequently. Dos Passos was a tall myopic man, the illegitimate son of a prominent New York lawyer, who had been educated at the Choate School and Harvard University and had written five novels by the time he and Ernest became friends; factors that would have normally gone against him with Ernest, but "Dos" was friendly and unpretentious and serious about his art. Ernest "was always looking for someone who could really talk with him on his level and with the same interests," remembered Hadley. "They had a lot to say to each other."[4]

Dos Passos had served as a Red Cross ambulance driver in Italy during the war, but the two did not meet then. They had met in Paris, where at a dinner together with Ella Winter, the fiancée of Lincoln Steffens, Ernest assured all at the table that anyone could write if they set their mind to it. "It takes it all out of you," he said, "it nearly kills you; but you can do it."[5] Hemingway knew about writer's fatigue. He had lately begun a long short story about a wounded soldier returning to the country to fish and restore his spirit. He was trying his theory of omission again:

2. *The Transatlantic Review, Vol. I*, May 1924.
3. EH to Hemingway family, May 7, 1924, *The Letters of Ernest Hemingway, Vol. 2*.
4. Hadley Mowrer, Alice Sokoloff tapes, Hemingway Collection, JFK Library.
5. Carlos Baker, *Hemingway: A Life*, 165.

the story contained no illusion to the young man's wounds or the war. In the writing, he was drawing on his personal experience of fishing the Fox River near Seney in the northern peninsula of Michigan. He changed the name of the river from Fox to Two-Hearted "not from ignorance nor carelessness," he wrote, "but because Big Two-Hearted River is poetry."[6]

Upon his return from Provence, Ernest wrote to Edward O'Brien in Rapallo, "I have ten stories done now and think it might be a good idea to have a literary agent or something peddle them around . . . What I would like to do would be bring out a good fat book in N.Y. with some good publisher who would tout it and have In Our Time in it and the other stories . . . How many would it take?"[7] Ernest knew how many stories it would take to make a book. He had counted pages in Sylvia's bookshop and studied Joyce's *Dubliners* as his model. *Dubliners*, like Anderson's *Winesburg, Ohio*, is a set of stories bound together by location, themes, and characters. Hemingway knew that setting could not be a unifier in his own collection because his stories were too geographically divided. In fact, he had not written the stories to be a whole, but he saw how Joyce had used the long story "The Dead" to bring *Dubliners'* themes together by placing it last to anchor the collection. Ernest needed a long story like that to end his book, a story that would bring together everything he had learned.

In the middle of May, Ernest pinned to the wall in front of his writing table a detailed, blue-tinted map of the northern Michigan peninsula. Every time he looked up, he saw it. He could see the sun turning silver on the chop of the water, smell the pine smoke again. If he ever had a true home, the cottage on Walloon Lake was it. To the east of the pine barrens ran the Black and Pigeon rivers, farther north, on the upper peninsula close to Little Two-Hearted Lake, was the Fox where he and two friends had caught big trout in the summer of 1919 after the war. He started the story about fishing a fictional river with a lone character named Nick Adams. Nick was in some of the other stories, and he would be in this last one holding the book together. Nick was like a twin

---

6. Baker, *Hemingway: A Life*, 166.
7. EH to Edward O'Brien, May 2, 1924, *The Letters of Ernest Hemingway, Vol. 2*.

brother to Ernest; he knew everything about him. Sometimes he could not tell himself and Nick apart, except Nick seemed to have experiences in a different way than his own. The story started in Seney after the war, with the town all burned out and gone; when Nick got off the train, Ernest got off with him, watching him study the clear water at the bridge where trout held steady in the current, almost invisible against the gravel bottom. Everything else faded in Hemingway's life when he worked on this story; each day the story grew, and it was so good it scared him. He didn't know how it would end, but neither did Nick. They were both there in the country and on the river every day. At night, he and Hadley went out along Montparnasse walking the warm streets, drinking and laughing, and returned home to sleep in their garret above the sawmill with open windows to catch the breeze. When Ford left the magazine to raise money, Ernest had to leave Nick alone and Nick waited patiently for his return. Ernest would call the story "Big Two-Hearted River."

Though Hemingway did not like Ford—nothing about the blustering, oversized, pink-faced writer, editor, and womanizer with the wheezing voice and officious manner pleased him—Ford liked and had confidence in Hemingway. "Ford Madox Heuffer wants to take me over to England to meet Joseph Conrad,"[8] Ernest wrote to his parents in early May. When Ford left for London to try to obtain more money for his financially foundering magazine, he did not take Hemingway; nor did Ernest ever meet Conrad, who would die in the coming summer; but when Ford sailed for America to persuade John Quinn to invest more money, he left Hemingway in charge. His review almost bankrupt, on the eve of embarking, Ford wrote a public announcement, "we . . . are leaving the helm of the review . . . in the hands of Mr. Ernest Hemingway, whose tastes march more with our own than those of most other men."[9]

As the acting editor of the *Transatlantic Review*, Ernest completely disregarded Ford's goal of bridging the writing of the old and the new and brought it as close to the creative heart of the Modern Movement as any magazine had ever yet been. He finished the July issue, which Ford had

---

8. EH to Hemingway family, May 7, 1924, *The Letters of Ernest Hemingway, Vol. 2.*
9. Baker, *Hemingway: A Life*, 166.

already mostly done, and edited the entire August issue. It was inconvenient to spend so much time editing a magazine and working without pay because he was absorbed in the creation of "Big Two-Hearted River," and he and Hadley were planning another trip to Pamplona, this time with friends, but Ford said if he didn't the review might go under, and so with help from Marjorie Reed, he assembled a table of contents for the August issue, weighing it more than before with American contributors and experimental literature.

Ready to use his experience from the *Co-operative Commonwealth*, Ernest was prepared to show what a literary magazine could be. In the all-but finished July issue, he seized upon the editor's absence to insert insulting remarks in Ford's editorial section about Tristan Tzara and Jean Cocteau, two French writers favored by Ford, and Gilbert Seldes, editor of the *Dial*, which was the most influential literary magazine in America. Hemingway wrote that Cocteau, who had translated *Romeo and Juliet* into French, "has a very good minor talent and a certain amount of intelligence," but was unable to read or write English, adding "with this example, however, we expect a translation of Marlowe by Mr. Tzara who is also ignorant of English." He then satirized Seldes, claiming he repeats the "mots of Mr. Tristan Tzara with childish enthusiasm and wonder at how splendid they are."[10] He did this not to hurt the magazine but to make Ford look like a fool, implying that no editor could take these writers seriously, much less put them into print.

For the August issue, which was his sole responsibility, he left out Ford's rambling essays and the serialization of his novel, *Some Do Not*, and instead published poems by Bryher and the eccentric Baroness Elsa von Freytag Loginhofen, whose work Ford had earlier vetoed, and assembled stories from his friends: Dos Passos, Nathan Asch, Guy Hickok, and Donald Ogden Stewart. William Carlos Williams wrote an appreciation of McAlmon's prose, there was an experimental story by English author Dorothy Richardson, and another installment of Gertrude Stein's massive *The Making of Americans*. Ernest did not publish any of his own new

---

10. *The Transatlantic Review*, Vol. II, July 1924.

fiction, which continued to receive rejections from American magazines like the *Dial*. During this time, he was visited by his cousin Frank Hines from southern Illinois, who stayed in the apartment, keeping away from Ernest in the mornings when he spent his time in the small bedroom writing and editing the magazine. But in the afternoons, they would box or play tennis with Ezra. Returning from the courts, Ernest pretended his racket was a bullfighter's cape and danced in front of trolley cars executing correct and incorrect passes. After his cousin left for Italy, the Hemingways began their second trip to Spain.

As spring progressed, Dos Passos and Hemingway became close in their friendship. Ernest had a very competitive nature that strongly affected his attitude toward other writers. He wrote about T. S. Eliot, a favorite protégé of Ezra, derogatorily in letters to Pound and would malign him in a satire in the *Transatlantic*. He may have done this because Eliot was making a name in poetry, a field that Ernest had tried and vacated, and also because he had gone to Harvard. Dos Passos observed that Hemingway "was a moody kind of fellow . . . sorry for himself. One of the things he'd get sorriest for himself about was not having been to college."[11] However, that was an attitude not so deeply sunk in, for he had been given the chance to go to college and did not take it, and when Dos once told him he may have been better off not attending university, Ernest jokingly acquiesced that it probably would have been his ruination. His attitude to people who had even a semblance of wealth and had been to prestigious schools, some of whom could offend Hemingway just by being nice, was in marked contrast to those whom he wanted to cultivate in the service of his career. However, with John Dos Passos in the spring and summer of 1924, their relationship was all friendliness.

Ernest read Dos Passos's 1921 war novel, *Three Soldiers*, and thought it "a swell book."[12] They thought they might have met as Red Cross ambulance drivers in the Dolomites but were actually there at different times, and Dos had a vague recollection of having lunch with Ernest and Hadley at Lipp's in Paris in 1922 and finding Ernest's acid estimates

11. John Dos Passos, *The Best Times*, 161.
12. EH to F. Scott Fitzgerald, December 15, 1925, *Selected Letters*, 176.

of Clemenceau and Lloyd George and Litvinow highly invigorating. He may have accompanied Ernest to some of the bicycle races in the Velodrome d'Hiver, for he wrote that Hemingway "had an evangelistic streak that made him work to convert his friends to whatever mania he was encouraging at the time," and that he "used to get himself up in a striped jumper like a contestant in the Tour de France and ride around the exterior boulevards with his knees up to his ears and his chin between the handle bars,"[13] as, despite his limited finances, Ernest didn't hesitate to buy an expensive bicycle. Both Dos Passos and Donald Ogden Stewart were coming along on the trip to Pamplona in early July. "Dos and Don Stewart . . . are both great guys," Ernest would write to Howie Jenkins. "Dos is like Bill [Smith] was before he started to go haywire."[14] In the weeks before leaving for Spain for the running of the bulls, Hemingway and Dos Passos had drinks together at the Closerie des Lilas and talked about writing and writers. They admired the wit of Don Stewart, who insisted that they should get to know "people that mattered,"[15] but were put off by his social ambitions.

Paris throbbed with the coming of another summer, a summer when the city, in addition to all else, would host the Olympics. In the first days of June, eleven liners docked in Cherbourg with American tourists packing into trains bound for Paris ready to burn their money. They would arrive like this throughout the summer, groggy from too much ocean drinking, to find the Left Bank boulevards daubed with color and strange behavior from odd people, gorgeous prostitutes and dancers, and free, unrestrained homosexual men and women putting on a show in front of the cafes for the gawkers from Indianapolis and Des Moines, appearing all the more extraordinary because of the country left behind: an America in a fundamentalist mood lead by Bible thumpers like Billy Sunday and Aimee Semple McPherson, a place where you couldn't legally drink wine or any other spirits, and that on the surface would mock and feel threatened by the new movement being generated through Modern

---

13. Dos Passos, *The Best Times*, 143.
14. EH to Howie Jenkins, Nov. 9, 1924, *The Letters of Ernest Hemingway, Vol. 2*.
15. Dos Passos, *The Best Times*, 145.

Literature. In Paris, the tourists got away from preaching and prohibition and indulged in the free and open exposure of pleasures denied back home. Ernest was there, too, steps away from the cafes on Montparnasse in his room above the sawmill on Notre-Dame-des-Champs with his mind across the sea, back in the good America that he loved, casting for trout on an imaginary stream somewhere in northern Michigan. He fished the river a little bit each day, and as the story continued to grow, he again became Nick on the river. He felt the coldness of the water as he struggled in the stream, a good struggle, and could see the fly line floating in the current. When the first trout hit Nick's line, Ernest felt the tug in his Paris apartment.

Life was commodious as friends came and went. McAlmon reappeared from the south of France just as his wife, Bryher, and her lover, Hilda Doolittle, arrived together from Switzerland; Bob sat silent and depressed in their presence at a dinner. Ezra and Dorothy brought William Carlos Williams and his wife over to the Hemingways' apartment. Williams, an obstetrician, examined Bumby, whose pallor he did not like. At nine months, the baby was still nursing and not on solid food. Williams told Ernest and Hadley to wean the child and have him circumcised. They all went to the fights together at the Cirque de Paris that night, and the next day Williams returned with his surgical instruments to remove the baby's foreskin. Ernest blanched when the scarlet blood flowed and his baby screamed.

By June 20, the August *Transatlantic* was ready for the printers and Ernest was eager for Spain and the running of the bulls at the ancient festival of San Fermin. A small, congenial group was finalizing plans to assemble there with them. Hadley, with help from a friend, put together a set of decent clothes for the holiday, sewing a homemade copy of a designer scarf, while Ernest, safeguarding his manuscripts, put aside the story about fishing in the river, not knowing how the tale of a war veteran's fragile and searching state of mind might end. That was the best part, not knowing how the story would conclude, and trusting that it would be there upon his return. For the month of their absence, they placed Bumby in the good hands of Marie Rohrbach and her husband Tonton.

It was late in June, with Hadley in borrowed clothes, when they boarded the evening express train to the Basque coast. Traveling south, Ernest read a rejection of "Cat in the Rain" from Carl Van Doren of the *Century Magazine* who said it "was suggestive of an ability"[16] they wanted in the magazine, but they thought the sketch was slight. Hemingway was certain that one day someone would understand his stories were not slight sketches. Early the next morning they caught the connecting train to Pamplona where they had reservations in the Hotel La Perla on the plaza, its cool, high-ceiling rooms darkened by heavy wooden shutters above the narrow back street where the bulls made their morning run to the Plaza de Toros. The town was quiet as they strolled through the square of the Plaza de la Constitución—the madness of San Fermín was ten days away—and on to the great bullring a hundred meters to the south. The next morning Ernest stood in a line to renew their seats to the bullfights and secured five new ones, most of them ringside, for the gang that was coming down: Chink, McAlmon, George O'Neil, Donald Ogden Stewart, and Dos Passos with his new girlfriend, Crystal Ross. There were five bullfights and a Prueba, which tested the bulls for fierceness of breeding. They then left Pamplona (not yet going to Burguete to fish for trout in the ageless mountain streams), taking the train to Madrid and attending bullfights late in the afternoons, eating late suppers in modest cafes with good wine and Spanish brandy, in the mornings drinking strong black coffee to start another day. Then they took the train back to Pamplona where their friends were waiting (Sally and Bill Bird coming down at the last moment) for the festival about to explode.

Beginning with a bang, the festival went nonstop for days. The weather was good. Ernest loved Spain and the people and the running of the bulls and encouraged all players assembled to enjoy the festival, watch the corridas, and participate with an enthusiasm to match his own. The Riau-Riau with the drumming and piping and parades of giant papier-mâché figures bobbing along every afternoon filled the streets. There were prolonged lunches and dinners with much wine, fireworks in

---

16. Michael Reynolds, *Hemingway: The Paris Years*, 211.

the square at night, and drinking and dancing in the street night and day. Sleep was not deliberate but happened when it happened, and then they were back on their feet drinking and eating and celebrating some more. Don Stewart caught the mood of the crowd and danced and clowned with a comic reverie understood by the Spaniards wearing garlands of garlic and drinking cheap wine from goatskin bags shaped like animals and small ships of the sea that they held at arm's length and squeezed into their mouths. In the melee the group from Paris lost each other, wandered with strangers, spilled red wine on their shirts drinking from proffered botas, and then, without effort, found each other on the plaza as if it were planned. The feverish activity matched Ernest's energy. The first *encierro* came when the bulls are released to run through the town down the narrow boarded cobblestone street to corrals by the bullring, closing the gap between the hundreds of boys and young men in red scarves and white shirts rushing ahead: "a few got butted or knocked against the walls by an excited and bewildered bull," remembered McAlmon, "but no one was badly injured or killed as is sometimes the case."[17] But on the last day of this fiesta one of the bulls did gore a twenty-two-year-old man from a nearby town, who died of his wound the next day.

Each morning, Ernest cajoled his friends into joining him in the amateur ring after the bull-run. Most of the men, not Bird and Dos Passos, were in the crowded arena by seven when the young or defective bulls with leather padded horns let the amateur bullfighters test their mettle. Ernest talked a lot about courage, believed he had to prove himself, and shouting "Huh, toro, toro," grabbed the padded horns of a bull calf and bulldogged the animal to the ground. Matadors Maera and Algabeno were standing by and coached Ernest and some of the boys in their efforts. George O' Neil took pictures and captured Ernest in action leading a bull with a cape. Hemingway claimed he was gored in a letter to O'Brien, but actually it was Don Stewart who got hurt when a young bull charged him full force and fractured two of his ribs. The story made the Madrid papers and was picked up by the *Chicago Tribune*, which

---

17. Robert McAlmon, *Being Geniuses Together*, 244.

headlined a front-page story of the incident, claiming, "BULL GORES 2 YANKS ACTING AS TOREADORS."[18] When Dr. Hemingway inquired, someone at the paper cabled him: "The Bull rushed for Stewart, lifted him on his horns, tossed him over, threw him into the air, and later tried to gore him. Hemingway rushed to rescue his comrade and was also gored, but saved on account of the horn bandages."[19] The *Toronto Star* printed a photograph of Ernest and Hadley with the same misinformation as the *Tribune*. Hemingway had only come to the aid of Stewart and neither had been gored; but, even before he was famous, such falsely reported incidents helped to build his legend.

The corridas began late in the afternoon. Ernest wrote to Ezra Pound, "The Plaza [de toros] is the only remaining place where valor and art can combine for success."[20] Sally was horrified by what she saw in the ring and wouldn't go again. Chink Dorman-Smith suffered from the sight of the horses gored at his first fight but then understood the spectacle was a death struggle on the sand in the ring and became deeply interested in the technical aspects. Dos Passos, Don Stewart, Bob McAlmon, and young George O'Neil each absorbed it in their own way, "but no one of us ever became the fervid enthusiast which Hemingway elected to become,"[21] wrote McAlmon.

From the *barrera* seats, Ernest could see the shadow crossing the matador's face as the bull closely passed and the bone whiteness of his face afterward. Not even Hadley understood how important the bullring was to Ernest, who after the fiesta wrote to Pound greatly exaggerating his participation in the bullring, saying Algabeno offered him a job as a picador. He lied out of his need to test himself and his admiration for bullfighters. With his bum right knee, Ernest was even more heavy-footed than when he had tried hard to be a football hero at Oak Park High, but part of him had never grown up and relinquished his boy's dream of heroic action. In the bullring, civilization and its charades fell away, leaving only a man and his skills fortified by courage and a sense of honor. Honor and courage were

18. *Chicago Tribune*, July 29, 1924.
19. Reynolds, *Hemingway: The Paris Years*, 214.
20. EH to EP, July 19, 1924, *The Letters of Ernest Hemingway, Vol. 2.*
21. McAlmon, *Being Geniuses Together*, 246.

something lost in the violence and brutality of the war, but there they were in the afternoon sun in the bullring, reinforcing his boyhood dreams of courageous action; dreams spawned by his grandfathers who had fought in the Civil War, by Teddy Roosevelt's Rough Riders, and the long shadows of the frontiersmen. It was not easy to explain this to his friends because many did not care about dying—and death was something Ernest had come close to experiencing and he knew it—and they felt sorry for the gored horses. In Pamplona, Ernest saw the art of bullfighting clearly: he understood it was the artistry of death, and he needed the bulls to study his own mortality. One could not face a mortar shell bravely: it simply happened. But in the ring, nothing happened simply; there, one's whole life was visible in the afternoon's artful death. As he studied the moves closely, getting to know them by heart, a story began forming in his head, an even longer one than the one on the river, but he wouldn't let it go too far yet.

McAlmon and the Birds left Pamplona early, taking an old bus to Burguete, the small Basque village in the Pyrenees by the ancient site of Roncesvalles, the setting of the twelfth-century epic *La Chanson des Roland,* near the French border about thirty miles northeast of Pamplona. The rest of the gang soon followed, their nerves frayed from the partying and their stomachs acidic from all the wine. There was only one small inn. The houses and buildings were white stucco with red roofs and shutters; sheep and goats grazed in the hills; peasants rode mules along the narrow roads and pine trees in the higher mountain reaches. After the melee of the fiesta, the country seemed unnaturally peaceful. They relaxed for five days, packing picnic lunches, taking long hikes, and visiting the metal-roofed monastery at Roncesvalles. One night, Chink discussed the tactics of Roland, who had died bravely in the high pass into France. Ernest proposed a fishing trip to the Irati River a few kilometers away. They hiked through a forest of thick-trunk beech trees and across mountain ridges to the river where in the cold stream the fishing was good. Ernest wrote to his mother, "Hadley and I got seven nice big ones one afternoon . . . The trout run from 3 to 15 pounds."[22]

---

22. EH to GHH, July 18, 1924, *The Letters of Ernest Hemingway, Vol. 2.*

Actually, Ernest was less happy than he might have been and showed a growing depression. Partly, it was a letdown from the week of unnaturally sustained high festival emotions, but it was also because he thought Hadley might be pregnant again, for her monthly flow of blood was late. He moped and made Hadley feel terrible, telling her that at his age it would be no fun if they had more children. Finally Sally Bird, angry and protective of Hadley, told him, "Stop acting like a damn fool and crybaby. You're responsible too."[23] Ernest retreated into oppressive silence. He continued to be grim company; there were tears in Hadley's eyes. The Birds left for Paris on July seventeenth, and on a final afternoon Chink, Dos Passos, young George O'Neil, and McAlmon set off on a hike to the principality of Andorra on the border about two-hundred-and-fifty miles to the east. Walking ahead as they left, Ernest waved back to Hadley who sat at a table on a terrace. After he passed, she overheard Dos Passos say to Dorman-Smith, "What a wonderful lad that was," and Chink answered, "Yes, Ernest was a wonderful lad." Hadley thought that "what Chink meant was he thought Ernest was going wrong, that he was changing, turning mean. And it made me sick because things like that began to be said about him."[24] After a few miles, Ernest turned back to be with Hadley, who everyone did think was pregnant. That evening her period began, much to her relief and to Ernest's chagrin for being such a bastard about it. No longer feeling guilty, she looked at Ernest in a new light. He had made her feel like a worthless drag on his life. It was not a good revelation, nor did the space between them immediately close.

Alone in Burguete and barely speaking to Hadley, Ernest vented his depression in a letter to Ezra. "The Spanish side of the Pyranees [sic]," he wrote, "is a good place to observe the ruin of my finances and literary career." He complained about a lack of money, which wasn't true, and blamed Ford for an inability to write. "I've tried and tried and can't go on with the thing [Big Two-Hearted River] that was 2/3 done and running smooth when he said I had to run the magazine . . . The Transatlantic killed my chances of having a book published this fall." Whipping

---

23. Reynolds, *Hemingway: The Paris Years*, 219.
24. Mowrer, Sokoloff tapes, Hemingway Collection, JFK Library.

himself deeper into a depression, he even complained about Joyce, "the more meazly [*sic*] and shitty the guy, I.E. Joyce, the greater the success in his art," (who, in actuality, was a gentleman if ever there was, and much admired by Hemingway), and also claimed, "I am going to have to quit writing and I will never have a book published." Ezra would remain his friend, but it's not known how he felt about the letter, and he must have wondered who Hemingway meant when he wrote near the ending, "These god damn bastards."[25]

For all his boyish charm and enthusiasm for life, Ernest also had a hair-trigger temper and mean habit of picking on those weaker, smaller, or more vulnerable than himself. Sometimes it was beyond his control, an irrational response for which he often apologized the next day. Moods came and went like a summer storm, an anger welling up in him, and those in the path of an outburst were stunned as if struck by lightning. Sometimes it was more of a darkness that grew slowly inside that he was unable to shake. Growing up, he had been frightened by the sudden mood shifts of his father, but he did not yet recognize how much his own temperament was becoming like his father.

With the departure of the summer men and the scare of Hadley's pregnancy, his mood dipped briefly and then bobbed up to another high, for after writing Ezra he unpacked the story of Nick on the river and began working again. This time he let Nick think out loud, putting into the draft all he knew about Paris and Pamplona and even his theory about writing. He would cut these thoughts from the final version, but it helped him move the story along. He let Nick think about the wonderful Cezannes on Gertrude's walls and the others he had seen in galleries and museums; he created the landscape by imagining how Cezanne might paint it and make it come alive with words. When Nick stepped down into the stream the water was cold and real and he waded across the stream as though moving through a painting. His stories were growing again, and as the fictional persona of Nick he wrote, "He wanted to get back to camp and get to work." For there was a desire to write about

---

25. EH to EP, July 19, 1924, *The Letters of Ernest Hemingway, Vol. 2*.

the old gang at Walloon Lake, the summer people he had lost when he married Hadley and pursued a career. In San Sebastián on July 27, the Hemingways boarded the train to Paris, tired, tanned, and missing Bumby. Ernest was over his depression and was eager to write and work on his book of stories.

Paris was hot and full of American tourists. Sweating profusely, Ernest carried their luggage up the stairs into the stifling apartment. The Olympics were over, and they had sublet the apartment probably for more than they paid in rent. Eating a light dinner in a café, Ernest read "Rambles through Literary Paris," Eugene Jolas's column in the *Sunday Tribune*, and found himself mentioned at the bottom of the page with a back-handed compliment from Ford Madox Ford, who was quoted as saying that most young American writers wrote with a kind of delusional disorder that "is the direct product of repressive legislation in the United States," which he thought would cease when such legislation was repealed, and he regarded "Mr. Ernest Hemingway as the most representative of the young American novelists writing today."[26] Ernest knew Ford talked indiscreetly, but he didn't like him talking about him and especially didn't like him calling him a novelist when he had not yet written a novel. The antagonism he felt toward Ford was one-sided, for, despite his drastic changes to the August issue of the *Transatlantic Review*, when they next saw each other, Ford was glad to see him. Nathan Asch thought that Hemingway personified "the image of the young bulls against the old bulls . . . who could not function unless he fought and destroyed older men."[27] Hemingway's need to attack others, especially in words, may have also come from his own divided self, for he was never easy in those early years with his own literary identity. Always he reached out for the active, physical life, refusing to give control to the sedentary, contemplative role of a writer.

Collecting his mail the next morning at Sylvia's, there was another rejected story returned from an American magazine. When he entered Bill Bird's print shop, he found Ford in a slump. Returning empty-handed

---

26. Reynolds, *Hemingway: The Paris Years*, 223.
27. Reynolds, 184.

from America, where John Quinn, the *Transatlantic*'s initial investor, was dying of cancer, the magazine was out of money. While Hemingway was in Spain, Ford had inserted a last-minute editorial note into the magazine wryly accusing Ernest of stuffing the August issue with an "unusually large sample"[28] of his young American friends and promising that future issues would resume the international content. Ernest was enraged. He felt he had made a considerable sacrifice helping Ford out when he left for America. But after all the rejections from American magazines, the *Transatlantic* remained Hemingway's best chance for publication and he also felt obligated to continue serializing *The Making of Americans*, and so when Ford came around to see him, mumbling an apology and pointing out that the magazine was almost broke and would become either a quarterly or cease publication, Hemingway swallowed his wrath and said he knew a man who might help. Krebs Friend, the strange and lonely man who had worked with Ernest on the *Co-operative Commonwealth* magazine in Chicago, had married a very wealthy almost elderly woman and was living in Paris and wanted to be part of the literary scene. Hemingway talked to Krebs, and he and his wife agreed to advance Ford two hundred dollars a month for six months. Krebs was named president of the review at a directors meeting in August, and so while Krebs and his wife wrote "letters" that were of no particular merit that appeared within its pages, the *Transatlantic* was able to continue on a little while longer.

Ernest begrudgingly agreed to write a "Pamplona Letter" for the September issue, though it was another interruption to his fiction. He had finished "Big Two-Hearted River" and was working intensely another long story about the summer people at the lake that he would soon finish and call "Summer People." In the middle of August, he wrote to Gertrude and Alice, "I have finished two long short stories, one of them not much good, and the other very good." The "very good" story was "Big Two-Hearted River," where "I'm trying to do the country like Cezanne and having a hell of a time and sometimes getting it a little bit. It's about 100 pages long and nothing happens and the country is

---

28. *The Transatlantic Review, Vol. II*, August 1924.

swell, I made it all up."[29] The one he said that was "not much good" was "Summer People," which, in fact, is a very good sensual story with much more character development than "Big Two-Hearted River," but he felt too personal about it to ever show to anyone during his life for it told of a fellow named Wemedge who has sexual intercourse with a girl named Katy in the woods under a hemlock tree, and though that may or may not have actually happened in the summers of his youth, his close friends would know the characters. "Isn't writing a hard job though," he continued in the letter. "It used to be easy before I met you. I certainly was bad, Gosh, I'm awfully bad now but it's a different kind of bad."[30] The Pamplona letter he wrote for Ford had personal complaints and was not very good; "when you destroy the valuable things you have by writing about them," he wrote, "you want to get big money for it,"[31] but Ford published it anyway.

On August 3, 1924, Ford's great collaborator and mentor, Joseph Conrad, died in England. Ford hastily gathered memorials from young contributors who happened to be in Paris to place as a supplement in the September issue of the *Transatlantic*. Some, like Robert McAlmon, regarded Conrad as part of the old literary establishment and felt no particular debt and had not much good to say, but not Hemingway, who loved the smooth scale of emotions and the testing of values in the old master's stories that were an important influence on his own ideals of fiction: take a man away from his supporting society, set him down in a foreign country, and see if his values hold up. Still, Ford's burst of sentiment made Ernest a little sick—why not let the man die with dignity instead of writing memorials he would never read—and the piece he wrote for Ford was a gut-level response that savaged critics who might think it fashionable to disparage Conrad now that he was dead. Citing how easy it was to make a mistake in their eyes, he slighted his friend, the experimental composer in dissonant music, George Antheil, by writing "I was made to feel how easily one might be dropped from the party . . . when

29. EH to Gertrude and Alice, Aug. 15, 1924, *The Letters of Ernest Hemingway, Vol. 2.*
30. EH to G & A, Aug. 15, 1924, *The Letters of Ernest Hemingway, Vol. 2.*
31. *The Transatlantic Review, Vol. II*, September 1924.

speaking of George Antheil that I preferred my Stravinsky straight," and insulted Pound's other great prodigy, T. S. Eliot, with the claim that some would now think him a better writer than Conrad, but "If I knew that by grinding Mr. Eliot into fine dry powder and sprinkling that powder over Mr. Conrad's grave Mr. Conrad would shortly appear . . . I would leave for London tomorrow morning with a sausage grinder . . . you cannot couple T. S. Eliot and Joseph Conrad in a sentence seriously . . . and not laugh."[32]

Ford Madox Ford did not quite know what to do with this sensitive, ebullient, and often overbearing young writer so quick to take insults, real or imagined. The editor ran the piece anyway, without changing a word, but in a subsequent issue did apologize for the blood thirstiness of the unnamed chronicler who had attacked Eliot, a public apology that infuriated Hemingway. Though he remained highly critical of the older writer/editor and would-be mentor, telling Gertrude and Alice that "Ford is an absolute liar and crook always motivated by the finest synthetic English gentility,"[33] it was practically impossible to avoid him because Ford, an inveterate party giver, was the center of expatriate life in Paris, and though bumbling in his affections, would never bear a grudge for long. When he returned from America empty-handed, he had every reason to dismiss his subeditor from the literary house on Quai d'Anjou after his barbed editorial insults, but instead, in his "Chronique" he wrote, "During our absence . . . this review has been ably edited by Mr. Ernest Hemingway, the admirable Young American prose writer,"[34] and would accept two more of Hemingway's stories for publication in the *Transatlantic Review*. Ford did have an attitude of superiority that often rubbed against people, especially Hemingway, but Ernest's editorial judgment was nearly always good, for Eugene Jolas declared in his literary column that the August number of the *Transatlantic* was "one of the best edited issues of this interesting magazine . . . for which Ernest Hemingway, the young romancer, is responsible."[35]

32. *The Transatlantic Review, Vol. II*, September 1924.
33. EH to G & A, Oct. 10, 1924, *The Letters of Ernest Hemingway, Vol. 2*.
34. Kenneth Lynn, *Hemingway*, 235.
35. Reynolds, *Hemingway: The Paris Years*, 231.

Before the Conrad supplement was printed, Ernest sent Antheil the proof sheet offering to cut his comment. "If you don't want this in about you," he wrote in the note that he dropped at Sylvia's, where George lived in the apartment above the shop, "bring it around to my place . . . and I'll cut it out . . . Figured that any publicity was publicity . . . You probably don't give a damn. But you might."[36] Igor Stravinsky, the modernist composer of the *Rite of Spring*, once George Antheil's idol, had become a nemesis against whose work the diminutive musician pushed his dissonant music to almost unbearable lengths. When he read the proof sheet from Ernest he was upset and angry and composed a letter that he gave to Sylvia calling Hemingway "a fake artist" and that "dumb people must have something to talk about and appear smart. Hemingway is among the dumbest."[37]

If Ernest learned about Antheil's remarks he didn't bother to reply. It was a snipe typical of the bitchy Left Bank interplay. For, despite Montparnasse's image of eccentric artists encouraging each other within a bohemian community, in reality it was a hotbed of gossip, backstabbing, and egotism. The Quarter's finer moments, with much retelling, have taken on a nostalgic glow that does not erase the dark rumors, snide remarks, and insulting behavior that always flourished on the Boulevard. Nor by the early mid-Twenties was it any longer an inexpensive haven for struggling artists, for American tourists and permanent expatriates were pricing it out of the artists' reach. The great cafes—the Dome, the Rotonde, the Dingo, and Select—were now part of the sow for Rotarians from Peoria, Illinois. The great and famous artists like Picasso, Pound, and Joyce were sighted and pointed out to hardware salesmen from Cleveland, Ohio, who didn't know their work. The truly outrageous among them, like Flossie Martin, became loud, drunken sideshows for the tourist to talk about in Topeka. Even McAlmon was known to vomit decorously in front of the cafes, and if he paled there was the sad-faced journalist Harold Stearns, reputed to be writing an expose of the Left Bank American colony, holding down his bar stool at the Select with

36. EH to George Antheil, August, 1924, *The Letters of Ernest Hemingway, Vol. 2*.
37. Reynolds, *Hemingway: The Paris Years*, 227.

unpaid saucers piling up before him. Sometimes a startled onlooker paid the bill so he could tell the story back home in the States.

Ernest worked hard at his writing amidst the world close around him. Bumby was cutting teeth and crying a lot more. Madame Chautard had found her small dog dead in the courtyard, and after accusing neighbors of poisoning the animal (an autopsy revealed it had been run over), had a taxidermist stuff and mount the dog as a sentimental trophy, never dreaming that one day soon her writer tenant upstairs would obliquely immortalize the creature in American Literature. Hemingway thought about the women he saw in the Quarter and how they would be in bed. Many brushed up against him in the dark and flirted at the Dome. Everywhere he looked there were desirable women. Fornication among those he knew appeared as casual as a shared drink.

Sometimes he played tennis with Harold Loeb on the small, rented court near the Sante Prison, where Ford sometimes joined in mixed doubles. Hemingway's game was based on strength, not agility. As Hadley remembered, "he couldn't run very fast because of his injured knee. Some of his shots were awkward because of his blind eye and every time he missed a shot he would sizzle."[38] Loeb reiterated, "He was a lousy tennis player and hated to miss a shot. But he was so exuberant you never had a lackadaisical game."[39] With Ernest, nothing was lackadaisical. As Henry Strater said, "He liked to win everything."[40]

Through August he worked on the review and on his own fiction. As the month ended in torrential rains, driving tourists away from the sidewalk cafes, Ernest could look out his window, rightly pleased with himself; despite his ranting during the summer, he had almost completed his book of stories. Of twelve stories written, several were brief and one, "Up in Michigan," was still unprintable. To lengthen the manuscript, he decided to interleave the stories with the vignettes from *in our time* and by mid-September would split "Big Two-Hearted River" into two parts and recast the vignettes about the nurse in Milan and the Bolshevik on

38. Reynolds, *Hemingway: The Paris Years*, 231.
39. Reynolds, 231.
40. Reynolds, 231.

the Italian train into stories, "A Very Short Story" and "The Revolution-ist," and in the hope of defeating censors, intended to publish "Up in Michigan" as the first story of the book. "I have written 14 stories and have a book ready to publish," he wrote to Edward O'Brien. "One of the chapters of the *in our time* I sent you comes in between each story . . . All the stories have a certain unity . . . and in between each one comes bang! the In Our Time – It should be awfully good I think."[41]

The book was experimental and very original, written with a tough, ironic style. Hemingway intended for it to be a structured book and not merely a collection of stories. Written under the influences of Paris and the great modern vanguard of Joyce, Pound, and Stein, it would take a distinctive place in Modern Literature. The invention of Nick Adams, whose life would roughly parallel but not intersect with the life of young Hemingway, was one of the most vital inspirations of his career. For through this character Hemingway could acknowledge fear and failure, lust and tenderness, and a more measured understanding of his parents; a sensitive and perhaps more intellectual persona that the author seldom allowed himself to be in life. Hemingway regarded "Big Two-Hearted River" as the climactic story of *In Our Time*; it would allow the readers to understand that Nick was the writer who had written the earlier stories and make them want to reread the whole collection with this in mind. Gertrude Stein wrote that she was glad he was doing a fishing story and wanted "awfully to read it."[42] She would be flattered by the influence he declared she had upon his writing. Modern writing, she thought, should not have traditional narrative forms or be concerned with a conventional beginning, middle, and end of a story. She claimed that in the three most important novels of her generation—Proust's *Remembrance of Things Past*, Joyce's *Ulysses*, and her own *The Making of Americans*—"there is, in none of them, a story."[43]

In Hemingway's fishing story, there is only the slow motion of description; moments of tedious compulsive detail followed by moments

---

41. EH to Edward O'Brien, Sept. 12, 1924, *The Letters of Ernest Hemingway, Vol. 2*.
42. James R. Mellow, *Hemingway: A Life Without Consequences*, 271.
43. Mellow, 271.

of surprising lyricism and the sense of ongoing immediacy; a continuous sense of presence that Stein claimed was another condition of modern writing. Nick Adams, the only human character in the story, is a man escaping his past, a man with a need to leave everything behind him, "the need for thinking, the need to write, other needs,"[44] and in meticulous detail Hemingway records the progress of his journey through the landscape. How he builds a camp and cooks a dinner. The moments of real action, such as when he loses a big trout in deep water, stand out sharply. In a story presumably without climax, the incident is the climactic moment. The story ends with Nick returning to the security of his camp perusing about the swamp he had decided not to fish that day: "There were plenty of days coming when he could fish the swamp."[45]

He completed the story in September, ending it with eleven pages of ruminations on life, art, and letters as Nick Adams remembers the Cezannes he had seen in Gertrude's studio and in museums. Nick, too, assessed his contemporaries: Joyce was too damn romantic and intellectual about his hero; it was easy to write if you used tricks, and Joyce had invented hundreds of new tricks. Nick also offers opinions on E. E. Cummings and Nathan Asch and then turns his sight on his own self as Hemingway: "It was hard to be a great writer if you loved the world and living in it and special people. It was hard when you loved so many places"[46] The ruminations reflect Hemingway: a writer borrowing experiences, situations, using the gossip of other people's lives, creating characters of his own. When Alice and Gertrude returned to Paris, Gertrude read his fishing story, and, referring to the ending as his "little story of meditations"[47] on writers and writing, told him "Hemingway, remarks are not literature;"[48] this, despite the flattering remark ("she'd know it if he ever got things right"[49]) made about her. And she was right that his reflections did not work in the story—years later, in the short story "The

---

44. Ernest Hemingway, *The Nick Adams Stories*, 179.
45. Ernest Hemingway, "Big Two-Hearted River: Part II," *Short Stories of Ernest Hemingway*, 232.
46. Hemingway, *The Nick Adams Stories*, 238.
47. James R. Mellow, *Hemingway: A Life Without Consequences*, 276.
48. Mellow, 276.
49. Hemingway, *The Nick Adams Stories*, 239.

Snows of Kilimanjaro," he would be able to bring the two streams of narrative together, the objective account and the ruminations, as Proust had done in *Remembrance of Things Past*—and he omitted the pages and wrote a new ending. "I got a hell of a shock when I realized how bad it was," he wrote to McAlmon, "and that shocked me back into the river again and I've finished it off the way it ought to have been all along. Just the straight fishing."[50]

---

50. EH to Robert McAlmon, Nov. 1, 1924, *The Letters of Ernest Hemingway, Vol. 2.*

Hotel Burguete

Donald Ogden Stewart

John Dos Passos

Joseph Conrad

Les cafes du Paris

Pamplona Square

George Antheil

Plaza de Toros, Pamplona

Running of the bulls

Transatlantic Review covers

IN OUR TIME

IN A review of *in our time* that appeared in the *Dial*, Edmund Wilson wrote that Ernest Hemingway was "strikingly original," had "almost invented a form of his own," that "his little book has more artistic dignity than any other that has been written by an American about the period of the war," and that along with Gertrude Stein and Sherwood Anderson, he had developed a special skill in using native language to convey "profound emotions and complex states of mind,"[1] and compared the vignettes of the bullfight scenes to Goya lithographs. Ernest wrote Wilson to thank him for the review. "I liked it very much . . . It was cool and clear minded and decent and impersonal and sympathetic," and told him "the stuff gets better. Have finished the book of 14 stories with a chapter [from the vignettes] between each story . . . to give the picture of the whole in between examining it in detail. Like looking with your eyes at something, say a passing coast line [*sic*], and then looking at it with 15X binoculars. Or rather, maybe, looking at it and then going in and living in it—and then coming out and looking at it again," and that the new collection "has a pretty good unity."[2]

What he told Wilson was true, but not really in the way he said it was, for the stories grew not from any rational level but from deep within young Hemingway. The unity came out of recurring violent images and conflict between men and women; a collection of fears and uncertainties done with a cool, ironic detachment, putting forth questions of the time. How should a man behave to be called a man? How can he deal with

---

1. Edmund Wilson, *The Shores of Light: A Literary Chronicle of the Twenties and Thirties*, 119-21.
2. EH to Edmund Wilson, Oct. 18, 1924, *The Letters of Ernest Hemingway, Vol. 2*.

his fears? What must he do to be brave? What is the proper relationship between a man and woman? And at the end, the last story, when Nick stepped into the water painted by Cezanne, the reader knows that Nick is the writer telling all the stories and is forced back to the beginning to read them again in a different light. The vignettes inserted between the stories were not a "picture of the whole"[3] but rose like small dense islands in the stream of the stories, providing a counterpoint to the tales. He was calling his new book *In Our Time*; unlike his book of vignettes, this time he capitalized the first letter of each word. When Don Stewart offered to try to sell it to a publisher, Hemingway sent the manuscript to him at the Yale Club in New York City. Dos Passos also arrived in New York carrying a copy of *Ulysses* along with Ernest's new book. Harold Loeb was eager to assist, too, and thought that if Horace Liveright published the book, as he had Loeb's novel *Doodab*, then he and Ernest could together be the rising stars of this literary firm.

Despite good notices—a laudatory review of O'Brien's *The Best Short Stories of 1923* in the September issue of the *Nation* praised "My Old Man" as "the finest in the collection," calling it "a Rembrandt study, rich of color"—Ernest continued to receive rejections from America. Jean George Nathan returned a story with a note saying, "this story [does not] fit into the general plan that we have for *The American Mercury*. But please don't be discouraged. Don't hesitate to send me whatever you write." Hemingway sent more stories, which were also promptly rejected: "Mencken and I cannot agree on the enclosed pieces of work," wrote Nathan, "but we shall continue to read with the utmost sympathy anything you send in to us."[4] He had sent "Soldier's Home" and "Cross Country Snow" to *Harper's Magazine* short story contest and both were rejected and returned. Daunted and a little depressed, he wondered: If Mencken and *Harper's* couldn't see that his stories worked then maybe they weren't as wonderful as he and Ezra thought. But as fall came upon Paris with cool nights and pleasant days, no matter how discouraged Ernest may have felt about the rejections, or irritated with his work at

---

3. EH to EW, Oct. 18, 1924, *The Letters of Ernest Hemingway, Vol. 2.*
4. Michael Reynolds, *Hemingway: The Paris Years*, 235.

the *Transatlantic*, he could always lose himself among the quays, browsing among the book stalls or watching fishermen bent over their long poles. Even with only small press and little magazine publications to his credit, Hemingway was a recognizable figure within the expatriate community of modern writers in the Quarter where people waved to him in the cafes or introduced themselves or their friends to his usual gracious acknowledgment.

Even where the Hemingways lived was becoming a significant address to those in the know. Jane Heap of the *Little Review* was dining at the carpenter's loft when a gift of Provençal apples arrived from Gertrude and Alice in St. Remy, and Ford and Stella Bowen moved into a place between the Hemingways and the Pounds, making Notre-Dame-des-Champs a most literary street accessible to the café crowd along Montparnasse. The Left Bank had changed since the Hemingways had first arrived. An American bought the old Dingo Bar on rue Delambre, just west of where the boulevards of Montparnasse and Raspail intersected, put in an American menu of hamburgers and chicken fried steaks with mashed potatoes, hired English-speaking waiters, and stayed open all night serving drinks. The hurdy-gurdy organs of the Quarter had vanished to be replaced by jazz bands as the boulevards were thick with Americans, swelling to maybe more than thirty thousand, many too young to have even been in the trenches and not caring what others before them thought, said, or wrote. A show of petticoat was nothing special to this "lost" generation for whom sex was an open topic of conversation. They enjoyed irritating their staid, conservative elders and defended their freedom of speech to say what they wanted, how they wanted, wherever they wanted to say it.

Thus, when to save printing costs at the foundering *Transatlantic* Ford decided to reduce Gertrude Stein's *The Making of Americans* to single type and single spacing, Hemingway pounded his fist on his desk. And when Ford returned the work to a double-spaced format, Hemingway still wanted to know where Gertrude's payments for the last two issues were, and so Ford saw to it that Gertrude was remunerated even though he was no longer a director of his own magazine, that having been taken away by the Krebs, who were funding the magazine on a tight, unworkable financial string. By October, the demise of the magazine was certain. "I believe the magazine is going to Go to hell on or about the first of Jan,"[5] Ernest wrote to Gertrude and Alice, blaming it mostly on Ford, who was probably relieved at the coming conclusion of his review. Ford's good manners wearing thin by continual harassment from Hemingway, his own rueful complaint to Miss Stein was that as editor he was "a sort of green baize swing door" that everyone kicked "on entering or leaving"[6] the office on the Quai D'Anjou. Still, on the surface, Ford Madox Ford continued to express admiration for Ernest Hemingway and published two more of his stories in the review.

Ernest was having a good fall. Amused by the good-natured skewering about his increasingly bohemian appearance when Marjorie Reed wrote in her "Paris Fashions" letter in the November *Transatlantic* that "some smart dressers are following the lead of Mr. Hemingway, the young American writer and mateodor [sic], who favors the beret for general use in literary circles,"[7] he knew that any publicity was good publicity. The same issue carried "The Doctor and the Doctor's Wife," and the December issue, which was the final issue, published "Cross-Country Snow." Hemingway found another outlet for his work in a German magazine, *Der Querschnitt (Cross Section)*, edited by a man named Count Alfred von Wedderkop, who liked some of Ernest's bawdy poems and bought four of them for the magazine. The Hemingways met Wedderkop in October at a dinner at the Pounds' and were impressed by his opposition to pretense in the arts. "[Wedderkop] I'm afraid is crazy but is a wonderful guy,"[8] wrote Hemingway to a friend. (Alas, Wedderkop, though he made fun of Hitler, did encourage the kind of anti-Semitism that led to the Holocaust.) Printing full-frontal nude photographs, satires, and caricatures of a curious German taste, *Der Querschnitt* was open and international in a way that the *Transatlantic* never had been. One of the

5. EH to Gertrude & Alice, Oct. 10, 1924, *The Letters of Ernest Hemingway, Vol. 2.*
6. Carlos Baker, *Hemingway: A Life*, 176.
7. Reynolds, *Hemingway: The Paris Years*, 240.
8. EH to Bill Smith, Jan. 9, 1925, *The Letters of Ernest Hemingway, Vol. 2.*

profane poems by Hemingway that it published was a satirical comment on perceived current fashions:

> Democracy is the shit.
> Relativity is the shit.
> Dictators are the shit.
> Menken is the shit.
> Waldo Frank is the shit.
> The Broom is the shit.
> Dada is the shit.
> Dempsey is the shit.
> This is not a complete list.

Hemingway's language could be blunt and vulgar. Harold Loeb's girlfriend, Kitty Cannell, found him personally attractive with very white teeth, rosy cheeks, and a sudden dimpled smile, and though outwardly they got on well, she never liked him. She thought he was a good companion with a wild sense of humor, except about himself, and his word portraits of fellow expatriates were both funny and devastating, but she felt beneath the attractive exterior there ran a streak of vicious cruelty. She warned Harold that he had a way of turning against those who befriended him and to be careful. Harold paid no heed; he thought Ernest was a natural man and remained his friend. At least once, when Loeb could get loose from Kitty, he went with Ernest to the fight at the Cirque de Paris. He didn't much enjoy the fight because it brought back memories of his boxing coach at Princeton, Spider Kelly, a memory he, no doubt, shared with Ernest, but he enjoyed the drinking afterward and listening to Ernest's post-fight analysis. Ernest absorbed everything and had a precise memory of details. He had recently read fight stories by Ring Lardner where there was always an angle or fix of some sort that made the fiction work, and he thought he could use it in his fiction too. Harold Loeb loved Hemingway and enjoyed their friendship. Maybe his good manners and Ivy League schooling took the edge off his sensors because he failed to see how competitive Ernest was. Harold beat him so regularly on the tennis courts that he must have thought Ernest always lost with grace. He could not have been more wrong.

When New York publishers Boni & Liveright accepted Loeb's novel *Doodab*, he ecstatically told everyone, including Hemingway, about his good fortune. When the firm sent Leon Fleischman to Paris as a scout, Harold wanted to help Hemingway. It would be fine, he thought, for the two of them to be published by the same firm. So, one night, he and Kitty took Ernest to Fleischman's apartment off the Champs Elysees where his wife, Helen, answered the door and let them in. Ernest was dressed in his shabby patched jacket. "It seemed to me that Hem disliked Leon on sight," remembered Loeb. Ernest remained quiet and staring as Kitty and Helen made congenial small talk. "What a beautiful apartment" and "I'm sure you'll love Paris," declared Kitty. Finally, Fleischman opened up and said he had heard that Hemingway was a coming writer. "I would like to read your stories," he said, "and if they're as good as Harold says they are, I will send them on to Horace [Liveright] with my recommendation . . . Horace knows it pays to accept my advice." Hardly making a response, Ernest sipped his drink and grinned boyishly as the tension in the room kept building. "I squirmed," remembered Harold. "I seemed to be hearing Leon with Hem's ears, and everything he said sounded precious, supercilious, affected." Loeb told a joke to lighten the mood, and when they had left and were out on the street, said to Hemingway, "He wants to send your stuff on, all right;" Kitty adding, "Fleischman is quite intelligent, don't you think?"[9]

Ernest exploded. "Double god damned kikes,"[10] he muttered. As he strode away toward Montparnasse, Kitty and Harold were both upset. "Well, baby, there's your future friend," Kitty remembered saying to Harold. "Oh no," Harold replied. "If Hem thought of me as a Jew he wouldn't have spoken that way in front of me. He used the word as I might say mick or dago. It doesn't mean a thing." Kitty wasn't at all so sure, but Harold, further defending Hemingway, thought Fleischman had been too patronizing. "Patronize your superiors if you like," he said,

9. Harold Loeb, *The Way It Was*, 226-7.
10. Reynolds, *Hemingway: The Paris Years*, 242.

"but not some poor bloke who has come to you with his life's efforts . . . You can write without a publisher, but you can't publish without a writer," adding, "Leon talks down to people probably because of an insecurity he developed in childhood. It isn't fair, but there's no fairness in nature. Justice is a human imposition."[11] Ernest did send Fleischman a copy of his manuscript and, probably without reading it, Fleischman sent it on to Horace Liveright.

In the *Transatlantic*, Ernest published the poems of a raunchily dressed twenty-year-old scion of a wealthy Philadelphia family named Evan Biddle Shipman, whose excuse for hanging around Paris was that a magazine called *The American Horse Breeder* had asked him to serve as European correspondent. An alcoholic, Evan had a casual elegance that Ernest enjoyed, and they drank together and became close friends. Hemingway also patiently poured over the short stories of Nathan Asch and had them published in the *Transatlantic*, too. But few in Paris escaped his barbs, and behind the backs of Shipman and Asch, he told McAlmon a malicious tale about a fight they supposedly had for half an hour with each emerging unmarked. He continued to be hard on T. S. Eliot, alluding to the heavy uncut pages of his quarterly, the *Criterion*, even changing the name of his short story about the infertile homosexual marriage to "Mr. and Mrs. Eliot." He also poked fun at his dear friend Ezra by gleefully noting that when the Pounds gave up their studio down the street to move to Rapallo, Ezra contrived a small nervous breakdown to avoid the work of packing up.

A strong motivation for creativity was Hemingway's disdain for pretentious, inadequate behavior, an unendearing trait that was as powerful as its opposite emotion, the admiration he had for courage such as Chink Dorman-Smith fighting at Mons, or Maera killing bulls in the Plaza de Toros. Many fragments of the literature of gossip found their way into his blue notebooks. He wrote about Ford and Stella bickering over the wine at the Negre de Toulouse; the overweight girl who had come to Paris on their boat from New York City to study piano and, if possible,

---

11. Bertram Sarason, *Hemingway and the Sun Set*, 148.

have an affair, but after a year she was still a virgin listening through the wall of her apartment to the sounds of others making love. And he did a sketch about Bertram Hartman, an American painter friend who met a German girl who made hooked rugs from Bertram's designs that remained unsold because the prices were too high. As Edmund Wilson had shrewdly observed in his review, "Mr. Hemingway [was] not a propagandist even for humanity."[12]

As chilly rains swept through November, Ernest continued his busy literary life with almost manic energy. The mail brought *Harper's* rejection of "Cross-Country Snow" and delivered the newest *Querschnitt* with two of his poems, "The Soul of Spain" and "The Lady Poets with Footnotes," which he had written in Rapallo the previous year after listening to McAlmon's gossip. He continued writing well, sometimes in the evening at home, sometimes at his back table at the Closerie des Lilas. By Armistice Day, November 11, Ford had given up on the *Transatlantic* and scornfully wrote in his last editorial "we issue what we will as irritatingly as possible style a Children's Number,"[13] for Hemingway's editorial clout had increased as Ford's diminished and young American writers overran the final issue. Ernest published two poems by Evan Shipman, his own short story, "Cross-Country Snow," (which began "The funicular car bucked once more and then stopped. It could not go further, the snow drifted solidly across the track"[14]), and stories by Don Stewart, Nathan Asch, Bob McAlmon, Ivan Beede, and Jean Rhys (a beautiful young novelist whom Ford, despite his desultory position with the review and situation with Stella Bowen, managed to seduce, to Hemingway's surprise and wonder, after coaching her in the finer points of creative writing).

In the middle of the month, Eugene Jolas published "An Open Letter to Ernest Hemingway" in his weekly *Tribune* column, "Rambles Through Literary Paris," giving further good notice to Ernest Hemingway. "Dear Hemingway," Jolas wrote, "you have one of the most genuinely epic

---

12. Baker, *Hemingway: A Life*, 176.
13. *The Transatlantic Review, Vol. II*, December 1924.
14. Ernest Hemingway, *Short Stories of Ernest Hemingway*, 183.

talents of any youngster writing in English today . . . in our opinion, you were destined to create a new literature on the American continent . . . To be brief, we like most of your stories . . . Now, we have just picked up Der Querschnitt and noticed two of your poems . . . We ain't able to follow you there . . . Please give us another 'My Old Man' and let it go at that."[15] Such praise, even when backhanded, thrilled the Hemingways, making them feel more certain their financial situation would improve through his writing.

Ernest, trying to keep his caustic tongue in check, answered in the column with an open letter of his own. "The two poems . . . were not intended to be serious and were written three years ago and a year and a half ago respectively. So if my writing is going bad it must have been going bad for some time . . . I have a son who was born in Canada. Perhaps he is the Hemingway you were thinking of when you referred to talented youngsters . . . If you would like to read some new stories in manuscript to ease your mind as to my present spiritual and mental state . . . there is a long bullfight story you might like."[16]

The bullfight story, "The Undefeated," he began in September and completed by November 20. It tells the story of the aging matador, Manuel Garcia, wanting to make a comeback in the Plaza de Toros in Madrid in the hot summer of 1918. In his comeback the matador is destroyed but not defeated, a theme in which Hemingway very much believed. It was a much longer story than usual, a distillation of all he had learned about bullfighting, and Ernest was full of shy admiration for it. He had worked on it a while and wrote it with subtle repercussions that reflected the reality of life being hard and unglamorous though often seen as otherwise. His spirits were buoyant, his writing seemed to improve each week, and he thought the stories would never stop coming. At Sylvia's there was always a warm stove and literary magazines and conversation to catch up on. With the *Transatlantic Review* dead, he saw little of Ford and that was fine. He could always find a chair at Gertrude's late in the

15. Baker, *Hemingway: The Paris Years*, 245.
16. EH to Eugene Jolas, mid-November, 1924, *The Letters of Ernest Hemingway, Vol. 2*.

afternoon. Alice was less and less cordial, but he was always polite, never failing to mention how sweet and fine were her cookies and cakes.

By mid-November, Hadley's dividend checks replenished their bank account. They repaid small loans from McAlmon and Gertrude and had enough to keep going until the next summer. Ernest performed one of his customary but usually unremembered kindnesses by being tender and supportive to Dorothy Butler (Lewis Galantiere's fiancée, whom neither he nor Hadley liked) when her mother died: "I was touched with your sweetness and sympathy,"[17] wrote Dorothy in return. With Bumby still cutting teeth, Ernest read books on the sleepless nights, often about explorers on the North Pole risking their lives, for, despite the war's disillusioning affect about heroes and heroism, in his mind, the age of heroic action was never dead, a feeling he would express more subtly in the realism of his fiction.

McAlmon wanted a new unpublished short story for his *Contact Collection of Contemporary Writers*. Hemingway complained to McAlmon that after finishing "The Undefeated" he was "having a period of not being able to do anything worth a shit"[18]: he knew that to be in the same book as Joyce he would have to publish something so good that reviewers would compare him favorably to the Irish prince of Modernism. He was not worried; there were no dark moods this time, for soon he would be high in the Austrian Alps in the little town of Schruns, where he was told by his friend, Bertram Hartman, the living was cheaper than Switzerland and there were far fewer tourists. There was plenty to do before leaving Paris: the apartment had to be sublet for the three months they would be gone, Mme. Rohrbach needed payment, and he had to set up a way for forwarding mail. His book of short stories was being considered in New York, and he did not want to miss any publisher's letter.

As the wet weather continued into December, Hadley and the baby came down with colds and Ernest began dreaming of the magical combination of snow and Alpine mountains. "We've only got one time to live," he wrote Howie Jenkins, "and so let's have a hell of a good time

---

17. Reynolds, *Hemingway: The Paris Years*, 249.
18. EH to Robert McAlmon, Nov. 20, 1924, *The Letters of Ernest Hemingway, Vol. 2.*

together."[19] There wasn't as much money as before, but in the village of
Schruns in the Austrian Voralberg, just off the main line between Zurich
and Innsbruck, with a family hotel called the Taube, the food was good,
the skiing was excellent, and because Austria was gripped by runaway
inflation, it was also very cheap. He reserved two rooms at the Taube for
less than thirty dollars a week, and they would sublet the Paris apartment
and spend three months in the snowy mountains. Meanwhile, they spent
more time with Archibald and Ada McLeish, who lived in an apartment
on the Boulevard Saint Michel near Luxembourg. They had met earlier
in the year; Ernest was browsing in Shakespeare and Company when
Archie, a nice-looking man, entered the store and Sylvia promptly introduced them. Archie was from Chicago and had a law degree from Harvard; he had abandoned the law to come to Paris and follow his calling
as a poet. He and Ernest drank together in the Closerie des Lilas where
Hemingway avoided conversations about aesthetics and mostly talked
about sports. When Ernest claimed he had grown up on the wrong side
of the tracks, Archie saw through it and was amused.

Hemingway also began working with Ethel Moorhead and Ernest
Walsh, whom he had met in Ezra's studio two years before, on a new
review called *This Quarter*, intended to rival *The Dial*, and replace the
defunct *Transatlantic Review*. Ernest had once thought Walsh pretentious
but now said he was a "pretty nice guy."[20] With the *Transatlantic Review*
about to expire, Hemingway needed a new outlet for his work. Their
new magazine could provide it, and he began going to their rooms in the
Venetia Hotel bubbling with talk about writers and artists. Walsh was
a talkative young poet in poor health due to a war injury as an aviator.
Ethel Moorhead was a wealthy, plain, middle-aged Scotswoman who had
taken him up and cared for him. Hemingway bombarded them with
suggestions for contributors and editorial content. Learning that they
planned to pay contributors on acceptance, Hemingway sent them "Big
Two-Hearted River" and wrote that payments were "the absolute secret

---

19. EH to Howie Jenkins, Nov. 9, 1924, *The Letters of Ernest Hemingway, Vol. 2.*
20. Baker, *Hemingway: A Life*, 178.

of getting the first-rate stuff."[21] He spread the word about the new publication to Stein and Evan Shipman and informed many of his other literary friends in Paris, and also, likewise, he promoted the talents of his friends to Walsh, many of them appearing in the first and second issues of the quarterly. Walsh dedicated the first issue of the magazine to Ezra Pound, asking Ernest to contribute an homage, which he would start to write in Schruns.

He became close, too, at this time with Janet Flanner, a handsome reporter for *The New Yorker* magazine. Originally from Indianapolis where her family owned a funeral home, Ernest would come to her room on the rue Bonaparte and sit and talk. Flanner liked his "friendly, observant, bright agate-brown eyes." At a boxing match she watched him yell advice and insults in rough Parisian slang and thought he was "a natural quick linguist who learned a language first through his ears because of his constant necessity for understanding people and for communicating."[22] And, along with finding new friends, an important person from the past reached out and reentered his life.

During his visit to Arles in the spring when Ernest had happened to read in a Marseilles paper that the distraught attorney Wanda Stopa had tried to murder Y. K. Smith, it must have conjured up memories of Bill and Katy Smith and Horton Bay and the months he spent in Chicago. It may even have prompted him to write "Summer People," the other inaccrochable story set in northern Michigan. Bill Smith had never really left Hemingway in mind and spirit. He cropped up in a couple of the stories of *In Our Time*, "The End of Something," and "Three-Day Blow," and there were remembrances of Bill and their fishing trips in the deleted coda to "Big Two-Hearted River." The violent debacle that happened to his brother must have softened Bill's heart toward Ernest, who had always spoken against marriage infidelity, and he wrote him a letter from St. Louis that arrived in Paris by early December. "Is my arm long enuf to reach an olive branch clear across the Atlantic? If so grasp it," asked Bill, and he apologized for the angry letter two years before. "I realize

21. EH to Ernest Walsh & Ethel Moorhead, Jan. 7, 1924, *The Letters of Ernest Hemingway, Vol. 2*.
22. Baker, *Hemingway: A Life*, 178-9.

quite well . . . that my last scroll was a savage, bitter thing and if you care to fling it into the division of dead letters (from dead writers) perhaps we can again capture some of what was once ours."[23] Bill's letter was like a piece of Walloon coming through the mail. The lake had always been Ernest's real home—he always missed it terribly whenever summer approached—and he immediately replied to his once best friend in a long letter filled with warmth and love.

"I haven't felt so damn good since we used to pestle them on the Black," he wrote, and he apologized, too: "I had made a more than offensive bludy [sic] ass of myself with Y.K. . . . The only feeling I have about the boy is feeling sorry I acted so shitty to him." The country that he and Bill had known in their boyhoods was on his mind all the time: "almost everything worth a damn I've written has been about that country . . . the Bay, the farm . . . fishing, the swell times we used to have with Auntie [Mrs. Charles] at the farm, the first swell trips out to the Black and the Sturgeon and the wonderful times we had with the men and the storms in the fall . . . and the whole damn thing." He wrote that "Hash hasn't lost any looks and gets better all the time," and told him about *In Our Time*, which he hoped would soon be published, and wanted Bill to "come over and we'll go down to Spain in June . . . drive down all through France and over the pass of Roland. Fish the Irati . . . and then go to Pamplona for the big bull fight week."[24] He would continue to write Bill long letters every week or so, full of enthusiasm for a most valued shared legacy of their past, and beneath it all, the wisecracks, the bawdiness, the brag, there was a genuine sense of affection and relief at having regained a needed friendship, one whose loss he had deeply regretted.

As the days in December further disappeared into rain and chill, Hemingway continued to write letters and worked on a review of Sherwood Anderson's new book, *A Story Teller's Story*, for which he was writing a column in the Paris *Tribune*. "He is a very great writer," wrote Ernest about Sherwood, saying as much about his own writing as that of Sherwood Anderson, "and if he has at times in other books been unsuccessful

---

23. James R. Mellow, *Hemingway: A Life Without Consequences*, 279.
24. EH to BS, Dec. 6, 1924, *The Letters of Ernest Hemingway, Vol. 2*.

it has been for two reasons. His talent and his development of it has all been toward the short story or tale and not toward that highly artificial form, the novel."[25] That he would call the novel a "highly artificial form" was because not only had he not yet written a novel, but he did not yet even understand how one could write a story that he could not hold completely in his head. Encouraged by Gertrude, and reinforced while writing "Big Two-Hearted River" as he lived each day with Nick on the river not knowing how the story would end, he completely distrusted planning. If, as people told him, novels needed planning, then he would know how it would end before writing it, and what joy could there be in that? He had not yet submitted an acceptable story for McAlmon's anthology, which was scheduled for publication in 1925. He had mailed "The Doctor and the Doctor's Wife," which had just been printed in the *Transatlantic*, but McAlmon wanted unpublished stories. Djuna Barnes, Joyce, and Hilda Doolittle were sending work that had not appeared elsewhere, "you'd better too," McAlmon told him, and, privy to what Ernest had been writing, asked, "how about the Smith Story, or O'Neil, or Krebs? They're around 5000 words aren't they?"[26] Hemingway would soon send him the Krebs story, "Soldier's Home," from the collection of *In Our Time* that had not yet been accepted by a publisher, telling Mac that "Gertrude thinks its [*sic*] a good story."[27]

While Ernest wrote letters and worked on his book review, Hadley mailed a large, framed portrait of Bumby to Oak Park, their Christmas present to his family. Her gentle politeness became more and more the link between Ernest and his parents. He was her future and everything she believed in. She would do whatever he needed, and whatever he wanted she wanted too: boxing, drinking, bullfights, skiing, fishing. When Bertram suggested Christmas in Austria for the excellent exchange rate and mountain slopes, she was as eager to go as Ernest, and for her the added benefit of exercise would help her to lose the excess weight she still carried from childbirth. At thirty-three, Hadley was an ample,

25. Reynolds, *Hemingway: The Paris Years*, 253.
26. RM to EH, December 1924, Hemingway Collection, JFK Library.
27. EH to RM, Dec. 18, 1924, *The Letters of Ernest Hemingway, Vol. 2*.

attractive woman with full breasts and wide hips. She did not turn many heads in Paris in a year when thin bodies and flat chests were the vogue. Ernest looked at other women, young and old, and received attention from them, but Hadley did not need to worry. When they were in bed with her holding him in her arms against his dark dreams, her amplitude was all he needed and wanted.

As Christmas approached and the dark came early, they finished packing and made their rounds of cheerful farewell. Gertrude and Alice sent them off with books and a present for Bumby. At Shakespeare and Company, they checked out Turgenev, Trollop, and Wilkie Collins. They looked for but could not find the winter issue of the *Little Review* that carried "Mr. and Mrs. Elliot." With their apartment sublet until the end of March, on the evening of December 19, they splurged on a taxi to the Gare de l'Est. A dense fog had transformed the Quarter into a strange, unrecognizable place; streetlamps were mere halos in the dark, casting tiny circles of pale light. Leaving late and proceeding at a crawl, their train slowly moved through the fog-bound suburbs out of Paris.

At Bludenz, Austria, the Hemingways transferred to an electric train on a branch line that carried them up the Montafon Valley to Schruns. The weather was as warm as September; cows grazed in the meadows; only the higher peaks were covered with snow. A porter at the station took them to the Hotel Taube, a large white stucco building on the town square. From their rooms on the second floor, Ernest could lean out his window and see ten mountain peaks rising above a fir-covered valley with pastures and small farms. It was beautiful country. After months of keeping house and caring for Bumby in their dingy Paris apartment, Hadley was thrilled by the ease of life at Schruns. Big breakfasts were brought to their rooms and the hotel had a piano for her to play Bach and Haydn. A lovely teenage girl named Mathilde Braun, who lived in the house next door with her mother, fell in love with Bumby and would take care of him for a pittance.

Ernest spent the first days in bed with a sore throat and did not shave or cut his hair. As he got better his appetite became enormous. The owner's wife, Frau Nels, supervised the kitchen serving great roasts of beef, browned potatoes with gravy, jugged hare, venison chops, soufflés, and homemade plum pudding, and always there was red wine and varieties of beer. The small town was joined together by wooden bridges across a fast-flowing stream. The villagers were friendly, tipping their hats to strangers. Ernest's beard grew black and full, and with his flowing locks, as he and Hadley took walks, he heard with pleasure the villagers calling him "the Black Christ."[28] He wondered how he could have ever thought of Austrians as the enemy.

Don Stewart sent a Christmas letter with an enormous check "to keep up our morale I think," wrote Ernest to Harold Loeb. "He's a swell guy." But the news from Stewart's publisher was disappointing. "Mr. Doran felt they couldn't go all the way with me on the matter of sex in a book of Short Stories," complained Ernest. The real reason was that a book of short stories was a hard sell in the current market; however, the publisher would be interested in a novel. Stewart then gave the manuscript to Mencken in hopes that he would recommend it to Alfred Knopf. "Well," wrote Hemingway, "Mencken doesn't like my stuff and . . . that will probably end in horsecock too."[29]

After the feverish production of the previous months, Ernest's writing went into an eclipse. He started a few exploratory stories that went nowhere. "Need a big town to write in," he wrote to Loeb. Ernest had hoped Harold could join them in Schruns if Kitty would let him go. "Tell Kitty you will be pure because there is only one beautiful girl in the village and she eats garlic for breakfast."[30] Instead, Loeb wrote that he was going to New York to look after the editing of his novel *Doodab* and promised to put in a word about Ernest's manuscript with his publisher, Harold Liveright. "We're all sad as hell this morning that you're not coming,"[31] replied Ernest. Harold would be doing him a very good deed, for his best hope for publication was with Boni & Liveright, a firm eager to sign the Moderns. Liveright had published Eliot's *The Wasteland*, Faulkner's *Soldier's Pay*, and Hart Crane's *The Bridge*. Ezra

28. Gloria Diliberto, *Hadley*, 183.
29. EH to Harold Loeb, Jan. 5, 1925, *The Letters of Ernest Hemingway, Vol. 2.*
30. EH to HL, Dec. 29, 1924, *The Letters of Ernest Hemingway, Vol. 2.*
31. EH to HL, Jan. 5, 1925, *The Letters of Ernest Hemingway, Vol. 2.*

Pound, even with his anti-Semitism, spoke of Liveright as a "pearl among publishers."[32] Liveright had been paying Ezra $500 a year since 1922 to send good American writers his way. He had probably mentioned Ernest and urged Liveright to publish him, but until that fall Ernest had not had enough stories for a commercial book.

Snow began falling in Schruns at last, at first high in the mountains and then blanketing the village and surrounding area. The Hemingways met Walter Lent while playing bridge in the evening by the fireplace in the hotel dining room. Lent, a demanding ski instructor and a good companion who fully enjoyed life, scorned the local hills and would take his pupils to snow huts high on the slopes of Alpine peaks. There were no mechanical lifts and no way to ski down the slopes without first climbing up. Hurling themselves into life on the mountains, Ernest and Hadley joined his ski school and began making exhausting treks to the high snows above the valley with sealskins on their skies to grip the snow and rucksacks on their backs to ski from one hut to another. Along the way up they sighted deer and chamoix and fox. They climbed the steepest slope on a cut-back trail at the head of the valley into Madlener Haus, an Alpine club that served simple meals and slept sixteen in dormitory bunks. From there, under Lent's guidance, they climbed 500 meters higher to ski back down across the Silvretta-Stausee with its broad snow fields of fine powder over a solid base. At day's end they returned to the hut to beer and hearty stew and the warmth of a porcelain stove. Outside, with snow piled half as high as the roof, the winds howled off the corners of the building and the slopes were radiant in the moonlight. Bedding down in the troughs in their sleeping bags, Ernest had no bad dreams up there, nor did he think about publishers.

During the months at Schruns, Ernest read Paris papers and magazines and kept up with the sporting world. In a small separate room at the Taube, he set up a writing table to answer letters and work on his fiction undisturbed. He wrote a lot of letters, many to Bill Smith. In the letters to Bill Smith the main concerns were sports and writing, which were not

---

32. Mary Dearborn, *Ernest Hemingway*, 173.

separate concerns to Hemingway. In his privately developed metaphysics, bullfighters and boxers and painters and writers were brothers in art. What he would write or say about a bullfighter in the ring would apply as well to a writer, sometimes metaphorically, sometimes directly. Both were skilled professionals whose best moves were not understood by the masses; in the practice of their art, they could not fake anything or it would show. He also urged Bill to get away from the States and come to Paris where there were jobs he suggested that he might work. Encouraged by his old friend, Bill began to unburden his private problems. After many disappointing years, Bill no longer had the confidence that he used to have, and Ernest saw that some of the problem was sexual and gave him much advice on the subject: "Non serious yencing [fornication] should be devoid of consequences over entanglements. Entanglements are what ruin yencing. You ought to yence. Yencing is a great conditioner. Makes a male see clearer, good for the corpo. If you get a chance to yence without entanglements and feel like yencing yence."[33] How he knew this, or how he thought he knew it, was through observation; for he was a man faithful to his wife, and yet for a man faithful to his wife, to suggest this to a friend, he had to have given a lot of thought to philandering.

Ernest seldom wrote letters when his creative well was full of fiction, and the three months in Schruns were mostly a dry spell that would deepen into the spring and beyond to the start of summer. After finishing "The Undefeated" at the end of November 1924, he would write but one good story during this time. He tried to write others, but the stories just weren't there. The stories he started would not end. Usually, they were about an artist's relationship with his art—often in the guise of a boxer—and women and money causing his decline. Despite his artistic acceptance in literary magazines, Hemingway was concerned about his artistic demise, especially when the stories weren't flowing, because his family could not live indefinitely on Hadley's fixed income and there was no word from New York about his manuscript of short stories. He wrote a few sketches about the friends staying with them, about how they

---

33. EH to BS, Feb. 17, 1925, *The Letters of Ernest Hemingway, Vol. 2.*

might be in bed, but he put them away knowing they could never get published—and Ernest Hemingway did not want to be an experimental writer in Paris growing old and unpublished like Gertrude; or living off patrons like Joyce, who wrote about masturbation; or in exile in Rapallo like Ezra. Ernest Hemingway wanted to be published and paid a lot and read by multitudes of people.

Late in February, they again hiked six-thousand feet up to the Madlener Haus Alpine hut from where they made glorious ski runs, soaring five miles down a glacier in twelve minutes. Hadley was actually a better skier than Ernest. Lent was critical of Ernest's technique but marveled at his courage on the slopes. "Ernest knew no fear," said Lent. "He just pointed [his] skis downhill and flew."[34] Returning at nightfall weary and wind burned, they slept well and returned to Schruns where there awaited two telegrams sent from New York, one from Stewart and the other from Loeb, both bearing the ecstatic news that Horace Liveright had agreed to publish *In Our Time.* "Hurray for you and the news," Ernest wrote to Harold Loeb. "I couldn't realize it at first and then couldn't believe it and when I did I got very excited and couldn't sleep."[35] The telegram from Liveright arrived in Schruns on March 5, accepting the book and offering a $200 advance against royalties. Ernest cabled: DELIGHTED ACCEPT. There had been other good news for Ernest. *Der Querschnitt* accepted "The Undefeated," a story he had failed to place in America with *The Saturday Evening Post*, and earlier when Ernest Walsh and Ethel Moorhead wanted a story for their new review *This Quarter*, promising payment, he sent them "Big Two-Hearted River," which they accepted and paid him a thousand francs ($50). He could have saved it for the American market, but he wanted and needed the money.

The news from Liveright came when the Hemingways' money was at low ebb. Their sublet tenants had jumped their Paris contract, leaving the Hemingways with two rents to pay if they stayed another month in Schruns, and a check for $2500 from George Breaker, Hadley's old friend who had embezzled her money, had thrice been returned for insufficient

---

34. Diliberto, *Hadley*, 185.
35. EH to HL, Feb. 27, 1925, *The Letters of Ernest Hemingway, Vol. 2.*

funds. So, they put up their skis and said their goodbyes, promising to return to Schruns next winter. The train trip down the valley to the main line seemed longer than coming up. On March 13, they passed through Swiss customs and arrived in Paris early the next morning. A light snow was falling that turned to rain when they reached Notre-Dame-des-Champs with only their cat there to greet them.

In the pile of mail waiting for Ernest at Shakespeare and Company was a letter that had arrived a few days before from an editor at Scribner's named Maxwell Perkins. Perkins had earlier received a tip about "a young man named Ernest Hemmingway" in a scrawled note sent by F. Scott Fitzgerald the previous October from a villa in the south of France where Scott was engaged in completing *The Great Gatsby*. Fitzgerald had read some of the stories in the *Transatlantic Review* and the collection of vignettes. "I haven't it here now," Fitz wrote to Perkins, "but it's remarkable and I'd look him up right away," adding, "He's the real thing."[36] Determining that the short pieces were published by the Three Mountains Press, Perkins ordered a copy from Paris and read it and was very impressed, writing to Fitzgerald that the vignettes were "presented with economy, strength, and vitality. A remarkable tight, complete expression."[37]

There were actually two letters from Perkins to Hemingway: the first letter had been misaddressed and returned; Perkins then got Sylvia's address from John Bishop Peale, who had made Hemingway's acquaintance in Paris, and wrote a second letter and included the first one. In his letters to Ernest, Max noted "the power in the scenes and incidents pictured, and by the effectiveness of their relation to each other." Carefully approaching a new author he wanted to sign, he mentioned the difficulty of obtaining the book, a subtle reminder of the difficulties of a small press. He also acknowledged that, as much as he liked the book, the vignettes made too slender a volume for booksellers to make a substantial profit and therefore the trade would have little interest. "This is a pity because your method is obviously one which enables you to express what

36. Kenneth Lynn, *Hemingway*, 274.
37. Lynn, 274.

you have to say in a very small compass." And he wrote that he had heard that Hemingway "would be likely to have material for a book before long. I hope this is so and that we may see it. We would certainly read it with promptness and sympathetic interest if you give us the chance."[38]

Ernest well knew about the publishing house of Charles Scribner's Sons in New York City, and he knew about F. Scott Fitzgerald, whose novels Hadley had read—though he didn't yet know that it was Fitzgerald who had brought him to Perkins's attention, but he had accepted Horace Liveright's offer, and the contract was before him. When he replied to Perkins in April, he wrote that "Boni & Liveright . . . have an option on my next three books." There was, however, a possibility that he might switch because "unless they exercise this option to publish the second book within 60 days of the receipt of the manuscript their option shall lapse, and if they do not publish the second book they relinquish their option on the third book." Ernest wanted to work with a man like Maxwell Perkins and would not break the tentative cord established between them. "I do want you to know how much I appreciated your letter and if I am ever in a position to send you anything to consider I shall certainly do so." He mentioned the possibility of someday writing a big book about bull fighting with wonderful pictures, but he wasn't yet interested in writing a novel. "I like to write short stories . . . the novel seems to me an awfully artificial and worked out form but as some of the short stories are now stretching out to 8,000 to 12,000 thousand words maybe I'll get there yet." He signed the letter "very sincerely,"[39] and gave 113 Rue Notre-Dame-des-Champs as his permanent address.

---

38. Mellow, *Hemingway: A Life Without Consequences*, 283.
39. EH to Maxwell Perkins, April 15, 1925, *The Letters of Ernest Hemingway, Vol. 2.*

Archibald and Ada MacLeish

Book stalls along the quays

Hemingway and Smith in Michigan

Maxwell Perkins

Hotel Taube

Hemingway in beret

Misty December night in Paris

EXPATRIATE*J*

T HE LATIN Quarter, where the Hemingways returned in the
late winter of 1925, was filled with unfamiliar faces, and the
gossip seemed strange. All of Paris was under the siege of gray, cold,
drizzling weather that kept most people away from the cafes. Even the
Americans there felt under siege with the use of a new word, "expatriate,"
used to describe them. Those in America "go too far when they speak of
Americans living in Europe as 'expatriates,'" they proclaimed in angry
letters. "The word . . . means one who has changed his allegiance . . .
France harbors few Yankees who are other than Americans."[1] But the rotten weather keeping people indoors was good for Ernest because he had
work to do on *In Our Time*. Liveright thought the stories were splendid,
but he wanted "Up in Michigan" replaced because of the explicit sex
scene and parts of "Mr. and Mrs. Eliot" rewritten.

Going through his manuscripts looking for something to replace "Up
in Michigan," Ernest reread the opening lines of a story he had started
earlier that winter: "Nick stood up. He was all right. He looked up the
track at the lights of the caboose going out of sight around the curve." It
would be the story of Nick's encounter with a punch-drunk fighter and
his "Negro" companion in their camp just off the tracks. Their meeting starts friendly and then quickly becomes scary. "I'm crazy," the old
boxer tells Nick, and informs the Negro when he arrives with food that
Nick has never been crazy. "He's got a lot coming to him,"[2] replies
the Negro. Ernest knew that well. He had seen his own father behave

1. Michael Reynolds, *Hemingway: The Paris Years*, 275.
2. Ernest Hemingway, "The Battler," *Short Stories of Ernest Hemingway*, 97.

strangely, changing moods so quickly it left him feeling helpless. The old boxer was that way, but only worse, talking friendly at first and then suddenly turning assaultive when Nick won't give him his knife. The Negro gently taps out the boxer with a blackjack, explains the situation, maybe not well enough but as best as he can, gives Nick a sandwich, and kindly sends him away. Hemingway knew it was a good story: no thinking, no conclusion, but something was learned as Nick moved out into the dark toward the next town. The story was called "The Battler."

Clarence Hemingway read "The Doctor and The Doctor's Wife" in the November *Transatlantic*, and impressed by Ernest's accurate details, wrote to his son that he got out "the old Bear Lake Book and showed Carol and Leicester the photo of Nic Boulton and Bill Tabeshaw on the beach sawing the old beech log. That was when you were 12 years old and Carol was born that summer." Ernest remembered that summer clearly. It was the year before his father turned strange, gave up the Agassiz Club, and took his first cure alone in New Orleans trying to get his nerves under control. It was a long time ago, and he didn't want to think about it. "Wish, dear boy," his father continued, "You would send me some of your work often."[3]

Ernest wondered if his father had missed the point of the fictional doctor's cowardly behavior, or maybe he understood and didn't want to acknowledge it. He replied to his father, "The reason I have not sent you any of my work is because you or mother sent back the In Our Time books." He wanted to prepare them for his next collection of stories. "You see I'm trying in all my stories to get the feeling of the actual life across—not just to depict life—or criticize it—but to actually make it alive. So that when you have read something by me you can actually experience the thing. You cant [*sic*] do this without putting in the bad and the ugly as well as what is beautiful. Because if it is all beautiful you cant [*sic*] believe in it. Things aren't that way . . . So when you see anything of mine that you dont [*sic*] like remember that I'm sincere in doing it . . . If I wrote an ugly story that might be hateful to you or to

3. CEH to EH, Mar. 8, 1925, Hemingway Collection, JFK Library.

mother the next one might be one that you would like exceedingly."[4] Reading his son's letter, Clarence may have wondered what he meant for he was less shocked by his son's stories and more supportive than Ernest might ever know.

At the end of March, Ernest returned the signed contract to Liveright along with the requested new story and an accompanying letter: "It is understood of course that no alterations of words shall be made without my approval . . . as the stories are written so tight and so hard that the alteration of a word can throw an entire story out of key." If he now sounded less than enthusiastic it was because he knew he could have signed with Scribner's.

He continued:

> As for the books selling or not selling, I don't look on it in any
> way as a lost cause . . . The classic example of a really fine book
> that could not sell was E. E. Cumming's Enormous Room. But
> Cumming's book was written in a style that no one who has not
> read a good deal of 'modern' writing could read . . . My book will
> be praised by highbrows and can be read by lowbrows. There is no
> writing in it that anybody with a high school education cannot read.

And then he gave a bit of a lecture. "If cuts are made outside of possible necessary elimination of obscenities . . . it will be shot to pieces as an organism and nobody will praise it and nobody will want to read it." Perhaps a telegram could have canceled the contract, but Ernest had given his word and felt committed. "The new story makes the book a good deal better. It's about the best I have ever written . . . I do not need to tell you how pleased I am to be published by Boni & Liveright." He signed "with best regards"[5] and awaited the proofs. His first commercial book, which he dedicated to Hadley, would soon be published.

Hemingway almost daily haunted the Imprimerie of Herbert Clarke on rue St. Honore using his experience to attend to the arrangements for

---

4. EH to CEH, Mar. 20, 1925, *The Letters of Ernest Hemingway, Vol. 2.*
5. EH to Horace Liveright, Mar. 31, 1925, *The Letters of Ernest Hemingway, Vol. 2.*

the first number of *This Quarter*. When "The Undefeated" was rejected by the *Dial*, Walsh decided to publish it in the second issue of his review and Ethel wrote Ernest another check for a thousand francs. He happily wrote back, "We are going to pay the rent with it. Pay a first installment on a suit of clothes. Buy a lot of groceries and go to the six day bicycle race."[6] He procured a Man Ray photograph of Pound to be used for the frontispiece and assembled some photos of Brancusi sculptures and paintings by Bertram Hartman and Miss Moorhead for illustrations within its pages. "It's going to be a damn fine review and the only one alive,"[7] he wrote to Walsh in April.

Yet he spent so much time editing, reading copy and proofs, sending out galleys, taking crowded buses to the printer on the rue St. Honore, the same one he had worked with on the *Transatlantic*, that he voiced his complaints to the absent Walsh: "I've found out how much damned time it takes . . . and I have to have my mind clear to write the stuff I'm working on now."[8] Over dinner one night with Walsh and Moorhead, Hemingway pushed hard for Bill Smith, soon to join him in Paris, suggesting he take the job for a thousand francs a month. Walsh became irritated and balked: no one had asked Hemingway to work for free; he had volunteered. Hemingway wrote to him the next day, "You seem suspicious that I'm just inventing some way to do you out of money. Well, I'm not."[9] Despite their disagreements, their relationship had a symbiotic quality. Hemingway needed the money and exposure their review could provide, for Walsh and Moorhead had cheerfully bought and paid for two long stories he had not been able to sell in America. And, along with his energy and connections, the review needed the growing prestige that Ernest Hemingway could provide, for in March, Ford Madox Ford had written in the New York *Evening Post* that "the best writer in America at this moment (though at this moment he happens to be in Paris), the most conscientious, the most master of his craft, the most consummate, is my young friend Ernest Hemingway."[10] And so, for another year, until

6. EH to Ernest Walsh and Ethel Moorhead, April 4, 1925, *The Letters of Ernest Hemingway*, Vol. 2.
7. EH to EW, April 12, 1925, *The Letters of Ernest Hemingway*, Vol. 2.
8. EH to EW & EM, April 4, 1925, *The Letters of Ernest Hemingway*, Vol. 2.
9. EH to EW, April 19, 1925, *The Letters of Ernest Hemingway*, Vol. 2.
10. Jeffrey Meyers, *Hemingway*, 127.

Walsh finally hemorrhaged to death in the south of France, they continued an air of camaraderie.

It was a memorable spring for Ernest in Paris. Harold Stearns returned from a brief visit to New York and took his place in the cafes on Montparnasse, reporting that he remained an American but could no longer live there again happily because "Everybody was dissatisfied . . . nobody was happy."[11] April brought six-day bike races, production of *This Quarter*, tennis games with Harold Loeb—sometimes with Hadley and sometimes not—and strolls along Montparnasse Boulevard. At Sylvia's bookstore one afternoon, he listened to the new gramophone recording of Joyce reading a portion of *Ulysses*. As the weather turned nice, Ernest spent a lot of time at the Dome loafing. He heard that Ford had finished a novel in the country, which gave Ernest pause to reflect; it had taken him six years to perfect his short-story form (and in coming years he would write some even better), but he had not written his own novel and had no ideas for one either. He bought tickets to the bike races where he and Hadley took enough wine and food to last well into the night. Ford visited the apartment one evening, and at Ford's suggestion, instead of the planned visit to Gertrude and Alice, they all took a taxi to the Bois. His fiction was still not flowing, so he wrote letters instead, lots of thank you letters to his friends who had helped get his manuscript accepted (with so many friends pulling Horace Liveright's strings, Ernest wondered if the quality of his fiction had anything to do with the contract). His life would soon take another significant expansion, always there were changes, as three new women entered his life that spring: Duff Twysden, Zelda Fitzgerald, and Pauline Pfeiffer.

Soon after returning from the mountains, Kitty Cannell invited Hadley to afternoon tea at her apartment near the Eiffel Tower to meet two sisters who had grown up in St. Louis, Pauline and Virginia Pfeiffer. Kitty remembered the sisters as "petit [*sic*] with bright black eyes and black bobbed hair cut straight across the forehead like Japanese dolls. Their bones were as delicate as those of small birds . . . they were more

---

11. Reynolds, *Hemingway: The Paris Years*, 286.

than twice as cute as if there had been only one of them. The one who was a little older [Pauline] benefitted by the looks of the younger, and Virginia shone in the witticisms of the one who was a little brighter."[12] They came from great wealth. Their father, who with his brothers owned Warner Pharmaceuticals in St. Louis, on a restless urge had purchased sixty-three thousand acres of bottom land in northeast Arkansas and moved his family there when the girls were in their late teens. There in the town of Piggott he built a twelve-room white frame house on Cherry Street; a room downstairs was a chapel where the mother, Mary, a devout catholic, had Mass said every Sunday. Paul Pfeiffer owned the Piggott Bank, the land office, and the Piggott Custom Gin Company that processed the cotton grown by the farmers who leased fields on his land.

Pauline Pfeiffer graduated from the University of Missouri in 1918 with a degree in journalism and was soon covering fashion for *Vanity Fair* in New York City where her intelligent, lively stories attracted the attention of *Vogue* editors, who offered her a position on the French *Vogue* in Paris as the assistant to the editor. She had been engaged to a man in New York, with whom she was not in love, and took the job in Paris in part to escape from her fiancé. There she settled into an elegant apartment on the rue Picot, off the Avenue Foch, at the center of a wealthy American enclave. She was joined by her sister, Jinny, who had vague ambitions to write, and they soon met Kitty, also a fashion writer who lived in comfortable circumstances, though not nearly so wealthy as the Pfeiffers. Their childless Uncle Gus, part owner of the Richard Hudnut Cosmetics, adored the girls and would pay any extraordinary bills if they needed them paid. But Pauline had more than enough to pay her own bills, for in addition to her *Vogue* paycheck she had trust funds that produced $3600 a year. With her boyish looks and fashionable clothes, looking much younger than the thirty she soon would turn, Pauline seemed to embody the flapper's dash and frivolity. In fact, she was a serious young woman who worked hard at her job and attended Mass regularly. Some said she was there to meet a husband—she could afford to look over men, and she

---

12. Bertram Sarason, *Hemingway and the Sun Set*, 146.

looked over both Hemingway and Harold Loeb—and some said she was spoiled, but no one ever called her stupid, and she usually got what she wanted. She told Kitty she had heard much about the Hemingways from Katy Smith, with whom she had been close at Missouri, and wanted to meet them.

It was a cool, glorious day in March as the season was changing from winter to spring. Hadley arrived at Kitty's apartment at four in the afternoon and was introduced to the two dark, slender, exquisitely dressed women with bobbed hair. "Pauline had on a new chipmunk coat from a top Paris designer," remembered Kitty. "It was the only one any of us had seen."[13] After tea, Hemingway and Loeb joined the party, fresh from tennis or boxing. The sisters provided light smart talk and Ernest took part with his usual geniality. At this first meeting, the Pfeiffers were sympathetic to Hadley, but not so much with Ernest. Ernest thought Jinny was the prettier of the two and joked to Loeb after they left, "I'd like to take Virginia out in Pauline's coat."[14] (Jinny was not interested in him, and maybe he knew she was a lesbian, or maybe not, but Ernest, like many men, was attracted to good-looking lesbians; the stunning Margaret Anderson said Hemingway got so "gooey eyed"[15] over her that she tried to avoid him in Paris.) Like Kitty, Pauline felt sorry for Hadley in her dowdy clothes, and a few days later she and her sister visited her in the warren of rooms above the sawmill. While there she caught a glimpse of Ernest, unshaven, unkempt, and apparently uninterested, lying in bed reading, paying little attention to the women in the front room. She was shocked by the conditions Ernest imposed upon his wife and baby in the name of art, and when Kitty next saw Pauline and her sister "they remarked with delicate shudders that they found Ernest so coarse they couldn't see how a lovely girl like Hadley could stand him."[16]

But Pauline did like Hadley. Admiring her new friend's warmth and dignity, she visited her often in the evenings after work and, along with Jinny, was drawn into the Hemingways' social circle. They joined them

---

13. Sarason, *Hemingway and the Sun Set*, 146.
14. Sarason, 146.
15. Reynolds, *Hemingway: The Paris Years*, 288.
16. Sarason, *Hemingway and the Sun Set*, 146.

for dinners at the Negre de Toulouse, had drinks with them under the chestnut blossoms at the Closerie des Lilas, and attended art openings and boxing matches. Occasionally they rode bicycles in the Bois as Ernest was thoroughly taken up with the six-day bike races. He wore the striped jerseys favored by the racers and rode around the outskirts of Paris on his bike. Archie McLeish was almost as competitive as Ernest and would sometimes race against him. Dos Passos recalled how they would all meet at a stall on one of the market streets and buy "a quantity of wine and cheeses and crunchy rolls, a pot of pate and perhaps a cold chicken and sit up in the gallery to watch the races. Hemingway knew all the statistics and the names and lives of the riders. [He] used to make poor Hadley sit there all night, but I would sneak out . . . when I got sleepy."[17]

Although it didn't seem so on the surface, the Hemingways' marriage had quietly begun to deteriorate. Lack of money had been a serious problem since Ernest had given up newspaper work, along with the depletion of Hadley's funds. George Breaker had sold nineteen-thousand dollars of Hadley's railway bond (about a third of her capital) for eleven-thousand dollars and sent her a check for twenty-five hundred dollars that had repeatedly bounced. After months of tortuous negotiations by mail, Ernest had managed to recover about a third of what they had lost. Meanwhile, without much income for several months, Hadley could not afford to have her shoes repaired, and her worn, old-fashioned clothes were a dismal contrast to her chic American friends like Pauline Pfeiffer and Kitty Cannell. Ernest dressed no better with his patched jacket and baggy pants, but, even poor, he managed to keep his integrity (John Bishop Peale saw him turn down an offer from an editor from Hearst that would have supported him handsomely for years) and his mind focused on fiction.

That spring, Hemingway was preoccupied with the coming publication of *In Our Time* and spent mornings writing letters and plotting career moves; in the afternoons he played tennis with friends. Many noticed he was becoming less considerate of Hadley. One woman remembered

---

17. John Dos Passos, *The Best Times*, 143.

running into him in the Luxembourg Gardens: Ernest "had put on flesh, grown a little moustache . . . his baggy tweed suit was patched at the elbows and the pocket of his coat was torn from the notebooks jammed into it. With [Bumby] astride his hip and Hadley following him as silently as a squaw, he strode along, his head down, kicking at the gravel with his sneakers."[18] Their age difference was becoming more prevalent too. After the birth of their baby, Hadley looked more and more matronly and, finding it difficult to keep up with the activities of her energetic husband, wanted a quieter life. Gradually exchanging the role of wife for that of a mother, she was awfully nice, but Ernest, living among the bohemians of Paris, desired someone more sophisticated and exciting. He had written a number of stories about troubled relationships—"The End of Something," "Out of Season," and "Cross-Country Snow"—but when he wrote the story "Cat in the Rain," about a bored and restless wife dissatisfied with her transient life and her marriage to a self-absorbed, disinterested husband, he had shown he was still sensitive to Hadley. Soon there would be even more open and troubling signs of a rift in their marriage.

When Bill Smith arrived in Paris in April, Ernest was overjoyed. One of his oldest and most valued friends was completely back in his life, healing the estranging quarrel about Doodles and Y. K. from five years before. Bill had suffered a nervous breakdown, and with much compassion, Ernest wanted to help him to a full recovery. Smith arrived flat broke and moved into a small study in the apartment for several weeks, an act of generosity—"There's a lot of that aspect of Hemingway that doesn't come out,"[19]—that Bill would remember. Hemingway described bullfights, wanting him to come along to Pamplona, and took him everywhere in the Latin Quarter and introduced him to his friends. Don Stewart, who was in town with Bob Benchley, his friend from the Round Table at the Algonquin Hotel, often went to the prize fights and bicycle races with Ernest and Bill. Ernest spent mornings writing at a table in the Closerie des Lilas, and in the afternoons he and Bill would play tennis

18. Gloria Diliberto, *Hadley*, 196.
19. Sarason, *Hemingway and the Sun Set*, 156.

with Harold Loeb and Paul Fisher whenever the courts were dry enough. When he introduced Bill to Pauline Pfeiffer, it seemed to Bill that she was working hard to get Ernest's attention. "I was talking to someone about you," she would say, and then Ernest would answer, "Oh? And what did he say?"[20] If Pauline didn't yet interest him, it may have been because another even more exotic woman had entered his life.

Often to satisfy the deep undercurrents of his being, consciously or not, Ernest would look for and find the germ of a good story in the people he met, and he always had a knack for attracting who or what he needed to further his career and reputation. As long as Hadley had known him he had always been bantering and affectionate to attractive women, and it had never troubled her because she knew he was faithful and was secure in his love. She remembered "He was then the kind of man to whom men, women, children, and dogs were attracted."[21] Many men were impressed by the youthful Hemingway: the aggressive grin, the opportunities for man-to-man talks, and the sense of a literary man who was completely down-to-earth. Loeb had been completely struck by his friend: "I admired his combination of toughness and sensitiveness, his love of sport and his dedication to writing . . . It was a good sign that men like Hemingway were taking up writing."[22]

Women liked him, too, and that spring in Paris there was an unsettling shift in his feeling that was no mere flirtation—and the woman he sought, a tall slim English woman named Lady Duff Twysden, was also sought by Harold Loeb. Harold was introduced to her at a cocktail party and then saw her again at the Select where, while working on a manuscript, "I heard a laugh so bright and musical it seemed to brighten the dingy room," and then sauntered over to McAlmon's table. McAlmon, "who knew everybody soon after they arrived in the Quarter,"[23] said her name was Duff. She reminded Loeb of a mysterious heroine in his favorite novel by W. H. Hudson. It was probably Robert McAlmon, too, ever a habitué of Parisian cafes, who introduced Hemingway to this woman

20. Kenneth Lynn, *Hemingway*, 301.
21. James R. Mellow, *Hemingway: A Life Without Consequences*, 295.
22. Harold Loeb, *The Way It Was*, 194.
23. Loeb, 249.

who made a home of the cafes—maybe even more than McAlmon—carrying along with her an interchangeable entourage of mostly gay men.

By nearly all accounts, Lady Duff Twysden was sexually liberated and had immense natural charm. She was striking in appearance, rather pretty with a long, lovely neck, expressive eyes, and, despite heavy drinking, a fresh complexion. She wore her hair cropped close and brushed back like a boy and had an excellent figure that she mannishly clothed with tweed skirts worn with sweaters under blazers. Often she wore berets or soft felt hats that sometimes had long brims under which she could alluringly cast her gray eyes. She turned thirty-three in Paris that spring (an age Hemingway then liked in women) and was living with Pat Guthrie, a tall, dissipated Scotsman some thought was her cousin. They mostly lived in a series of fleabag accommodations in the fifth arrondissement but sometimes had rooms in the Ritz Hotel, depending on the irregular flow of remittance from home.

That Duff had a live-in bed partner did not prevent her from becoming involved with other men. She would go to bed with some of them but seemed to adhere to a code of husbands being off limits. People were drawn into her orbit, mostly men, particularly gay men, surrounding her like bees on a hive. Unlike Pat, who would get silly or sullen, Duff had a great capacity for drink and held her liquor gallantly. She enjoyed enchanting and controlling the men around her, using her ability to make them feel attractive and important and compete for her favor. Since she and Pat were always short of cash, she would cadge money from people and let them pay her bar bills. A well-known homosexual couple, the artists Sir Cedric Morris and Lett Haines, was often in her company, as was Ernest Hemingway, who was smitten very soon after meeting her. Her language was as profane as Ernest's, a trait that endeared her to him. And at late parties in the Quarter he sometimes took Hadley home early to disengage the babysitter and then returned alone to be with Duff.

Duff was born Dorothy Smurthwaite to a Yorkshire wine merchant and a socially pretentious mother who claimed aristocratic ties. She had studied art in Paris and was presented at Buckingham Palace using her mother's maiden name Stirling. Her first marriage was to an older man, and when he went off to the war, she found herself unwilling to fend off the advances of the young officers she met through her courier work with the British Secret Service and was soon divorced for adultery. A few weeks later she married a royal naval commander who was a baronet (the only British heredity title that is not peerage) named Sir Roger Twysden, thereby giving her the title Lady Twysden. Even after Duff gave birth to a son, her mother-in-law continued to despise her as an unprincipled social climber and an alcoholic who led her son into debauchery. Duff remembered the marriage differently: Sir Roger was a drunk who got ugly in his cups and may have even beaten her. She finally fled to her grandmother's castle in Scotland and into the arms of her would-be cousin, Pat Guthrie, whose alcoholic drinking occasionally required him to "dry out" in a hospital.

Pat had a history of bisexuality (some think it was he who attracted the homosexuals in the Paris cafes) and a habit of leaving large unpaid bills, expecting his mother to bail him out. He had a temper and a ruthless personality that struck an answering chord in Duff. They ran off to Paris together and became a fixture in the Left Bank cafes, leaving her child in the care of her husband's grandmothers as he filed for divorce. When she and Guthrie swept into the night spots with their entourage, everyone paid attention. Her defiantly androgynous appearance, combined with aplomb, made her seem independent and above Montparnasse's edgy sexual fray, but not everyone admired her: Robert McAlmon thought her "generally stinko with brandy, terrified of life economically, a mess generally."[24]

Duff had wit and a hearty sense of humor. "When she laughed," Hadley recalled years later, "the whole of her went into that laughter. Lots of broad language, certainly, but it went over with all kinds of people." People remembered her throaty laugh and her ability to joke with the "chaps"[25] as she called them. Many also remembered a legendary love life that probably wasn't as legendary as some people thought since for a woman to be promiscuous there must be promiscuous men and she

---

24. Sarason, *Hemingway and the Sun Set*, 225.
25. Hadley Mowrer, Alice Sokoloff tapes, Hemingway Collection, JFK Library.

constantly surrounded herself with homosexuals, which was a safe way for an attractive woman to drink herself blind in the Quarter. Ernest Hemingway grew up in a house of Anglophiles and would have been impressed by a titled English woman, especially a young, attractive, available one, and was instantly and completely fascinated: "the title seemed to electrify him,"[26] remembered McAlmon. She was the stuff stories were made of and Ernest listened to the cadence of Duff's throaty lilt carefully when she talked and wrote down notes of what she said: "We can't do it. You can't hurt people. It's what we believe in place of God"; "It is like living with fourteen men so no one will know there is someone you love"; and "I have to have it and I can't have what I want with you so I'm going to take this other thing"[27]: snippets of conversation maybe overheard, but too intimate for bar talk. Most people think Duff never let him into her bed but used him to pick up bar tabs Ernest could not afford, or as a foil to keep other men at a distance if that was needed.

It was a dangerous spring for Ernest. He was distracted and less than attentive to his wife and to his fiction. Hadley was accustomed to his sexual magnetism and was generally passive about his infatuations, but now she was watching the onset of a behavior pattern that would haunt his life: an exciting new woman apparently in reach and him with a wife in tow. When he took Duff to their apartment, she was charmed by Bumby and felt sorry for Hadley, and like Kitty and Dossie Johnston, gave her dresses and other clothes. Apparently Duff had assured her she did not prey on husbands, and Hadley admired her brass behavior. "[She was] a man's woman with delightful manners," remembered Hadley; still, she was deeply distressed by Ernest's relationship with her. According to McAlmon, sometimes with Hadley along on a drinking expedition in Montmartre he would flirt so openly with Duff that Hadley would cry, and he would ask someone to take his weeping wife home while he stayed with Duff, both liking the charm and romance of flirting knowing it would never go far. Hadley, though upset, was not openly worried. "[Duff was] wonderfully attractive . . . with no sexual inhibitions . . .

---

26. Sarason, *Hemingway and the Sun Set*, 227.
27. Reynolds, *Hemingway: The Paris Years*, 290.

[Ernest] just adored her, but I'm sure they didn't have an affair."[28] Yet Ernest had expressed in a letter to Bill Smith a desire to "yence"[29] without complications, and Duff, though not really attracted to Hemingway, liked his attentions and may have seemed available even if she really wasn't.

As the Hemingways made new friends like the Pfeiffer sisters and Duff Twysden, some of their oldest Parisian friends were falling away. Ezra and Dorothy Pound were now living full time in Rapallo and would rarely see them again. And later in 1925, their friendship with Gertrude Stein ended. One day after dropping in at Gertrude and Alice's apartment Ernest returned to the sawmill in a grim mood. He said he had overheard a shocking lovers' quarrel between the two women, who were upstairs in their bedroom. "Ernest said he had never heard such language," recalled Hadley. Without giving details, he said, "Well, I'm just not going to have anything to do with them anymore." Hadley was still fond of the two great lesbian women and wanted to continue to see them. One afternoon coming home from the Luxembourg Gardens with Bumby, she stopped at 27 rue des Fleurus. A maid came to the door, told her to wait outside, and returned a few minutes later saying coldly in French, "Madame, they do not know you today." Hadley felt "cut to the quick." She believed Stein was too embarrassed to face her. "I think Gertrude was aware of what Ernest heard. And she couldn't bear for anyone to hear it, especially anyone like Ernest, who was such a good reporter. Ernest never forgave them, and they never forgave him."[30]

However, the real reason behind their rift went much deeper. Alice jealously guarded her relationship with Gertrude and quickly became wary of anyone else who might get too close. From the start she was wary of Hemingway and came to dislike him more and more. She did not like that Gertrude loved him and she did not like that he loved Gertrude, but she knew that Gertrude needed him because mentoring was very important to Gertrude, and Hemingway was someone Gertrude wanted and needed to mentor, and when the time had come when the mentoring

28. Reynolds, *Hemingway: The Paris Years*, 289-90.
29. Reynolds, 269.
30. Mowrer, Sokoloff tapes, Hemingway Collection, JFK Library.

and favors that were to be done between them had run their course and been completed—and by 1925 Gertrude's influence on Hemingway's writing was thorough and complete, and Hemingway had seen that Gertrude was published and paid for her work—Alice exerted her very strong will upon her lover and mate, and Hemingway was dropped from their lives. And though Gertrude Stein would write of him, "he looks like a modern and he smells of the museums,"[31] which was not without truth, for Hemingway's writing would enter the mainstream of culture, the affection between them never entirely abated, as Gertrude in *The Autobiography of Alice B. Toklas*, taking Alice's point of view, wrote about Alice and herself and her feelings for Hemingway, "However, whatever I say, Gertrude Stein always says, yes I know but I have a weakness for Hemingway,"[32] and years later when they saw each other in Paris near the end of World War II, they again declared their love for one another. But before the break with Gertrude, the Hemingways met and befriended another great literary couple: a remarkable American named F. Scott Fitzgerald and his beautiful but strange wife Zelda.

---

31. Gertrude Stein, *The Autobiography of Alice B. Toklas*, 204.
32. Stein, 208.

Cycling

Pauline Pfeiffer

Portrait of Ernest Walsh

Expatriates

Duff Twysden (lower left) at the Dingo Bar

CHRONICLER OF
THE JAZZ AGE

*Scott Fitzgerald is always described as a representative figure of the
1920s, but the point has to be made that he represented the new
generation of ambitious college men rising in the business world much
more than he did the writers. He earned more money than the other
serious writers of his generation, lived far beyond their means—as well
as living beyond his own—and paid a bigger price in remorse and
suffering for his mistakes. Like the others, he followed his own path
through life, and yet when all the paths are seen from a distance they
seem to be interwoven into a larger pattern of exile (if only in spirit)
and return from exile, of alienation and reintegration.*[1]

— MALCOLM COWLEY

ANY YEARS after they knew each other Hemingway would
write of Fitzgerald, "His talent was as natural as the pattern
that was made by the dust on a butterfly's wings. At one time he understood it no more than the butterfly did and he did not know when it was
brushed or marred."[2] Hemingway was right that Fitzgerald's talent was
natural, but he was wrong about him not understanding it. Scott Fitzgerald knew well that his talent came from his Irish blood, and he knew that
the reasons he wrote were from the pain of social consciousness and that
he was always helplessly falling in love. What he didn't understand was
the money he made from writing, and he made a lot of it.

---

1. Malcom Cowley, *Exiles Return*, 292.
2. Ernest Hemingway, *A Moveable Feast*, 147.

The differences between Hemingway and Fitzgerald were striking, but their similarities went deep. Like Hemingway, Scott was a son of the American Midwest, growing up among the affluent in St. Paul, Minnesota. He was christened Francis Scott Key Fitzgerald, named after the cousin who had composed the national anthem, and began writing almost as soon as he could think, intrusively so, as a means of defining himself and trying to make logic from the frightful confusion of the surrounding world. Like Hemingway, Fitzgerald had an ineffectual father whose failures Scott tried to reason away, and a strong mother who wore big hats and stood out for being rather eccentric. After the emotional trauma of losing her first two children in infancy, Mollie Fitzgerald coddled and cosseted her only son, a very good-looking boy, making him more self-absorbed than other youths, a tendency he may have had anyway, and perhaps more emotionally vulnerable. In company, she would dress him up and show him off, and to further receive their admiration, he would recite speeches from Shakespeare's plays, which developed into a theatrical bent as he began writing plays as an adolescent, reserving the best parts for himself when they were acted out in the neighborhood. So thoroughly spoiled was Scott that until he was fifteen, he "did not know anyone else was alive."[3] He was unpopular among boys, but the girls always liked him.

Intense about courtship, which he considered to be a competitive game, as a young writer he obsessively ranked his standing with various girls and the reasons why they were what they were. "I didn't have the two top things—great animal magnetism or money," he wrote in a notebook. "I had the two second things, tho', good looks and intelligence."[4] At nineteen, he wrote a ten-page treatise to his younger sister Annabel, coaching her on social skills and how to win the admiration of young boys. To truly play the game successfully, one had to put themselves in the place of the competitor and of the opposite sex. Here young Scott had an advantage for he could think like a girl. "I'm half feminine," he

---

3. James R. Mellow, *Invented Lives*, 21.
4. Scott Donaldson, *Fool for Love: F. Scott Fitzgerald*, 44.

once said, "at least my mind is."[5] Naturally, the first time he really fell in love was with a beautiful rich debutante from Chicago who carried on multiple romances, never really took him too seriously, and left him devastated with a broken heart.

He attended Princeton, where he threw himself into the Triangle Club musicals, both as an author and sometimes actor, portraying a chorus girl so effectively that men asked for dates (which he declined). He left without graduating in 1917, joining the army in the hope of seeing combat in the war overseas and was commissioned a second lieutenant. At Fort Leavenworth, Kansas "Every Saturday at one o'clock when the week's work was over I hurried up to the Officers' Club and there in a corner of a room full of smoke, conversation and rattling newspapers, I wrote a one-hundred-and-twenty-thousand word novel on the consecutive weekends of three months."[6] The work was titled *The Romantic Egotist* and was little more than a grab bag of stories, poems, and sketches recounting the author's coming of age. Entrusted to a friend, it found its way to Charles Scribner's publishing house in New York City where the young editor Maxwell Perkins took a keen interest and wrote to Fitzgerald, "no ms. novel has come to us for a long time that seemed to display so much vitality."[7] Perkins pointed out a lack of cohesion and wanted him to rewrite it with more intensity and promised "we shall then reread it immediately."[8] Scott rewrote it and sent it back, but Perkins could not at this time muster enough interest for publication. Scott was too distracted to be very disappointed because again he had fallen deeply in love. Stationed at Camp Sheridan in Montgomery, Alabama, in the summer of 1918, when he saw eighteen-year-old Zelda Sayre at a country club dance everything inside of him melted. She was short with blue eyes, a wonderful figure, smooth flawless skin, and beautiful golden hair; she also had a fine creative mind, playing the mating game as well as Fitzgerald but without all the thought and writing.

5. Mellow, *Invented Lives*, 37.
6. James West, *F. Scott Fitzgerald*, 3.
7. Mellow, *Invented Lives*, 53.
8. A. Scott Berg, *Max Perkins: Editor of Genius*, 13.

Zelda, the youngest of six children, was spoiled by her mother. "I was a very active child," she remembered, "and never tired, always running with no hat or coat even in the Negro district and far from my house. I liked houses under construction and often I walked on the open roofs; I liked to jump from high places . . . in the tops of trees . . . I had great confidence in myself," and "did not have a single feeling of inferiority, or shyness, or doubt, and no moral principles." She behaved well at school through the primary grades and then became bold and sassy, discovering education not in the classroom but by reading whatever she found at home: "books chosen by accident in my father's library: a life of John Paul Jones, lives written by Plutarch, *The Decline and Fall of the Roman Empire* by Gibbons, and fairy tales a lot." She read Wilde and Galsworthy and Kipling "and all I found about the Civil War . . . The fairy tales were my favorite."[9] She chafed against restraints, and as she grew older, drank and smoked and could be quite provocative: driving past the local whorehouse, she would flick a spotlight on the boys she knew as they entered and left the building. She felt herself suffocating in the small arena of Montgomery, Alabama. Her release came when the United States entered the war in Europe and thousands of soldiers and aviators poured into Montgomery to train at the camps just outside of town. The most handsome, and to her the most captivating, was F. Scott Fitzgerald.

Clothed like an ephemeral butterfly, she was always surrounded by beaux, and before their courtship turned serious, she carefully kept other suitors dangling within sight because she instinctively knew it further enticed Scott, who was himself playing the game between them quite well and didn't fall inextricably in love until well after a month. Zelda's family had been at the center of the old Confederate establishment; a great-uncle had been a general during the Civil War and afterward served in the United States Senate for thirty-one years. They were not rich but were more prominent than the Fitzgeralds had ever been in the north and were still prominent during the courtship. In the evenings, as they swayed together on the creaking swing at the far end of the "gallery" on

---

9. Nancy Mitford, *Zelda, Part 1: Southern Girl.*

the wide front porch of Judge Sayre's house on Pleasant Street, the judge himself, a rather distant father who was a justice on the Supreme Court of Alabama, would be reading his paper by the light from a window, while the mother, "Miss Minnie," chatted with others who came calling on the large family.

With a self-effacing candor, Fitzgerald would later admit to being the worst lieutenant in the entire American army. And while he lacked military logic and was never a leader of men, he understood personalities and administration and most of the officers liked him. In his smart tunic and polished boots he did make an impression, and as a supply officer he was sent north late in October with overseas orders to help prepare for the embarkation of his division to France. He may have had thoughts of death on the battlefield, for he told Zelda before leaving, "Here is my heart."[10] However, the war ended while he was in New York. As inept a soldier that he was, except in his snappy uniforms, the Armistice denied him the glory of combat, and he drank to assuage his disappointment. Unlike Hemingway, who was only an ambulance driver for the Red Cross, Fitzgerald was an officer in the United States Army; and unlike Fitzgerald, who returned to Camp Sheridan unscathed, Hemingway was almost killed on the front lines in Italy and decorated for courage.

Waiting out his discharge, Fitzgerald continued to court Zelda, nights she remembered as soft and gray with the scent of pines. She committed to him in ways that lovers understand; even when she flirted with and dated other men, she did so to make him jealous and increase her value in his eyes, but she held him off because he had no money and the life of a writer with a new attitude toward his craft seemed to have little promise. Finally, with the demobilization of troops, late in the winter of 1919, he took the train to New York in the hope of becoming a journalist like his college friend Bunny Wilson. His parting from Zelda had not been easy: she was restless and provocative, and he was anxious. "My affair still drifts," he wrote to a friend. "Still, she is remarkable."[11]

---

10. Mellow, *Invented Lives*, 55.
11. Mitford, *Zelda, Part 1: Southern Girl*.

In New York, he accepted a job writing advertising copy. He was good at the work but unhappy with the low pay, living in a drab room, broke most of the time, plodding to work with cardboard in the sole of one of his shoes. "I walked quickly from certain places . . . wearing the suit from before the war."[12] Though he could hardly afford it, he made monthly trips to Montgomery to see Zelda, who had consulted a spiritualist who "told us to be married—that we were soul-mates."[13] On a last visit Scott pressed for an answer to his proposal of marriage, but she would not give it. Back in New York, he went on a binge that lasted three weeks. Disgusted with himself and unhappy about Zelda, "I got roaring weeping drunk on my last penny and went home."[14]

In a third-floor room in his parents' house on Summit Avenue in St. Paul, Fitzgerald stayed sober and dug in and rewrote the work Scribner's wouldn't publish into a longer, more focused novel. Donald Ogden Stewart, living in a boarding house farther up the avenue, recalled: "Scott showed me a shoe box full of handwritten-in-pencil manuscript of a novel called *This Side of Paradise*. Fortunately, I liked it very much."[15] By the end of July Scott wrote Max Perkins: "This is definite attempt at a big novel and I really believe I have hit it."[16] Perkins received the manuscript in August, read it, and wrote Fitzgerald in the middle of September that the book was enormously improved—"It abounds in energy and life and seems to me to be in much better proportion"[17]—and accepted the book for publication. The author's mood soared. He stopped cars in the street to tell them the news and sent letters to his friends. Edmund "Bunny" Wilson, who he knew would be an exacting critic, took a long, scathing look at the work and expressed what he thought were its flaws, "Your hero as an intellectual is a fake of the first water," but he also praised the style: "You do have a knack of writing readably, which is a great asset."[18] The prose of F. Scott Fitzgerald is clear and poetic, the words and phrases

12. Mellow, *Invented Lives*, 61.
13. Mellow, 68.
14. Mellow, 71.
15. Mellow, 71.
16. Mellow, 72.
17. Mellow, 73.
18. Edmund Wilson to FSF, Nov. 21, 1919, *Wilson's Letters*.

musically rise from the pages, and the novel he wrote in the summer of 1919 told about a new generation, its mores and music and promiscuity, that was entirely different from all the ones before them.

It was as if a large door had suddenly swung open; what had been hard was now easy, and he wrote with much more confidence. *Scribner's Magazine* bought two of his stories: "The Cut-Glass Bowl" and "The Four Fists"; *The Smart Set* bought "Dalyrimple Goes Wrong" and a one-act play named *Porcelain and Pink*. Jean Paul Nathan wrote that Fitzgerald had an uncommon gift for dialogue and advised him to keep writing plays. Recalling that "first wild wind of success" when it seemed impossible to do anything wrong, Scott wrote, "the postman rang and rang, and I paid off my terrible small debts, bought a suit and woke up every morning with a world of ineffable top loftiness and promise."[19] His feelings for Zelda were also rekindled, and in October he broke his silence and wrote her about the publication of his novel. She wrote back and warmly acknowledged, "I don't feel a bit shaky and do-don'tish like I used to when you came—I really want to see you—that's all."[20] It was never easy between them, but his stories kept selling, and he had money and could return to Montgomery as a success. In the New Year, he sold "The Camel's Back," "Bernice Bobs Her Hair," "The Ice Palace," and "The Offshore Pirate" to *The Saturday Evening Post* for fees that rose from four hundred to five hundred dollars. Then, in February, Metro Studios paid the staggering sum of twenty-five hundred dollars for the movie rights to his *Post* story "Head and Shoulders."

On trips to New York, Scott, pulling hundred dollar bills out of his pockets, drank and spent recklessly. He sent Zelda an expensive platinum and diamond watch. "O, Scott," she wrote, "It's so be-au-ti-ful."[21] Even though success bred more success, especially in the movies where options were sold for two more stories, Scott was not artistically satisfied: he considered his stories meretricious and commercial. When he sent Zelda an orchid corsage, she wrote meaningfully to him: "Our fairy tale is almost

19. Mellow, *Invented Lives*, 73.
20. Mellow, 78-9.
21. Mellow, 85.

ended, and we're going to marry . . . I'm sorry for all the times I've been mean and hateful . . . You deserve so much, so very much."[22] They were married in Manhattan on April 3, 1920, in the rectory of St. Patrick's Cathedral. The nation was about to go on "the greatest, gaudiest spree in history,"[23] and the groom in the small wedding would not only write about it, but with he and his bride living a life so creative and wild, leave a strong, indelible, personal imprint.

F. Scott Fitzgerald loved New York City: the lights of battleships on the dark Hudson at night drifting like "water jewels," the fashionable crowd moving like a river along Fifth Avenue, the quiet of a Sunday, and the lights at night in distant buildings flickering like stars. He would speak of its "flashing, dynamic good looks, its tall man's quick-step," and keenly sense the rhythm of a weekend: "its birth, its planned gaieties and its announced end." Days and nights were as "tense as singing wires."[24] Staying mostly in Manhattan on an extended honeymoon, the mayhem of the Fitzgeralds' first year together was astounding. Young, brilliant, and beautiful, making up their own rules, they got drunk and went from party to party where Zelda would often undress and take baths in the bathtubs. At a comedy they laughed at their own jokes and not the playwrights; the actors complained, management asked them to leave, and Zelda stormed off in a huff. They played games in the revolving door of the Commodore. When hotels asked them to leave, they'd pack their bags and move to another. Zelda plunged into a public fountain; not to be outdone, Scott jumped into the fountain outside the Plaza. Dorothy Parker first glimpsed them riding on the top of a taxicab. Scott did little serious writing, but *This Side of Paradise* was a bestseller, and the stories he had written before they were married continued to sell at even higher prices. So, they partied and fought, spent extravagantly, made the gossip columns, and found themselves the spokesmen for a new generation of gilded youth.

The writing was harder to do. Zelda went off with friends, mostly men who were friends of Scott, leaving him alone and worried about

22. Zelda to FSF, Feb. 1920, Correspondence.
23. Cowley, "Introduction", *The Stories of F. Scott Fitzgerald*.
24. Mellow, *Invented Lives*, 91.

her fidelity. She worried about him too. He had promised Max Perkins a second novel by November, but he finished it late in the following winter. *The Beautiful and the Damned* is about a young wealthy couple whose indulgent, destructive behavior destroys the love between them and ruins their lives. Edmund Wilson read the manuscript and wrote to a friend, "though I thought it was rather silly at first, I find it developing a genuine emotional power . . . It's all about him and Zelda."[25] Fitzgerald was an autobiographical novelist, but he was also objective and knew how to make a story work, and like all gifted writers, the characters in his books are creations and not real people. As Scott put the finishing touches on his second novel, Zelda discovered she was pregnant and left to see her parents. When he joined her in Alabama, they packed their bags again and left on an extended trip abroad.

In England, they enjoyed a luncheon with Lady Randolph Churchill, Winston's American mother and aunt of Scott's old friend Shane Leslie, and visited Oxford, which Scott thought was the most beautiful spot in the world. But they continued to move from hotel to hotel, drinking heavily and leaving the rooms in disarray. The Fitzgeralds were too American to integrate themselves into older foreign cultures and cared little for Italy and France. "Goddamn the continent of Europe," Fitzgerald wrote to Wilson from Rome. "It is merely of antiquarian interest."[26] In Paris they looked up Edna St. Vincent Millay, there to escape her many suitors in America, one of whom was Bunny Wilson, who soon appeared in Paris but missed the Fitzgeralds, who had returned to London. "The truth is that you are so saturated with twentieth-century America," wrote Wilson with keen insight, trying to bring them back to Paris, "so used to hotels, plumbing, drugstores, aesthetic ideals and vast commercial prosperity of the country that you can't appreciate those institutions of France . . . which are really superior to American ones."[27]

In August they returned to St. Paul to await the birth of the baby. Their daughter, Frances Scott Fitzgerald, was born in a hospital on

---

25. Mellow, 133-4.
26. Mellow, 138.
27. Mellow, 139.

October 26, 1921. As Zelda awoke from the anesthesia, Scott wrote down her remarks: "I hope it's beautiful and a fool—a beautiful little fool."[28] They moved to a house not far from his parents. Scott began to write again, renting an office downtown to work on proofs of *The Beautiful and Damned*. He wrote stories, book reviews, and a play for the local Junior League. On a trip to New York at the end of the long winter, Edmund Wilson found them changed, "particularly Zelda, who had become more matronly and rather fat,"[29] and liked her better for it. He also noticed a strain between them because, apparently, Zelda was pregnant again and this time wanted an abortion.

In an essay written about Fitzgerald for the March issue of *The Bookman*, Wilson thought that Scott had the Celtic gift for turning language "into something iridescent and surprising."[30] *The Beautiful and Damned* sold thirty-three thousand copies in its first month of publication and the critical response consolidated Fitzgerald's growing stature, but Scott was not satisfied. He had written a play called *The Vegetable* that he thought was going to be a huge Broadway success and was "going to make me rich forever."[31]

Back in Minnesota, Scott kept busy revising his play and wrote a story about a man who grows younger and younger, ending as an infant, called "The Curious Case of Benjamin Button." He also selected eleven stories for a collection called *Tales of the Jazz Age*, which included "May Day" and "A Diamond as Big as the Ritz." They returned to New York in September 1922, stayed at the Plaza Hotel, and scoured the countryside looking for a house to rent. Edmund Wilson visited them and was astonished by their good looks and sobriety: "Fitz goes about soberly transacting his business and in the evening writes at his room in the hotel."[32] While at the Plaza they met John Dos Passos, who had liked Fitzgerald's review of *Three Soldiers*. At a lunch in their room, Scott introduced Dos Passos to Sherwood Anderson. Dos Passos and Anderson plunged into a

---

28. Mellow, 143.
29. Edmund Wilson to Stanley Dell, Mar. 25, 1922, *Letters on Literature*.
30. Mellow, *Invented Lives*, 149.
31. Jackson, Bryer, Margolies, Prigozy, *F. Scott Fitzgerald: New Perspectives*, 259.
32. Wilson to J. B. Peale, Sept. 22, 1922, *Letters on Literature*.

literary discussion that may have been in self-defense against Fitzgerald's incriminating questions. "I used to kid Scott about his silly questions," remembered Dos. "They were like the true or false lists psychologists used to make up. Even that first time I couldn't get mad at him and particularly not at Zelda; there was a golden innocence about them and they both were so hopelessly good looking."[33]

After lunch, Dos accompanied Zelda and Scott in a rented touring car with a chauffeur. They went to Long Island to meet with a real estate agent. Having broken their sobriety during the boozy luncheon, their behavior disgusted Dos Passos. They were rude to the agent, dropped him off, and visited Ring Lardner, who lived in a house with his wife and four sons in Great Neck. Lardner was too drunk to carry on a conversation, and so they left and stopped at a carnival along the way. During a ride on the Ferris wheel, Dos sensed an edge of madness in Zelda: "The gulf that opened between Zelda and me, sitting up on the rickety Ferris wheel, was something I couldn't explain . . . Though she was so very lovely, I had come upon something that frightened and repelled me, even physically."[34] On the ride back to the Plaza, Zelda sulked and Scott was drunk. Dos felt relief at departing.

They found a beautiful, rather large Mediterranean-style house on a quiet curving street in Great Neck, New York. Great Neck is on the north shore of Long Island in an area then called the Gold Coast. During the twenties, this was the haven of millionaires, successful and famous writers, artists, and theatrical personalities. At one time or another, Eddie Cantor, Ed Wynn, Jane Cowl, Leslie Howard, Basil Rathbone, and George M. Cohan had homes there. Ring Lardner (whose alcohol benders lasted for weeks) had an impressive view of the neighboring estate and sprawling grounds of Herbert Bayard Swope, executive editor of the *New York World* and an inveterate and extravagant party-giver. Sometimes guests would wander into the Lardner "cottage." Nearby, on the western shores of Hempstead Bay, the Guggenheims and Vincent Astor maintained baronial mansions. Small in comparison to the grand

33. John Dos Passos, *The Best Times*, 128.
34. Dos Passos, 130.

estates, the Fitzgeralds' home was the scene of continuous and expensive weekend partying.

Going to parties among the rich and famous, Scott boasted to a cousin that Great Neck was "most amusing after the dull healthy middle west."[35] If he expressed any interest in the Round Table in the dining room of the Algonquin Hotel in Manhattan, he never attended. His friend Bunny Wilson found the people at the Round Table too shallow for his tastes—they were from the hinterland and suburbs and had all been brought up with the same standards of gentility, played the same games, read the same children's books, and were now in the business of mocking their provincial upbringing by way of an acquired New York sophistication—and said, "I found this rather tiresome, since they never seemed to be able to get above it."[36] Ring Lardner was revered by the Round Table literati but kept his distance. "He never mingled with them. . . . he was somehow aloof and inscrutable, by nature rather saturnine, but a master whom all admired, though he was never present in person."[37] When Bunny served as managing editor of *Vanity Fair*, Fitzgerald wrote an homage to Ring Lardner, who he idolized: "Because he is quite unaware of the approval he is receiving in erudite circles . . . because he has a rare true ear, he has set down for posterity the accents of the American language."[38]

Bunny Wilson, Scott's old friend from Princeton, was one of the most influential vanguard critics of the period, an early champion of T. S. Eliot's *The Waste Land* and James Joyce's banned *Ulysses*. Of *Ulysses* he wrote, "It contains some of the most brilliant and some of the dreariest and dullest writing of the age, but it has already been accepted as a sort of divine revelation by the intelligentsia—most of whom have not read it."[39] He wrote to Fitzgerald that some of the drunken episodes had an uncanny resemblance to the "drunken-vision"[40] scene in his play *The*

---

35. FSF to Cecilia Taylor, Autumn 1922, *A Life in Letters*.
36. Wilson, *The Twenties*, 45.
37. Wilson, 48-9.
38. Mellow, *Invented Lives*, 173.
39. Wilson to Stanley Dell, May 26, 1922, *Letters on Literature*.
40. Mellow, *Invented Lives*, 175.

Vegetable. Fitzgerald read *Ulysses,* but rather than any resemblance to his play, it reminded him his own middle-class Irish background and made him feel "appallingly naked."[41] Probably through Bunny Wilson the Fitzgeralds met Esther Murphy, whose father, Patrick Francis Murphy, had turned his leather goods company, Mark Cross, into a lucrative business and lived in a home in Southampton where the servants intimidated his wife so much that she was afraid to fire them.

During Prohibition, the literary and artistic gatherings in New York City flowed with liquor. Conde Naste, owner of many slick magazines, hosted luxurious parties in his thirty-room penthouse at 1040 Park Avenue where high society and royalty mixed with show business types, artists, designers, and photographers. Fitzgerald attended at least one of these parties and thought they "rivaled in their way the fabled balls of the nineties."[42] Sometimes Zelda and Scott arrived at parties very late and so very drunk they passed out at the table with bowls of soup laid before them. A sense of disorientation, a kind of bibulous haze, hangs over many recollections of the period. Fitzgerald, trying to be the chronicler of his age, was actually one of its most active participants. He so picked his way through foggy memories of gay nights and mornings after, of continuous parties that traveled from dimly remembered apartments to vaguely recollected speakeasies, that he wrote years later, "even now I go into many flats with the sense that I have been there before."[43]

The most durable friendship Fitzgerald made at Great Neck was the one with Ring Lardner. A very tall man, Lardner was thirty-seven (Fitz was twenty-six) and, when sober, unusually taciturn. He could hold an audience captivated with stories, though never smutty ones for he had an old-fashioned sense of propriety. Ring had been a heavy drinker since the age of twenty-five, and in the deeper reaches of a binge would turn incommunicable. By the time they met, Lardner was a confirmed alcoholic. He could handle liquor much better than Scott and took pride in being a two-bottle man. Fitzgerald was also an alcoholic by this time

---

41. Mellow, 175.
42. F. Scott Fitzgerald, *The Jazz Age*, 25.
43. Mellow, *Invented Lives*, 182.

and probably knew that in Lardner he saw his own dissipation down the road. Ring Lardner's son wrote of Fitzgerald: "He probably felt satisfaction that he could sleep off a drunk and get back to work with much more ease than his older friend, but he must have known he was heading in the same direction."[44]

Lardner had been a highly paid sportswriter who approached baseball as if it were one of the most serious professions in the world and had been terribly shaken by the White Sox scandal of 1919. During the years in Great Neck, he had settled down to being a short story writer, but he still collaborated with cartoonist Dick Dorgan on a highly profitable syndicated comic strip, "You Know Me Al." He was an avid theatergoer, liked musical comedies, wrote skits for the Ziegfield follies, and was friends with a number of rising comedians like Ed Wynn, Eddie Cantor, and Groucho Marx, who lived in the Great Neck area. In his peak years, whatever his amount of alcohol consumption, he earned approximately $100,000 a year: terms of success—and self-indulgence—that Fitzgerald must have found encouraging. They would frequently sit up all hours of the night (no doubt drinking), either at Fitz's house on Gateway Drive or on the porch of the Lardner house overlooking the Swope estate, discussing sports and literature. When their literary hero, Joseph Conrad, visited his American publisher, Frank Nelson Doubleday, at his estate on nearby Oyster Bay in May 1919, Lardner and Fitzgerald did a hornpipe dance on the publisher's lawn in the hope that Conrad would look out the window and know of their admiration. (For their effort, the caretaker unceremoniously told them to leave.) Ring's wife, Ellis Lardner, was put off by the Fitzgeralds' exhibitionism and probably regarded Scott as an encouragement to her husband's drinking. But the four Lardner sons, who were then children, liked the Fitzgeralds heartily.

Almost immediately, Scott began promoting Ring to Max Perkins and badgered Lardner into putting together a collection of his stories to be published by Scribner. Lardner was so indifferent that Fitzgerald, stunned by his friend's lack of self-editing, had to gather copies of the

44. Ring Lardner Jr., *The Lardners*, 164.

stories from local libraries. Fitz even came up with the title of the book: *How to Write Short Stories*. The entire fruitful project was carried out by Fitz and Perkins with little help from the author. Scott's concern for Lardner's better stories like "Champion" and "The Golden Honeymoon" and his effort to get Scribner's to bring out the volume of collected stories was an act of generosity from one writer to another in the highly competitive literary profession. And there was reciprocity in their literary relationship: Fitz introduced Lardner to the work of Gertrude Stein, specifically *Three Lives*, a book he had learned about from Bunny Wilson (perhaps reading "Melanctha" was an influence on Lardner's dialect), and Lardner introduced Fitz to Dostoevsky's *The Brothers Karamazov* (and possibly Dickens's *Bleak House*), a book Scott claimed was an important influence on his writing, later telling Mencken he had resorted to its masculine influence when writing *The Great Gatsby* rather than the feminine one of Henry James's *The Portrait of a Lady*.

The summer of 1923 was a hot summer in Great Neck. But, despite the heat, despite the distracting hope for the production of his play, despite the rounds of parties and trips to and from New York along the shimmering highway past the slums and ash heaps in Flushing, Scott began to feel the stirring of his imagination, some sense of the undercurrent beneath the surface of uneventful days and stalled opportunities. There were chance impressions. One evening, an acquaintance from one of the golf clubs told him that as a fourteen-year-old boy in lower Brooklyn he had warned a wealthy yachtsman that his boat could be damaged in the running tides of Sheepshead Bay. Consequentially, the rich man hired him, and he lived on the yacht for three years. Scott frequently encountered a neighbor who fondly called him "Old Sport."[45] There was also the chance meeting of Arnold Rothstein, the notorious gambler who had had a hand in fixing the World Series in 1919. Other impressions came together in Scott's mind that summer: the carnival along the highway where he had sat in the car while Dos and Zelda rode the Ferris wheel, the dazzle of wealth and fame at the Swope and Naste parties,

---

45. Mellow, *Invented Lives*, 194.

the unrelenting heat and memories of New York apartments,—all of which would hover around the composition of *The Great Gatsby*, which he began in the house in Great Neck that summer.

He worked on the book with such earnestness that Zelda complained to friends, "Scott has started a new novel and retired into strict seclusion and celibacy."[46] Scott apparently did equate celibacy with a means of preventing Zelda from absorbing all his time and emotion, and he could not rid himself of the Catholicism he had grown up with in his family as he had apparently first thought to put a Catholic element in his novel. Although Great Neck provided the setting for much of *The Great Gatsby*, he did not complete his novel there, and his intention of the Catholic element was later discarded—out of the husk of which he did shape the story "Absolution." That fall, his play *The Vegetable* failed in Atlantic City. He had thought it was one of the funniest plays ever written and that it was going to make him a fortune. The sobering disappointment sent him back to work with a new sense of seriousness. He retired to his room above the garage; watching his drinking and consuming coffee, he produced ten saleable stories, the most important being "The Sensible Thing" about his and Zelda's courtship. In the spring of 1924, Scott's period of sobriety was coming to an end. Wearying of Long Island, he wanted to finish his novel in Europe.

They sailed for France in early May 1924, with seventeen pieces of luggage. In Paris, they met Gerald and Sara Murphy. Gerald was eight years older than Scott and the older brother of their friend from Great Neck, Esther Murphy. Gerald had a quicksilver temperament and was occasionally given to black moods. Sara was calm and unflustered, sensible, and not especially profound. Archibald MacLeish once described her "like a bowl of Renoir flowers."[47] The Murphys and the Fitzgeralds took to each other on very short acquaintance and planned to meet again in the summer. From Paris they moved to Hyeres on the Mediterranean coast, where Scott read about Byron and Shelley. Zelda did not like the atmosphere, so they moved farther east up the coast to Valescure and

---

46. Mellow, 195.
47. Mellow, 203.

rented a clean, cool villa perched on a hillside with the blue Mediterranean stretching below. They planned to stay until the first of November.

F. Scott Fitzgerald settled down to work on his novel. He wrote to a friend, "I am perfectly happy."[48] Zelda, however, was restless with little to do. The house had servants to do all the chores, and Scottie—as they called Frances—was looked after by a nanny who complained when Zelda interfered. So, Zelda spent a lot of time on the beach getting suntanned and met Edouard Jozan, an aviator from the nearby airfield, to whom she was very attracted. With Scott concentrating on writing his novel, she spent much time with this man on the beach and in the casino in the evening. The Murphys, who were on the Riviera to see about the renovation of the villa they had bought at Antibes, thought something was going on between them and that Scott was too busy to notice. It wasn't until later that Scott's suspicions were aroused, and if anything actually had happened between Zelda and the aviator it remains in the shadows of time and circumstances. Friends like Gilbert Seldes and his bride, who visited later in the summer, saw no signs of marital discord. However, the sense of betrayal in *The Great Gatsby* may have come from this brief fling.

Fitzgerald wrote to Perkins, "I feel I have an enormous power in me now," and throughout the summer sent progress reports on both the novel and himself—"I've been unhappy [Jozan Affair?] but my work hasn't suffered from it. I am grown at last,"—and became more enthusiastic as the summer progressed: "I think my novel is about the best American novel ever written."[49] He finished the novel and sent it to Perkins late in October after a visit from Ring and Ellis Lardner on the Riviera. He had several titles in mind and apparently was undecided up to publication, finally deciding upon *The Great Gatsby*. At the end he was feeling sad and old, even at the age of twenty-eight. He and Zelda planned to spend the winter in Italy and something of the end-of-summer mood had crept into the novel. "I feel old too, this summer," he wrote. "I have ever since the failure of my play a year ago. That's the whole burden of this novel—the loss of those illusions that give such color to the world so that you don't

---

48. Mellow, 205.
49. Mellow, 215; bracketed note from Mellow.

care whether things are true or false as long as they partake of the magical glory."[50] But, as the last line of his novel indicates, the dream that is in *Gatsby* is a dream that will never die: "So we beat on, boats against the currents, borne back ceaselessly into the past."[51]

In Rome, Scott wrote some more stories. Dissatisfied with his commercial efforts, he wrote to Perkins asking for more money and wanting to know his opinion of the novel. Perkins was magnanimous: "I think the novel is a wonder . . . It has vitality to an extraordinary degree and glamour . . . And as for sheer writing, it is astonishing." He became more enthusiastic after a second reading, impressed by Fitzgerald's use of symbols; "In the eyes of Dr. Eckleburg various readers will see different significances; but their presence gives a superb touch to the whole thing: great unblinking eyes, expressionless, looking down upon the human scene. It's magnificent!"[52] Fitzgerald's response was heartfelt: "Your letters make me feel like a million dollars—I'm sorry I could make no better response than a telegram whining for more money. But the long siege of the novel winded me a little."[53]

The Fitzgeralds took in the nightlife of Rome, became friendly with the film crew shooting *Ben Hur*, and then fled to Capri where Scott finished reading the galley proofs of *Gatsby*, making some changes, and felt uneasy about all the homosexual men surrounding him on the island. He also began writing "The Rich Boy," which he would finish in Paris in the summer. Toward the end of their island visit Scott wrote, "The cheerfullest things in my life are first Zelda and second the hope that my book has something extraordinary about it."[54] As the publication date for *The Great Gatsby* approached—April 10, 1925—Fitzgerald became nervous and hopeful. They booked passage aboard a steamship from Naples to Marseilles, transporting their Renault back to France. At some time en route, Perkins cabled that the sales were doubtful but the reviews were excellent. Driving from Marseilles to Paris, the car broke down in

---

50. Mellow, 216.
51. F. Scott Fitzgerald, *The Great Gatsby*, 159.
52. Mellow, *Invented Lives*, 225.
53. Mellow, 226.
54. FSF to John Peale Bishop, April, 1925, *A Life in Letters*.

Lyons; they left it in a garage and went on by train. In Paris, they found an apartment near the Eiffel Tower and moved in around the middle of May. Soon after arriving, Scott wandered off alone and in a café on the Left Bank met Ernest Hemingway, who he had wanted to meet since first reading Edmund Wilson's copy of *in our time* in the early spring of 1924.

Hemingway, who had rugged good looks, remembered F. Scott Fitzgerald as

> a man then who looked like a boy with a face between handsome and pretty. He had fair wavy hair, a high forehead, excited and friendly eyes and a delicate long-lipped Irish mouth that, on a girl, would have been the mouth of a beauty. His chin was well built and he had good ears and a handsome, almost beautiful, unmarked nose. This should not have added up to a pretty face, but that came from the coloring, the very fair hair and the mouth.[55]

The accounts of their first meeting vary, but it's certain they did meet on a spring evening in Paris in one of the cafes along Montparnasse. And, as one story has it, it may have happened at the Dingo on rue Delambre, just off the Boulevard, while the Hemingways were at a table with friends, which may have included Duff and Pat, and Scott came over and introduced himself. He was "only a little drunk," remembered Ernest in an unpublished sketch, "and when he sat down with us I found he had great charm and seriousness."[56]

Fitzgerald's third novel, *The Great Gatsby*, had just been published, and he made good money writing short stories for glossy New York magazines. "I was very curious to see him and I had been working very hard all day and it seemed quite wonderful that here should be Scott Fitzgerald." Scott ordered champagne and talked a lot. "I was embarrassed by what he said," Ernest wrote in *A Moveable Feast*, "it was all about my writing and how great it was." Hadley grew bored with the intense literary talk and

---

55. Ernest Hemingway, *A Moveable Feast*, 149.
56. Ernest Hemingway, unpublished sketch, item 486, Hemingway Collection, JFK Library.

told her husband that she would wait for him on the brightly lit sidewalk outside a nearby café. Scott started asking some very direct and personal questions about his sex life with Hadley before they were married and then "a very strange thing happened." As he sat there talking "the skin seemed to tighten over his face until all the puffiness was gone and then it drew tighter until the face was like a death's head."[57] Scott passed out and Ernest put him in a cab and rejoined Hadley, who had liked Fitzgerald, though he asked a lot of questions, and when told of the way he passed out, wondered if there was something wrong with his heart.

Scott and Zelda soon visited the Hemingways in their rooms above the sawmill. "Fitzgerald was around yesterday afternoon with his wife and she's worth seeing so I'll bring them around Friday afternoon unless you warn me not too [sic],"[58] wrote Ernest to Gertrude and Alice. He took them to the studio on rue de Fleurus, where Scott gave Gertrude a copy of *The Great Gatsby*, which Gertrude read and soon wrote to Scott expressing her admiration. A few days later, Ernest probably did meet Scott at the Closerie des Lilas where they had a few drinks as Ernest told him why he liked this café, and Scott liking it, too, and asking more questions and telling Ernest "about writers and publishers and agents and critics" along with the gossip and money earned as a successful writer. "He was cynical and funny and very jolly and charming and endearing," and he spoke about his new novel and wanted Ernest to read it as soon as he could get his last copy back from someone to whom he had loaned it. "To hear him talk of it," remembered Hemingway, "you would never know how good it was, except that he had the shyness about it that all non-conceited writers have when they have done something very fine, and I hoped he would get the book quickly so that I might read it." As they sat outside on the terrace watching it get dusky and the people passing by, Scott did not ask embarrassing questions, nor get drunk and pass out, but "acted as a normal, intelligent and charming person,"[59] and when he invited Ernest to join him on a trip to retrieve his car in Lyon,

---

57. Hemingway, *A Moveable Feast*, 149-52.
58. EH to Gertrude & Alice, May 1925, *The Letters of Ernest Hemingway, Vol. 2*.
59. Hemingway, *A Moveable Feast*, 153-54.

Ernest gladly accepted the offer, and they arranged to meet at the train station the next morning.

Though they were saving their extra money for Pamplona, Hadley thought it would be good for Ernest to rest from work and take the trip. When Ernest arrived at the station Fitzgerald was not there and had still not arrived when the train pulled out. "I had never heard, then, of a grown man missing a train," wrote Ernest in *A Moveable Feast*, "but on this trip I was to learn many new things."[60] Ernest went alone and cabled Zelda when he got to Lyon: "SCOTT MISSED TRAIN PLEASE WIRE HIM CARE GARAGE I WILL BE AT HOTEL BRISTOL LYON WIRE ME CARE OF GARAGE THERE."[61] Fitzgerald showed up the next morning full of apology. They had a big breakfast in the hotel and ordered a big expensive lunch to go. Scott had been drinking, and they had another drink in the hotel bar and then went to the garage where Ernest discovered the small Renault had no top. The top had been damaged in Marseilles and Zelda ordered it cut away. Driving back to Paris they were halted by rain several times, seeking shelter under trees or in small cafes. "Didn't miss one vintage from Montrachet to Chambertin. Elaborate Trip,"[62] Ernest wrote to Ezra. The lunch from the hotel was excellent, Ernest bought several bottles of wine, and Fitzgerald began worrying disproportionately about his health. They stopped at a hotel along the road where Scott lay on the bed and badgered Ernest about his dire condition. "I was very tired of Scott and of this silly comedy,"[63] but took his temperature and assured him he wasn't going to die, and then they went downstairs for dinner. Scott again passed out from drink at the table and was helped up to their room. "It was obvious that he should not drink anything,"[64] thought Ernest.

The next day was sunny, and they drove through the country with the air freshly washed and the fields and the vineyards all new. Scott was cheerful and happy and healthy and told Ernest all the plots of Michael

---

60. Hemingway, 157.
61. EH to Zelda Fitzgerald, May 1925, *The Letters of Ernest Hemingway, Vol. 2.*
62. EH to Ezra Pound, June 8-10, 1925, *The Letters of Ernest Hemingway, Vol. 2.*
63. Hemingway, *A Moveable Feast*, 166.
64. Hemingway, 174.

Arlen's books. When they parted in Paris, Ernest was happy to see Hadley again but felt troubled and uncertain about F. Scott Fitzgerald. When Scott brought his new book over a couple of days later Ernest read it and, greatly moved, pondered his friend's alcoholism: "I knew that no matter what Scott did, nor how he behaved, I must know it was like a sickness and be of any help I could to him and try to be a good friend . . . If he could write a book as fine as The Great Gatsby I was sure that he could write an even better one."[65]

A few days later, the Hemingways lunched at the Fitzgeralds' apartment on rue de Tilsitt near the Champs-Elysees. The building was expensive looking, but their pre-furnished flat was dark, and for Ernest and Hadley, conjured up stuffy images of Henry James and Edith Wharton. Fundamentally generous, Scott wanted his friend to share in the writing bounty and talked to him about technique and what to charge for stories, showing Ernest the ledgers he meticulously kept that detailed the sums he received from magazines. Zelda appeared lovely but ravaged; she had a hangover, and her eyes would go blank during the lunch remembering some episode of the previous night. "She was very spoiled," wrote Hemingway, "and what she said did not make good sense to me."[66] Hadley thought Zelda was a lovely and charming southern girl, "I enjoyed looking at her,"[67] and also frivolous. But Zelda and Ernest discovered a strong dislike for each other: she thought he was phony, and he thought she was jealous of Scott and erratic and kind of crazy.

At dawn the next morning, they were awakened by Scott drunk and banging on the gate of the sawmill yard. "That used to happen a lot," Hadley recalled. "[Scott and Zelda] would come at these outlandish hours after drinking, and they did foolish things like taking a roll of toilet paper and standing at the top of our stair landing and unraveling it all the way down."[68] Ernest didn't seem to enjoy these episodes, but he never told them to leave; he, too, drank a lot, but, unlike Scott, could control himself, and they would all sit around in their nightgowns and

---

65. Hemingway, 176.
66. Ernest Hemingway, unpublished sketch, item 486, Hemingway Collection, JFK Library.
67. Hadley Mowrer, Alice Sokoloff tapes, Hemingway Collection, JFK Library.
68. Mowrer, Sokoloff tapes, Hemingway Collection, JFK Library.

pajamas and talk. Zelda didn't like being in her husband's shadow, and recognizing it was a role Hadley had accepted, said to her, "I notice in [your] family you do what Ernest wants."[69] Hadley recalled that "Ernest didn't like that much, but it was a perceptive remark."[70]

Though Ernest didn't like Zelda, he liked Scott a lot and their friendship deepened. Fitzgerald made and spent more money in the past year than the Ernest and Hadley had lived on during their first five years of marriage. As writers, it was like they were alter egos, each one wanting what the other had: Scott the overnight precocious success, Ernest the struggling artist accepted only among the avant-garde. Ernest wanted Scott's commercial success; Scott wanted to write for the intellectuals. Hemingway was flattered by the attention paid to him by Scott, who always had time for literary advice. They became close, especially that spring and early summer; the jokes good, the laughter genuine, together frequently eating, drinking, and talking the writing game. In June, Ernest wrote to Max Perkins, "Scott Fitzgerald is living here now and we see quite a lot of him. We had a great trip together driving his car up from Lyon through the Cote D'Or. I've read his Great Gatsby and think it is an absolutely first rate book."[71] Fitzgerald, too, spoke glowingly about their trip telling Gertrude Stein, "Hemingway and I went to Lyons . . . to get my car and had a slick drive through Burgundy. He's a peach of a fellow and absolutely first-rate."[72]

Hadley kept an open house for Ernest and their friends through the spring and summer before they left for Pamplona. Duff would come by on occasion. Scott Fitzgerald did not like her, but Ernest remained impressed by her looks and style, her insouciance, British accent, and capacity for drink. His scorn for the floaters of Montparnasse lost some of its edge when he talked with her. He was not among the narrow circle of her amours but felt possessive enough towards her to resent Loeb's steadily increasing infatuation. Bill Smith and Scott did not much like each other. Bill did like Harold Loeb, who Hadley thought was handsome

69. Mitford, Zelda, 116.
70. Gloria Diliberto, Hadley, 193.
71. EH to Maxwell Perkins, June 9, 1925, The Letters of Ernest Hemingway, Vol. 2.
72. Kenneth Lynn, Hemingway, 282.

and much more athletic than Ernest, and Harold liked Bill Smith. Despite Bill's quiet ways, Loeb discovered he "had a wit which expressed itself in cynical wisecrack and that he was loyal, discreet and reliable."[73] Bill also became friends with Kitty Cannell and Pauline Pfeiffer.

Zelda, too, was part of the crowd. Hadley remembered, "She needed to feel that she could do something as well as Scott, and she did have talent."[74] She wrote good letters and painted and studied ballet. Hadley thought she was graceful and even had a flair for dance. As Ernest watched Zelda that spring, she seemed to confirm his worst fantasies about the destructiveness of some wives; and as she watched Ernest, he seemed to her a fake, swearing too much and insisting too loudly on the beauty of killing bulls. Most members of their opposite sex were drawn to them, but together the two were bad chemistry from the start. For all of her charm, Zelda was aging early, her face hardening and her eyes beginning to dull from too many parties and drinks and nights without sleep. She got to Hemingway at his softest spot, accusing him and her husband of a homosexual affair. Ernest would say that Zelda was crazy. He was becoming acutely attuned to mental problems, perhaps realizing his own periodic ups and downs were not so healthy.

Ernest knew he needed to write a novel, but he did not really know how to write one. His only attempt had been stolen off the train two and a half years before with nearly all his early manuscripts. In his letters he had called it an artificial form, but he knew better. George Doran, when rejecting *In Our Time*, had told him he needed a novel, and Fitzgerald told him in the cafes that short story collections don't sell unless the author has made his reputation with a novel. With his fiction not working well that spring, he returned in his mind to the war in Italy and his wounding and talked about the war with Fitzgerald and with Loeb: the explosion, the hospital in Milan, the beautiful nurse and their nights together and how she sent him home to jilt him, which tore him apart. Fitzgerald, a fool for thwarted love stories, urged him on; Loeb was impressed, too, for he never thought Hemingway had suffered in love. It was the same

73. Harold Loeb, *The Way It Was*, 247.
74. Mowrer, Sokoloff tapes, Hemingway Collection, JFK Library.

story he had told without the details of the wounding in three pages in "A Very Short Story" and he wondered if he couldn't reshape the material in a longer form with the tools developed for the short story. All he had to do was to start writing it one word after another.

And one morning Ernest did surprise himself by starting to write in his blue notebooks something tentatively titled *Along with Youth* that started aboard the troopship *Chicago* as it neared the French coast. The main character was named Nick, and apparently Hemingway expected to follow him to Italy where the focus of the story would alternate between scenes of war in the mountains and the valleys of Veneto and scenes of romance in Milan with a nurse named Agnes. He was trying again to set down the war story that he so much wanted to write, but this time it didn't work either. After reading *The Great Gatsby*, his dialogue sounded heavy and childish alongside Fitzgerald's poetry, so he stopped on the twenty-seventh page and put it in his drawer of busted fiction, not then knowing that what he had done had been a real start at something longer than anything he had ever done.

Max Perkins was still interested in publishing Hemingway's work and wrote him a letter in May, sending along his copy of *in our time*, which Ernest said could not be found in Paris. But Sylvia Beach sold copies and he bought one and signed it and sent it to Max in June. Max seemed more concerned about his future than Horace Liveright, who finally sent the advance check along with notice that "Mr. and Mrs. Eliot" had been rewritten to avoid obscenity charges. Apparently, in New York it was obscene for a couple to "try" to have a baby and the deleted first lines of first paragraph had been so butchered that it destroyed the rhythm and humor of the story. If "tried very hard to have a baby" was obscene in New York, then how could people there quote Shakespeare or Chaucer? Ernest worked with the proofs as best as he could to restore what he could to the story. If Eugene Jolas, in a review praising "Big Two-Hearted River," could understand the importance of his details, then why couldn't his publisher? Ernest was becoming less and less pleased with Boni & Liveright, who had also just signed Sherwood Anderson. Ernest could deal with Harold Loeb, whose books weren't nearly as good as his own, but it was more difficult to work against Sherwood, who didn't like Hemingway's review of *A Story Teller's Story*, and through Gertrude Stein had let him know it was a better book than Ernest had given credit.

In June, angry and depressed and writing no fiction, Hemingway again showed signs of the dark disposition of his father. At a café with Fitzgerald and a visiting Princeton professor, discussing influences upon early work, Hemingway became particularly vehement over the need to be free from outside influences. He wrote to Jane Heap of *The Little Review* about a story he wrote that was cut without comment—"was it because the piece you had asked me to write wasn't considered good enough"—and offered a strange solution: "Going down to Spain looking for something this month and if I find it do me a nice one like you did Amy Lowell"[75]—the "nice one" being the obituary of Amy Lowell, whose death, he wrote, pleased him. Many things unduly upset him: Fitzgerald's talent was depressing, wanting Duff and not being able to have her was depressing, Liveright's revisions were depressing. But these were the symptoms, not the causes for his deep despondency, a behavior in his father that would soon push the doctor to suicide. This was only the second or third time Ernest had fallen into this darkness. Hadley may have sensed a pattern, but she could do nothing, and it was frightening for both of them. Ernest did not know this was a cycle, and in his private midnight he again thought he might never imagine another story.

One June 12, they dressed up for Joan Miro's first one-man show at the Galerie Pierre. In a festive crowd he could disguise the darkness within beneath a smiling face. Among the paintings along the walls was one called "The Farm"; halfway between cubism and surrealism, this large canvas captured for Hemingway the essence of rural Spain, its colors covering a farmscape strewn with objects become icons. Priced at 3500 francs ($175) he could not afford it but bought it anyway, putting down 500 francs the next day with the promise to pay the rest before October. Miro was delighted, but Hadley was shocked. They had his $200 advance from Liveright, but that was to pay for their trip to Spain. They would

---

75. EH to Jane Heap, June 12, 1925, *The Letters of Ernest Hemingway, Vol. 2.*

have to be poor, and she would have to wear last year's clothes to Spain. "Hadley's a perfect fool to take it," Kitty Cannell bitched to Harold Loeb. "Her clothes are falling off and she can't even show herself on the street. And it's her money."[76] Ernest called it a birthday present for Hadley, but, the purchase being an erratic, spontaneous act of a depressed person, a momentary elation, artificial and unsustainable, he had bought it as much for himself.

76. Loeb, *The Way It Was*, 207.

Beautiful Zelda

Fitzgerald in Love

Young Scott with a crush

Scott and Zelda (pregnant) in Europe

Great Neck mansion

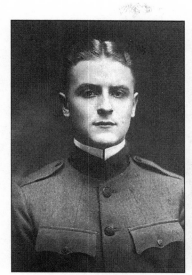

Scott in uniform

Scott at the time of meeting
Hemingway

The Fitzgeralds in Paris

Ring Lardner

The Farm by Miro

THE JUN ALJO RIJEJ

ERNEST HAD been dreaming of his third visit to the Fiesta de San Fermin all through winter and spring, and as the time approached for another trip his mood began to lift. Don Stewart, a welcome source of humor and companionship, arrived from New York and went to the fights with Ernest and Bill. By the end of the third week in June, Ernest had gathered the funds from his friends for train fare, bullfight tickets, and hotel reservations. They would stay at Juanito Quintana's Hotel Quintana on the square in the heart of the town. Juanito was a bullfight aficionado, and bullfighters often stayed at his hotel. Bumby was going with the Rohrbachs to Brittany, and Ernest and Hadley planned a week of trout fishing in Burguete before the fiesta where Bill Smith, Don Stewart, Bob Benchley, and Harold Loeb had plans to join them, but Benchley canceled completely and Harold decided to skip the fishing.

Loeb, wearying of the long-legged charms of Kitty Cannell, was as consumed by Duff as Hemingway but had the money to act on his desire and no wife to inhibit him, and so when Pat Guthrie returned to Scotland for a time, in his absence, without telling Ernest, he and Duff went off together to the coastal retreat of St.-Jean-de-Lux near the Spanish border. Duff returned to Paris and reunited with Pat, saw Hemingway, and decided to go to Pamplona too. She wrote to Harold, still in St.-Jean, "I am coming on the Pamplona trip with Hem and your lot. Can you bear it? With Pat of course."[1] Loeb, in his vanity, may have misunderstood her signals, and instead of being upset, arranged to meet Duff and

---

1. Jeffrey Meyers, *Hemingway: A Biography*, 156.

Pat in St.-Jean and proceed to Spain from there. Ernest, still in the dark about their affair, wrote to him also: "Duff and Pat are coming too . . . Pamplona's going to be damned good . . . I haven't felt as good since we came back from Austria."[2] Harold may have already decided that he and Duff had no future, but he still had strong feelings for her. When she and Pat arrived in St.-Jean, Pat was simmering with anger, which would only get worse. "I didn't like Pat," remembered Harold. "When he wasn't the life of the party he didn't exist. Now he was surly with good cause, but he might, I felt, make a little effort to conceal it."[3]

Ernest wanted to show his friends the world of bullfighting, from its arcane detail to the multiplicity of its meanings. In fact, it was almost his favorite type of situation: taking a trip with his buddies to do some serious celebrating, and then getting to explain to them an exciting subject in technical detail (just before the fiesta started, when they all walked out to the railroads to watch the bulls unloaded, Hemingway gave a lecture on the bulls). He had not counted on any romantic intrigue and was slightly proprietary about Duff, who had been something of a phenomenon in Paris that spring. His last days in Paris were busy meeting with an editor from Boni & Liveright, and on their final night, Sylvia Beach appeared on an errand from James Joyce asking where to send the section of *Finnigan's Wake* that was to appear in the second issue of *This Quarter*. Ernest stopped packing and penned a note to Walsh to have Joyce's work sent directly to the printer on rue St. Honore. Up at dawn on Thursday morning, June 25, exuberant and happy, they finished packing and caught the train to Pamplona.

Time collapsed when they crossed the border into Spain. Pamplona and Burguette became interwoven and inseparable. Everyone remembered it differently. On Saturday, June 27, Bill Smith's fishing license was issued and dated in Pamplona, and from there they took a rickety bus up the foothills of the mountains to Burguete where the woman in the inn shook her head and looked gloomy. Loggers had been working the forests, and the dark stream bed of the Irati was filled with loggers' trash.

---

2. EH to Harold Loeb, June 21, 1925, *The Letters of Ernest Hemingway, Vol. 2.*
3. Harold Loeb, *The Way It Was*, 284.

"We found our best stream which was full of trout last year ruined by logging and running logs down," Ernest wrote to Gertrude and Alice; "all the pools cleaned out—trout killed."[4] "The irony of it," declared Don Stewart. "The pity of it."[5] They fished for four days along the streams and caught nothing. But Ernest was undaunted. He felt happy there in the high country among the beech forests of Roland. "This is swell country," he wrote to Ezra. "Nice country to fight in. Ask Charlemagne."[6] The simple food combined with the good humor of Smith and Stewart made him feel whole again. On July 2, the fishing party took the rickety bus down the foothills to Pamplona to meet Harold and Duff and Pat.

It's not known when Ernest discovered Duff had taken Harold to bed, but when the gang gathered in Pamplona, the tension was obvious to all. Duff did not know Harold would behave like a lovesick loon in front of everyone, and Pat was miffed and barely civil. Duff told Loeb it was over between them, but she wouldn't tell him to leave, so he stayed on with a hangdog look, mostly sullen and sad. Pat Guthrie needled him at every chance as he wallowed in the humiliation. "Harold had a little genius for making a fool of himself," remembered Hadley; "The other boys were rough and tough and would catch him at these things."[7] Ernest, who hated not being in the know, simmered. He had no plans to sleep with Duff, but to him that didn't mean she was fair game for Harold. During the fiesta, Bill Smith warned Harold about Ernest. "You should have seen his face when [he learned] you and Duff had gone off." "You mean he's in love with Duff," asked Harold. "I didn't say that,"[8] replied Bill, leaving Harold worried about his friendship with Ernest, who treated Duff as if she belonged to him. Hadley stopped talking to Duff and wept with jealousy and humiliation while her husband seemed to court her. "It was a very upsetting summer for me," she remembered years later. "Ernest and I had not started to fall apart at that time . . . but

4. EH to Gertrude & Alice, July 16, 1925, *The Letters of Ernest Hemingway, Vol. 2.*
5. Carlos Baker, *Hemingway: A Life Story*, 193.
6. EH to Ezra Pound, June 29, 1925, *The Letters of Ernest Hemingway, Vol. 2.*
7. Michael Reynolds, *Hemingway: The Paris Years*, 302.
8. Loeb, *The Way It Was*, 291.

everybody was having affairs all the time, I found it sort of upsetting."[9] Donald Ogden Stewart noticed that Hadley seemed gloomy and silent much of the time.

The fiesta started and they were up at dawn to watch the running of the bulls through the street. One morning, Bill, Harold, and Ernest entered the ring for the amateur fights. Harold managed to grab on to a bull's horns and hang on while the bull carried him the length of the arena. Photographers took pictures and he became such a darling that barbers and shoeblacks wouldn't charge for their services. Hemingway probably felt overshadowed and that made him simmer some more. In an afternoon bullfight they saw the great new phenomenon, a nineteen-year-old from Ronda born Cayetano Ordonez but called Niño de la Palma, slim and straight as an arrow, in his first full season as a matador. Hadley immediately became an ardent admirer and Ernest shared her views.

As in former years, Ernest carefully watched the reactions of his friends. Don Stewart seemed genuinely fond of all phases of the bullfight; Bill Smith was shocked and horrified by the goring of the horses; Duff did not like the horses wounded but was excited by the bullfighters and the emotion of the spectacle. Harold Loeb found the whole proceeding distasteful and shameful. When they sat down at tables on the square for meals, Loeb, in his pastel sweaters, white duck pants, and round tortoise-shell glasses, looked out of place with the shabbily dressed Hemingways and the dissipated Duff and Pat, and was made to feel more out of place by Ernest, whom he had further angered with his disinterested attitude toward bullfighting. Bill Smith both liked and pitied Loeb, who, as an object of scorn to Hemingway and Guthrie, seemed at very low ebb throughout the fiesta. Stewart remembered Harold being a fanatic about searching out barbers in Pamplona for shaves. He also noticed a mean streak in Hemingway; whereas before he had been companionable, now he was assertive and smiled an aggressive smile. "You were not to disagree with the Master in any way from then on,"[10] said Stewart.

---

9. Gloria Diliberto, *Hadley*, 199.
10. Bertram Sarason, *Hemingway and the Sun Set*, 199.

The fiesta was noisy, hot, and insane as always and constantly going on with outrageous tipsy parades in the streets and the weaving about of huge heads of papier-mâché giants. Pat bought a goatskin bota that he kept filled with rioja and they all took turns squirting wine into their throats. Keeping up with Guthrie, a certified drunk, and Duff, not far behind him, required great capacity, especially when they began ordering absinthe—no wonder the fiesta blurred for the others. Don Stewart complained too many English and Americans were there that summer; "My God," he said, "even the American ambassador was there in a big car."[11] He remembered being in line at a brothel for two hours with somebody and was certain that wasn't Harold, who was different from everybody else, never getting truly drunk and always a little defensive because Ernest was turning against him. Someone, probably Pat, may have told Loeb to leave, but "obstinacy kept me there," remembered Harold. "Pat wanted me somewhere else and that made me want to stay. Also I was curious about Hem. It was hard for me to believe that things had changed so drastically between us."[12] He may have also not wanted to leave Duff. Hemingway and Duff flirted heavily, whispering in conversations and wearing matching berets. Their behavior did not anger Pat, who held his venom for Loeb. When Harold looked at Duff, not understanding her distress from two grown men acting like schoolboys in the presence of her drunken, surly fiancé, she would look away. His knowing remarks about her infuriated Ernest.

People were moved by Hemingway and wanted him to like them because of his charisma, a charisma that protected him from the consequences of his more outrageous actions. But anyone who spent time with Ernest Hemingway in the Quarter sooner or later saw his mean streak. Loeb knew about it. He had seen Ernest in the cafes say terrible things to strangers but never to a close friend like himself. At Pamplona, Ernest made Loeb feel like a rich Jew who did not belong to the party. It was like they had never shared meals and laughed together, played tennis, and read each other's work. Stewart remembered the viciousness well.

---

11. Reynolds, *Hemingway: The Paris Years*, 301.
12. Loeb, *The Way It Was*, 293.

"There's no explaining it particularly, it was just part of his character along with the rest of him . . . To look at it in a more charitable way, if Hem had been just plain mean you wouldn't have noticed it. But he wasn't mean; he was charismatic; and it was for this very reason that the mean streak startled you so when it came to the surface . . . he didn't have to have a reason to be mean. It was more of a mood thing."[13]

It was the same startling mood change of his father's that had scared Ernest as a child. At San Fermin that summer, Ernest's mood was volatile. Knowing he had no claim on Duff's affections, he continued to bend to her wishes, tutoring her on bullfight rituals and rhythms. Harold had taken her to bed while Ernest only got her sexy asides, leaving him uncomfortable and unrequited. Surfacing after a depressed period in which his writing failed him, his anger turned on Harold Loeb. Hadley, recognizing the signs but not the cause, retreated into her protective shell.

Once raised, Hemingway's anger did not subside quickly. On Friday evening, July 10, Harold managed to go off alone with Duff to a private club full of Spaniards who crowded around Duff, made her feel wonderful, and they all got very drunk. Loeb did not remember the end of the night, but the next day at lunch Duff appeared with a black eye. When Harold asked about it, Hemingway abrasively cut him off, saying she had fallen against a railing. Not even the spectacular performance by Niño de la Palma in the bullring on the last two days of the festival took his mind from Duff and Loeb. In the ring this young matador was graceful and effortless, moving the bulls artfully with the flow of his cape work. Discussing the bullring, Ernest kept calling the fights a tragedy. Loeb did not see bullfighting as an art; his sympathies lay too often with the bull, and the messiness of the gored horses turned his head away; the bull's death seemed shameful to him. The ritual was interesting but nothing to become religious about in the way that Ernest demanded. After watching Niño and Belmonte perform in the ring that evening, the last night before the festival ended, the final confrontation between Ernest and

---

13. Sarason, *Hemingway and the Sun Set*, 199.

Harold happened. Over brandies after dinner at a table on the square, Hemingway and Guthrie mercilessly baited Harold Loeb.

'Tomorrow will be swell," Loeb remembered Hemingway saying. "The bulls will be . . . the best in Spain." And then he turned to Harold. "I suppose you'd like it better if they shipped in goats."

"Goats have a sense of humor," quipped Harold, "but you've got me wrong. I don't dislike bullfighting; I just find it hard not to sympathize with the victims."

"Our sensitive chum is considerate of the bull's feelings," said Guthrie. "But how about ours?"

"Harold is very considerate," interjected Hemingway. "You should see him with Kitty. I've listened to him take it by the hour."

"I may be dumb," said Pat. "I may be useless. But I know enough to stay away when I'm not wanted."

Loeb, who disliked Pat but was hurt by Hemingway, retorted, "Is that how you got through school?"

"You lay off Pat," said Hemingway grimly.

"Why don't you get out?" said Pat. "I don't want you here. Hem doesn't want you here. Nobody wants you here."

"I will," said Harold, "the instant Duff wants it."

Duff turned her head and looked at Harold. "You know," she said, "that I do not want you to go."

"You lousy bastard," exploded Hemingway. "Running to a woman."

Harold stood up and challenged Hemingway to step down the alley to settle the matter. Hemingway rose from the table. When they got into the alley Loeb stopped and faced Hem and took off his jacket. "I was tremendously sad," he remembered. "It was my pattern, I felt, slowly, gradually, to acquire a friend and then have him turn in an instant into a bitter, lashing enemy . . . I felt excruciatingly lonely." He took off his glasses, put them into a pocket in his jacket, and looked around for a safe place to put the jacket. He then heard Hemingway say, "Shall I hold it for you," and saw that Ernest was smiling "the boyish, contagious smile that made it so hard not to like him."

"I don't want to hit you," said Harold.

"Me either,"[14] said Hem. And they put on their jackets and walked back to the table together, the others pretending not to notice their return.

On the last day of the festival, with only Don and Bill speaking to Harold, they crowded into the great bullring, where on the sand of the arena below the great throng of people the young matador Niño de la Palma performed brilliantly, killing three bulls, delighting the crowd with his grace, and outshining the great Juan Belmonte. "He did everything Belmonte did and did it better," wrote Ernest to Gertrude and Alice. "He stepped out all by himself without any tricks—suave, templando with the cape, smooth and slow."[15] Niño de la Palma was awarded the ear of a brave bull he killed, and he gave it to the bright-haired Hadley, who sat on the front row with Ernest, for Ernest in his broken Spanish had been cultivating the man all week. Hadley would wrap it in Don Stewart's handkerchief and leave it in a drawer in Madrid.

That night, in his room in Quintana's hotel, Hemingway wrote an apology note to Loeb and left it for him the next morning. He hated to leave the fiesta on this note, he wrote, and was ashamed of the way he had acted and the unjust, uncalled-for words. It was not his first or last apology to someone. If at times he lost control, he also had a sense of remorse after behaving badly. On Monday, July 13, the gang departed Pamplona. Duff and Pat were broke and could not pay their hotel bill; they were always confident someone would pick up their tab, and Don Stewart, always a soft touch, lent them the money he would never see again. Ernest and Hadley took the train to Madrid, Bill and Harold rented a car and with Pat and Duff drove to the coast, and Don visited Gerald and Sara Murphy at their villa on the Côte d'Azure. Nothing had turned out as Hemingway had planned, but as the train chugged across the open grasslands the lousy feeling he'd had began to lift. A young man in their third-class compartment had big sample jugs of wine from his father's vineyard near Tafalla to sell in Madrid, and opening jug after jug, continued offering drinks to everyone in the compartment "including 2

---

14. Loeb, *The Way It Was*, 294-7.
15. EH to G & A, July 15, 1925, *The Letters of Ernest Hemingway, Vol. 2*.

priests and 4 guardia civil," Ernest wrote to Gertrude and Alice. "It was the best party almost I've ever been on. . . . Hadley and the priests talked Latin."[16]

In Madrid, a creative seed burst inside as the words returned to Hemingway and he began to write and lift himself beyond everything else. They were staying in the Pension Aguilar and in the mornings would go to the Prado Art Museum and in the afternoons take in more bull-fights where they were again impressed by Niño de la Palma. Getting the proofs of *In Our Time* helped Hemingway along in his writing, for reading his stories that he could not exactly remember writing gave him an emotional lift. Madrid was quiet in the early afternoon with only a few street noises coming through the heavy shutters, and Ernest could quietly concentrate. Hadley was glad to have him back like this from wherever it was his mind had been for the last four months.

A story started that he began to write on loose leaf sheets of paper. He was not sure where the story was heading, but the tension of the past week was there to be used. At first it began with the meeting of a bullfighter in a hotel room in Pamplona. He was using real names: the bullfighter was Niño de la Palma and the room where they met was in the Hotel Quintana where Quintana is afraid that this young savior matador will be corrupted by rich American tourists. The ambassador's sexy wife wants to meet Niño, but the narrator, still named Hem, won't deliver the message; yet, later in a café, Quintana enters to see "Niño with a big glass of cognac in his hand, laughing, between me and two women, one with bare shoulders and a table full of drunks."[17] It was funny, Hemingway thought at first, then realized that it wasn't funny, and the true story started to jell. He began to see it clearly: the Paris crowd comes to Pamplona with their Left Bank values and corrupt the fine young bullfighter—who the Duff character seduces as she had Pat and Harold and even Ernest. He wrote late mornings and early afternoons before the bullfights, and as he continued writing he knew the story would not be short.

---

16. EH to G & A, July 15, 1925, *The Letters of Ernest Hemingway, Vol. 2.*
17. Reynolds, *Hemingway: The Paris Years*, 307.

On July 21, his twenty-sixth birthday, he wrote to Bill Smith, "Have been working like hell."[18] Before they packed up to follow the bullfight circuit to Valencia, he penciled across the top of his manuscript: "Cayantano Ordonez/'Niño de la Palma.'" Naming the story removed whatever depression remained as he entered the manic country of the truly blessed, an ecstatic high region where he had only been a few short times, once when he was writing "Big Two-Hearted River." This cycle would last through the fall and into the winter, producing two books and three new stories in twenty weeks. In Valencia, he wrote to Bill Smith again: "I've averaged about 1200 words a day since left Pamplona. Think some of it may be bludy good . . . I work from lunch until the bull fight starts. The story is fairly funny. Have Ford in it as Braddocks. The Master goes well as Braddocks."[19]

As he realized he could no longer use real names, nor all the people in Pamplona, the first of the story's scaffolding began to come down. Hadley disappeared, Bill and Don melded into Bill Gorton, and Duff became a woman named Brett Ashley. The most significant change was Hem, who metamorphosed into a new narrator named Jake Barnes, a newspaper man with a background belonging to Bill Bird. Jake was also a war veteran, an aviator wounded while flying. His wound was that he had lost his penis. Ernest knew about soldiers maimed that way; he had discussed it with other men who had been in the war. "What happened to me is supposed to be funny," Jake says in the manuscript. "Scott Fitzgerald told me once it couldn't be treated except as a humorous subject."[20] Apparently, Ernest had discussed the subject with Fitzgerald on walks they had taken together in the spring.

In Valencia, there was nothing between Ernest and his fiction. He moved from the loose sheets of paper, now on page thirty-seven, to the blue notebooks he had brought with him from Paris. He decided to shift the beginning of the story to Paris, for the reader had to understand about the Quarter to appreciate what happened in Pamplona, and wrote

---

18. EH to Bill Smith, July 21, 1925, *The Letters of Ernest Hemingway, Vol. 2.*
19. EH to BS, July 27, 1925, *The Letters of Ernest Hemingway, Vol. 2.*
20. Reynolds, *Hemingway: The Paris Years*, 308.

biographical details of the main characters thus far in the story, characters based upon what he knew about Duff Twysden, Pat Guthrie, and Harold Loeb. A lot that he put into this first draft he would have to take out later as all of his Oak Park revulsion with bohemian pretense boiled over and he archly wrote about gossip he knew. "Gertrude Stein once told me that remarks are not literature. All right, let it go at that. Only this time all the remarks are going in and if it is not literature who claimed it was anyway."[21] He took that remark out, too, for as he began to understand his narrator, that Jake Barnes was not the type to visit Gertrude and Alice, he began keeping himself out of the narration. Jake was a man who lived without complications—no wife, no kid, no cat—a passive, laconic man to whom things happened. The more Ernest learned about Jake, the better he liked him. He was living in the book each day now as he had with Nick on the river.

He worked in bed every morning. In the afternoon they would swim at the beach, catch the streetcar to the Plaza de Toros, and watch another heroic performance by Ordonez. The story began to take shape. Ernest was skilled and practiced enough in the literature of gossip that the new opening in Paris carried him along with wondrous momentum. He wrote for eleven straight days. Black ink stained his fingers. There was no time for letters, though he did write to Sylvia Beach about the book: "I've written six chapters on a novel and am going great about 15,000 words done already."[22] He knew he was writing a novel but still did not know exactly where the story was going. That was better because if he knew everything the story would be dead to him; it was better not to know, this way each day was an adventure where he could be with Jake. He got the opening scenes in Paris with the Bal Musette and Brett entering with homosexuals set just right, and he changed the title again, this time to "Fiesta."

Early in August, they returned to Madrid for a few days where Ernest continued to write in their room at the pension: "Have 8 chapters done on a novel," he wrote Bill Smith. "Going like wild fire. Ought to be a

---

21. James R. Mellow, *Hemingway: A Life Without Consequences*, 308.
22. EH to Sylvia Beach, Aug. 3, 1925, *The Letters of Ernest Hemingway, Vol. 2.*

swell novel."[23] The heat drove them out of Madrid. They took the train north to San Sebastián, where for two days they swam in the blue bay of La Concha, which is sheltered from the ocean by the small Isla de Santa Clara. From there they moved up across the border to Hendaye, where there were purple mountains and a long white beach embroidered with Atlantic surf. They lived easy in cheap pensions as Ernest wrote every day, nothing keeping him from his time with Jake. On August 11, Hadley returned to Paris to see Bumby, leaving Ernest alone with his notebooks. With almost eleven chapters on paper, he wrote in solitude for as long as he could. Boni & Liveright sent the dust jacket for *In Our Time*, and he didn't like the blurbs by all the authors put on the cover, but he must have been pleased that the book would be out in October. His writing went smoothly, but not his sleep. Without Hadley beside him in bed, the bad dreams and fear returned. Some nights he wrote to exhaustion; on others he woke in the dark and picked up his pen. He filled another notebook and thought the end was almost in sight.

On August 19, he returned to Paris. Maybe the money ran out or maybe he was tired of not sleeping. There the days were hot and muggy, and tourists filled the cafes. Bumby needed attention, and Madame Chautard, the landlord, smiled her witch's smile as she showed Ernest the repaired window and hideous new wallpaper in the dining room and said that she must up the rent. He threatened to leave but knew that he couldn't and set to work in their second bedroom and lived in his book. He was "working very hard," remembered Hadley, "disappearing every morning and night into that little room."[24] Making more of it up each day, characters and scenes came and went, but scenes like the sharp, humorous bantering between Jake and Bill Gorton as they fished on the Irati were written so well they stayed as they were. He wrote to Jane Heap that his book was "written very simply and full of things happening and people and places and exciting as hell." He thought it would take about another month to finish and then he would leave it alone and work on it again in the winter and no one would see it until it was finished: "I don't

---

23. EH to BS, Aug. 5, 1925, *The Letters of Ernest Hemingway, Vol. 2.*
24. Hadley Mowrer, Alice Sokoloff tapes, Hemingway Collection, JFK Library.

want all my great literary friends giving me good advice." Ernest had recently read Constance Garnett's translation of *War and Peace*, which made him more sensitive about his small books published in Paris. "That gave me a considerable jolt," he wrote. "That's when I stopped being satisfied with perfect small ones," and referred to his new novel as "a hell of a really swell big book."

Jane Heap had asked him if he was happy with Boni & Liveright. If he was not, she knew a publisher's representative eager to meet him (probably someone from Harcourt, or Alfred Knopf). Ernest told her that Boni & Liveright "have an option on my next 3 books—said option to lapse if they refuse any one book." Though *In Our Time* had not been released, but soon would be in the fall, Hemingway was already considering breaking the contract. "I can't talk business now but I would like very much to meet your friend and I wish you would bring him around. Because you can't ever tell what might happen."[25] Ernest was tired of the comparisons with Sherwood Anderson, his literary godfather, and did not want to be in the same publishing house. Also, Horace Liveright's letters were straight business with little praise for his work and no stroking of his fragile ego. He liked the letters from Maxwell Perkins that made him feel secure as a writer. Perkins really did like his work, but Ernest wasn't so sure about Boni & Liveright because it took pressure from several friends before they consented to publish his collection of short stories, and then they cut one story and rewrote another. Ernest wasn't yet ready to make the break with his first big publisher and switch to Charles Scribner's, but the idea was already there in August, and when he was ready to break his word, he almost always found a way to force the other party to make the first move.

He stayed out of the cafes as much as possible and few people called at the apartment because most of his close friends were out of town: Bill Smith and Loeb had left on a bike trip to the Rhine, Joyce and his family were on the coast near Bordeaux, Sylvia was in Savoie, Gertrude was in Provence, Ezra in Rapallo, the Fitzgeralds were in Antibes, and

25. EH to Jane Heap, Aug. 23, 1925, *The Letters of Ernest Hemingway, Vol. 2.*

McAlmon had remained in London. The only person who bothered him was Pauline Pfeiffer, who looked better than she had in the spring. When she came by she said it was to talk to Hadley, but she had taken a decided turn for Ernest. He was the true object of her visit, and he must have sensed it and did nothing to discourage her. He liked having admiring women around. It was a game he had always played with rules that had always been clear; like Izzy at Chamby or how it might have been with Duff if Loeb had not ruined Pamplona. Hadley was not worried yet. Pauline was "very bright, very quick and shrewd, especially about money,"[26] she remembered. Pauline, a small birdlike woman with delicate moves whom no one remembered as careless, left behind personal tokens to retrieve from attractive men. She was having a wonderful time in Paris and would very soon start leaving behind tokens with the Hemingways.

Ernest, once appalled by infidelity, was now curious, open minded, and ripe for an affair. Since writing to Bill Smith about "yencing,"[27] he had spent much idle time fantasizing about other women. With Duff Twysden he had been unfaithful to Hadley in everything but the deed itself, and apparently the reason was Duff's disinclination to have him. But Hadley had seen how her husband behaved in Pamplona and she was hurt. Affairs and adulteries burgeoned all around them and there were divorces aplenty. Far from the restraining values of Oak Park and St. Louis, the bonds of the Hemingway marriage were losing their meaning as more and more Ernest looked at other women and wondered how they would be in bed. But Pauline Pfeiffer was different. She had a deeply ingrained Catholicism controlling her life and was not one to be comfortable in an affair. She believed deeply that her soul would burn in eternal hell if she married outside the church. If she were going to take Ernest away from Hadley and marry him, she could not have pursued this of her own accord; she would have needed not merely encouragement but active collaboration from the other person.

In his notebooks, Hemingway kept Jake moving, talking, and letting the action flow. Though his life in Paris and the actual events of Pamplona

---

26. Reynolds, *Hemingway: The Paris Years*, 316.
27. EH to BS, February 17, 1925, *The Letters of Ernest Hemingway, Vol. 2.*

had inspired him, and some of his characters were closely based on his friends, the tale was completely fiction. He was beginning to realize the story was about Jake Barnes, just as Fitzgerald's *The Great Gatsby* was about its narrator, Nick Carraway. More than once in the manuscript, Hemingway had gotten into awkward interior discussions about who was the central figure; wondering who was the hero of the book, or if there was any hero at all; and perhaps he was right about there being no hero for his generation for whom, out of the trenches, there were no believable heroes. He kept making changes to characters and action and sequence; changes he would settle in the revisions. The story had started as the story of a bullfighter corrupted by the Paris crowd, but the bullfighter—who he would name Pedro Romero from a historical torero one hundred and fifty years before—would become the only uncorrupted character in the book. It would be the narrator, Jake, who would understand corruption and what had happened and come to know the enormity of the loss of his own true innocence.

Hemingway told Fitzgerald it was "a hell of a sad story,"[28] and one he knew himself, because the values he brought from Oak Park were not holding up in the Quarter, and he could see the tragedy. Filling his fourth notebook at the end of August, he had carefully brought the story back to the Quintana dining room where Jake and his drunken friends, Lady Brett with her shoulders bare, were sitting at a table with the fine young matador Pedro Romero, when Quintana walks in and cannot believe what he sees, not after Jake had agreed with him about Pedro's need to be protected from corrupting influences: "For one who had afición he could forgive anything. At once he forgave me all my friends,"[29] observed Jake Barnes. But with their glasses full of cognac and Romero next to bare-shouldered Brett, Jake's friends were no longer forgiven, and Quintana did not even bother to nod.

Despite Ernest's fear, when Loeb and Smith returned from the Rhine their presence did not slow him down. They had both booked passage for New York on September 5. The night before they left, Kitty Cannell

---

28. EH to F. Scott Fitzgerald, May 15, 1926, *The Letters of Ernest Hemingway, Vol. 3*.
29. Ernest Hemingway, *The Sun Also Rises*, 132.

gave a farewell party at a restaurant and invited Hadley and Ernest. Kitty thought that Harold, who she did not desire to marry, was blind to the way she thought Hemingway manipulated his friends. She disliked the clever Tom Sawyerish way Ernest obtained money and favors from people, appearing as if he was embarrassed by friends forcing favors on him, nor did she like the way he talked down Ford Madox Ford, who was her friend, and she deplored what she thought was his lack of consideration for Hadley, letting her live in the mean quarters they had and letting her dress the way she did: "She never had any new clothes."[30] Kitty, blonde and statuesque, was fashion conscious and could easily have misunderstood this aspect lacking in other people's lives. She liked Hadley very much, and when she took her shopping, buying her little gifts, it annoyed Hemingway and gave her pleasure.

Ernest had remained shrewdly silent about Kitty Cannell, never showing any resentment. But in his novel, he transposed her personality onto a bitchy, possessive character named Francis Clyne and wrote a devastating portrait of a desperate, no-longer-youthful woman who wanted the Jewish boob, based on Harold Loeb, to marry her. The fictionalized character of Kitty was brief, she only appeared in the opening chapters set in Paris, but his acid portrayal of Harold Loeb, who he had come to see as an obnoxious lovestruck literary pretender, appeared throughout the book as the rich, self-centered, and emotionally precious Robert Cohn. At Kitty's dinner, Harold, remembering Pamplona, tried not to show any anxiety as Ernest talked about bullfighting; he and Bill Smith would remain close friends, but after this dinner never again would Harold and Ernest speak person to person.

Ernest finished the first draft of what he was calling *Fiesta: A Novel*. Names still had to be straightened out and small parts of the story were still not right, but it was done. There were jokes and friendship and betrayal and loss. Near the end when the gang was in the lobby of the hotel paying the bill, "Montoya did not come near us," said Jake. "One of the maids brought the bill."[31] The bill for Jake was more than pesetas,

---

30. Mellow, *Hemingway: A Life Without Consequences*, 305.
31. Hemingway, *The Sun Also Rises*, 228.

for by leading the bullfighter to Brett, Montoya would no longer consider him a valued friend and aficiónado, and Pamplona would never be the same. Jake and his gang who went to Spain from Paris were all emotional cripples, left wounded by the war one way or another. In the end, when Brett wired Jake to come get her in Madrid she was not in real trouble, for the toreador she had run off with had paid her bills; she was in emotional trouble. Breaking away from a few much-needed restful days in San Sebastián, Jake did not quite know himself why he went to her aid, but, unable to stop himself, he did it anyway and found her in the kind of low-rent lodging where Duff Twysden would actually most often stay. In the back of a taxi Lady Brett says, "Oh Jake, we could have had such a damn good time together," and Jake replies, jaded and discouraged, "Yes, isn't it pretty to think so."[32] Jake was the biggest loser in the tale: not even Robert Cohn, who foolishly loses his temper and knocks down people with punches, takes as much emotional beating. Unlike Cohn, who lived by an unrealistic romantic code, Jake had held himself together as best as he could, but in the end faith and honor and hope were gone; perhaps charity was still with him, and since he had lost all his pride, maybe humility, too.

The drive to finish his novel left Ernest physically and emotionally exhausted. For nine weeks he had lived so intensely in the book that all else was irrelevant. Now he felt empty, anxious, and restless. The crowds in the cafes saw more of him, and they all knew about his new book. *In Our Time* had not yet been published, and no one had seen his new novel, but Bob Wilson, including Ernest among the "Bookshop Crowd" at Shakespeare and Company, wrote in *Paris on Parade* that he had "recently finished a new novel which is said to break new ground. While an admirer of James Joyce, Hemingway is in no sense an imitator of him; he pursues his own ways and his friends expect him to go far. He is a young man of vigorous health and physique who has been a soldier and war correspondent."[33] As he mingled with the crowd in the Café du Dome, he felt lonely and "tired as hell inside" and was drinking a lot.

32. Hemingway, 247.
33. Reynolds, *Hemingway: The Paris Years*, 324.

"Can drink hell's own amount of whiskey without getting drunk because my head is so tired," he told Ernest Walsh. He needed to get away. "Hate to waste the autumn in town."[34] Hadley couldn't go because of Bumby. Ernest wrote to his father that he might travel to Morocco with Dos Passos and may have considered joining the Fitzgeralds in Antibes where Floyd Dell, Max Eastman, and the Murphys also happened to be at the time, but, instead, taking along his manuscript, went off by himself to spend a long weekend in Chartres.

Chartres was quiet. Its great medieval cathedral had been an ancient place of pilgrimage, and Hemingway liked the permanence of its stone; the interior odors of age and incense; and the stained-glass windows of the ambulatory that told the story of Charlemagne taking Pamplona, depicting proud Roland at Roncesvalles dying by the Saracens. Catholicism appealed to him, its ritual and mystery. It was the religion of bull-fighters and royalty, and unlike the Congregational Church of his youth, held a strong emotional attraction. He wanted to clear his head, but his thoughts kept returning to his book where the narrator, Jake Barnes, was a Catholic. He did not do any rewriting in Chartres; he relaxed, and in his mind the dross of the book started floating to the top for skimming. He needed to focus the novel and find a better title than *Fiesta*, which meant little unless you had been to Pamplona. He thought to call it *The Lost Generation* from a story that Gertrude Stein had told: stopping in a garage in a French village with one of the valves in her Ford stuck, a very young mechanic fixed it quickly and efficiently, and asking the owner where he got such good workers, he told her he trained them himself; the young ones learned fast, he said, but those in the age group of twenty-two to thirty who had fought in the war could not be taught and "C'est une generation perdue." In Chartres, however, he went to the Bible, where others had found good titles, and made a list of possibilities in his eighth notebook, four from Ecclesiasties, one from Paul's First Epistle to the Corinthians:

---

34. EH to Ernest Walsh, Sept. 21, 1925, *The Letters of Ernest Hemingway, Vol. 2.*

The Sun Also Rises
Rivers to the Sea
For in much wisdom is much grief and he that increases
knowledge increaseth sorrow
Two Lie Together
The Old Leaven[35]

He returned to Paris still unsettled about a title, and more personally, his references to the Catholic Church, where many French writers found literary conversions, showed a need for some sort of ritual support in a life that had no winners. When Pauline Pfeiffer saw this side of him, she began telling him more and more about her religion. Ernest didn't care for Popes and bishops, the hierarchies of authority, but, since Pamplona, religion and its substitutes were on his mind. In his novel he would have Jake pray in a Catholic Church in Pamplona, or at least make an effort, and know enough about the sacraments to tell Brett that she couldn't listen to someone in confession. Duff was still on his mind, but mostly for literary purposes since one of his main characters was based upon her. He made no effort to see her and a note she left for him with the bartender at the Dingo asking for 3000 francs to help pay her bills probably went unanswered. His extramarital romantic gaze had shifted more to Pauline Pfeiffer.

What money Ernest had was used to buy the expensive painting that, ostensibly, was a gift for his wife. Dos Passos, back from spending time with the Murphys on the Riviera, visited the Hemingways in their sawmill apartment and was there when Ernest brought home *The Farm*, the large bright canvas by Joan Miro. (Evan Shipman had originally consigned to buy it, but on hearing Ernest wanted to give it to Hadley as a birthday present, magnanimously allowed him the honor. Ernest made a down payment in June and borrowed the rest from friends.) He arrived from the gallery in a taxi and hung the large painting above their bed as

---

35. Reynolds, *Hemingway: The Paris Years*, 326-7.

a surprise for Hadley, whose thirty-fourth birthday was soon approaching. Miro came to see it, content it had fallen into good hands. Ernest, ecstatic, said Miro was the only painter who could combine in one picture all that you felt about Spain when you were there and all that you felt when you were away and could not go there.

Hem and the gang in Pamplona

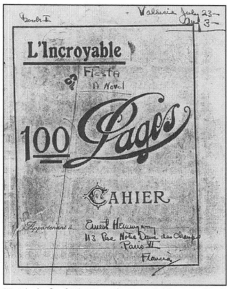

Hem's draft of *The Sun Also Rises* in blue notebook

Hotel Quintana

Pamplona Bullring, 1925 (Hemingway and Don Stewart on the right)

Matador

San Sebastián

Chartres cathedral

A CHANGE OF LIFE

ERNEST HEMINGWAY was a twenty-six-year-old barely known writer when his fiction made its American debut on October 5, 1925, with the publication of *In Our Time* by Boni & Liveright in New York City. The book, dedicated to Hadley Richardson Hemingway, was a masterful work certifying his connections with the vanguard of Modern Literature. Hemingway knew his work was very good. The vignettes and the stories counterpointing one another offered an innovative structure that impressed the critics, as did his distinctive declarative style. The brusque syntax and clean, clear use of words gave the short-story form a new vitality, a fact recognized by the more perceptive critics. "His language is fibrous and athletic, colloquial and fresh, hard and clean, his very prose seems to have an organic being of its own," wrote the unsigned reviewer in the *New York Times*, adding, "He makes each word count three or four ways."[1]

Though the reviews were very good, he did not like the continued comparisons to Sherwood and Gertrude Stein. The comparisons remained in critical essays that were otherwise excellent: "He shows influence of Gertrude Stein very strongly, that of Joyce almost not at all; he is also very strongly under the influence of Sherwood Anderson,"[2] wrote the reviewer in the New York *Herald Tribune*. Paul Rosenfeld's review of *In Our Time* in the *New Republic* on November 25 praised the prose for its "lyricism, aliveness and energy tremendously held in check" and likened his rhythms to "the trip-hammer thud" of Stravinsky's *Le*

---

1. James R. Mellow, *Hemingway: A Life Without Consequences*, 314.
2. Michael Reynolds, *Hemingway: The Paris Years*, 329.

Sacre du Printemps, but he also pointed out that the diction was akin to Anderson's vernacular and its "steady reiterations"[3] of certain words derived from Gertrude Stein. Ernest might have wondered if they had read Joyce's *Dubliners,* or any of Gertrude's work, for Gertrude had never really written a story. To Ezra he wrote, "Le Grand Gertrude Stein warned me when I presented her with a copy [of *In Our Time*] not to expect a review as she thought it would be wiser to wait for my novel . . . She is afraid that I might fall on my nose in a novel and if so how terrible it would have been to have said anything about this book no matter how good it may be,"[4] which was probably not a true interpretation of the motives of a friend who had been so close and caring.

Two of his books, *In Our Time* and *Three Stories & Ten Poems,* could be seen in the windows of Shakespeare and Company alongside Sherwood Anderson's new novel, *Dark Laughter,* also published by Boni & Liveright. Unlike *In Our Time*, which had a small printing and little promotion, *Dark Laughter* was well promoted, made a lot of money, and elevated Anderson to the most prized author of the publishing firm, which further haunted Ernest. He wrote to Ezra, "Sherwood Anderson has written about 350 pages of perfect diahorreah [*sic*] . . . and become a best seller," and he also complained that his friends Stein and McAlmon regarded him as a traitor "through the accident of having a book published by a so called regular publisher. It seems to have been the very worst way I could have betrayed them all."[5] But it probably mattered even more to him that his parents in Oak Park read the stories. He had written to them in September that the book would be out in October, and in October, after his book had reached Paris, he wrote to his mother, "Have you seen In Our Time yet?"[6] and then two weeks later to both his parents, "In Our Time was out in the States on October 10th and you have doubtless seen it."[7] He wanted his parents' approval (would Grace hear her own voice in "Soldier's Home"?) and he wanted the approval of Oak Park, but those

---

3. Kenneth Lynn, *Hemingway*, 306.
4. EH to Ezra Pound, Nov. 8, 1925, *The Letters of Ernest Hemingway, Vol. 2.*
5. EH to EP, Nov. 1925.
6. EH to GHH, Oct. 19, 1925, *The Letters of Ernest Hemingway, Vol. 2.*
7. EH to CEH & GHH, Oct. 29, 1925, *The Letters of Ernest Hemingway, Vol. 2.*

approvals would be a long time coming. Meanwhile, a final break with Stein and Anderson would come very soon and quickly.

Themes of duplicity and double-crossing began cropping up in his fiction as Ernest continued writing stories through October. In "Ten Indians" young Nick Adams' heart is broken when he learns from his father that his Indian girlfriend was thrashing about in the bushes with another boy, and the long story "Fifty Grand," which he began in October and finished in November, revolved around a fixed welterweight championship bout. A third story began on a cold snowy day with Nick entering a café: as he sits down and eats, two strangers enter and sit down, and then the story broke off to be resumed a few months later with the strangers becoming hired guns in town to avenge a double-cross by a boxer named Ole Andreson. He would name this story "The Killers." Hadley was sick in bed, and so when Ernest finished working, he looked for other company. Pauline was spending a lot of time at the carpenter's loft. That they shared Midwestern roots and a friendship with Katy Smith were comforting so far away from home. "Pauline was quick, hot and emotional,"[8] Hadley said. She was amused by her gossip about the world of couture, and the two became closer in their friendship—a friendship into which Ernest was drawn. "We've been seeing a lot of Pauline Pfeiffer,"[9] he wrote Harold Loeb in November.

Pauline was knowledgeable about books and interested in Modern Literature. She was "much more interested in the techniques of writing than I was,"[10] recalled Hadley, who was frequently ill with colds that fall and tired at the end of the day from chasing Bumby, who had just turned two. Often, she went to bed early leaving Ernest and Pauline alone together. They would talk and share a bottle of wine and he would walk her to the corner for a taxi home. Their friendship began turning into a romance. Pauline was a better drinker than Hadley and, unlike Hadley, could also pay the bar bills. Hadley seemed to accept the situation. With her husband's magnetic attraction, stray women seemed to

---

8. Gloria Diliberto, *Hadley*, 203.
9. EH to Harold Loeb, November, 1925, *The Letters of Ernest Hemingway, Vol. 2*.
10. Hadley Mowrer, Alice Sokoloff tapes, Hemingway Collection, JFK Library.

follow him home like lost kittens. She had seen this before. For Pauline it was a new experience, and each step she took was new and tentative, testing the thickness of the ice as Ernest, smiling, charming, and attentive, encouraged her.

By November, his enthusiasm for Boni & Liveright was evaporating. He wrote to Harold Loeb, "Sorry to hear they are not making any attempt to sell *In Our Time,*" and took note that "they are certainly putting Sherwood over big and will evidently make the boy a lot of money."[11] His own book with its small printing had poor distribution and, despite its excellent review, few sales. Searching throughout Paris, he could not find it in any bookstore other than Shakespeare and Company. Hemingway had thought that all 1,335 copies printed would quickly sell and was disappointed. He was also annoyed and disappointed by the continued comparisons to Anderson and Stein. An idea began to grow in his mind that if in a flash of inspiration he wrote a short parody of Anderson's bestselling novel, *Dark Laughter,* which he considered atrociously bad, and put in some remarks ridiculing Gertrude Stein, such a book could not only do away with the comparisons but also break his contract with Boni & Liveright, for as Anderson's publisher and friend, Horace Liveright would have to reject it and he could then sign with Scribner's or Harcourt, Brace, or some other house of greater distinction. It was a flawless plan as long as he didn't allow himself to remember how kind Anderson had been to him over the years, something which Hadley would not allow him to forget. She thought his idea detestable and told him so.

He wrote to Harold about his novel, "So far am calling it The Sun Also Rises," and though he felt the publisher had deceived him, "Evidently they made up their minds in advance that it was not worthy trying to sell a book of short stories," he tried to pretend he was still satisfied with Boni & Liveright, "it's up to them to keep me happy . . . I must have a good advance on the novel. I'm not sore but I'm annoyed they have done nothing in Chicago where hells own amount of books are

---

11. EH to HL, November, 1925, *The Letters of Ernest Hemingway, Vol. 2.*

sold." He told him about his "long boxing story called FIFTY GRAND," about an aging boxer who bets against himself not knowing the fight is already fixed, and when the challenger fouls him in the late round he won't go down and fouls the challenger. "It's a hell of a good story. Scott FitzGerald thinks he can sell it for me."[12]

To write such a tale Hemingway could call on an impressive knowledge about boxing. Not only had he been boxing since high school, but by hanging around gyms where professionals trained, he had picked up vast quantities of anecdotal lore. He had seen scores of fights in arenas on both sides of the Atlantic and had read follow-up accounts of countless others in the newspapers. Though he had an encyclopedic knowledge of boxing, he did not forget that less is more in fiction, and as Dorothy Parker would write of him in her *New Yorker* review when "Fifty Grand" came out in *Men Without Women* a few years later, his sense of selection in this story is "unerring."[13] The story bore a kinship to what Hemingway felt Harold Liveright was doing to his book of short stories—sabotaging it for something bigger. Perhaps he wrote it as a parable, for as the idea kept coming to write a tour de force to get back at Liveright and solve other associations of a literary nature, too, it made it all right for him to reply in kind by giving a book he knew Liveright couldn't publish.

Charged with energy and unable to slow down, Ernest remained busy through November, partaking of the life of Paris, intellectual and otherwise. He read Turgenev's *Torrents of Spring* and Flaubert's *Sentimental Education*. There were prize fights and gallery openings, and at a gathering at Shakespeare and Company, Paul Robeson sang Negro spirituals. One of the horses Ernest picked at Auteuil paid 73.50 francs on a ten-franc bet. The morning after his race winnings, Ernest returned to the lending library of Shakespeare and Company to check out Don Stewart's *Parody Outline of History* to see what a satire could be and that afternoon sat down at his typewriter with the intensity of a reporter up against a deadline. Not even Hadley and Bumby, sick in the next room with winter colds, could distract him. He wrote for ten straight days

12. EH to HL, November 1925.
13. Lynn, *Hemingway*, 309.

with little revision. Still angry that some critics compared his work to Sherwood Anderson, his parody of Sherwood's new novel *Dark Laughter* was coming out in good form. He had discussed Sherwood's book earlier with Hadley and Dos Passos, and they all agreed it was silly and sentimental. With his keen ear Hemingway could imitate anyone's stuff, and Anderson's Whitmanian style was particularly easy. The tale he wrote was of two men in Petoskey, Michigan, who had tangled love lives and were filled with the vague and inarticulate longings and pointless questions often had by Anderson's men.

The weather turned cold in Paris, and the winter setting of his satire was made more real to Ernest as he worked in a small room of the barely heated apartment. When *The Making of Americans* was issued by McAlmon's Contact Press, Ernest put Gertrude into the story and named the last part "The Passing of a Great Race and the Making and Marring of Americans." One night Fitzgerald showed up at the apartment drunk, and he put that into the book too. Late in November, borrowing the title *The Torrents of Spring* from Turgenev, Hemingway's novella, unplanned and unedited, was finished and ready for the typist. *The Torrents of Spring* is an adroit, original, and humorous tale that deserved the praise received in *The Nation* from Allen Tate, who called it "a small masterpiece of American fiction."[14] The effort was for Ernest a cathartic step toward full artistic independence. It was also the betrayal of a friend for, beyond stretching his literary muscles, the point was to write a short book that Liveright could not possibly accept and also make clear that Sherwood Anderson was no longer his literary role model.

Testing the material, he read aloud chapters to his friends. Dos Passos admitted to laughing when passages were read to him one autumnal afternoon at the Closerie des Lilas, but he considered it a bad move to double-cross an old friend like Anderson. Hadley had thought the idea behind the book detestable because it was such a vicious parody of their friend, and after reading it she felt even sorrier for Anderson, who had opened literary doors and written passionately in favor of Hem's stories,

14. Lynn, 304.

and she expressed the hope that her husband wouldn't publish it. She found herself in the awkward position of being a "thoroughgoing wet blanket,"[15] for there were others who considered it terribly funny and were totally for publication. Dos Passos likewise recommended that he keep the manuscript to himself, and when he tried to argue Hemingway out of publishing it Hemingway would turn evasive. "Hem," noted Dos, "had a distracting way of suddenly beginning to hum while he was talking to you."[16] Dos Passos thought "that In Our Time had been so damned good he ought to wait until he had something really smashing to follow it with."[17] There were good laughs in the new manuscript here and there, he conceded, but that it wasn't "quite good enough to stand on its own feet as a parody,"[18] and why chop an aging writer who at one time had written remarkable stories?

Pauline Pfeiffer, however, dropping by regularly during the writing to see Hadley and hear the latest chapter, thought it was great. She was a good listener with a wide interest in contemporary writing who looked and pretended to be younger than she was by all available means. She laughed heartily at the story and encouraged Ernest to send it to Liveright. Pauline probably wouldn't have been bothered by the disparagement of Sherwood Anderson, with whom she had no personal connection. *The Torrents of Spring* can also be understood as a counterpart to Hemingway's developing marital crisis, not yet reaching its peak nor maybe even known yet to Hadley, with two women hovering around him as he wrote it and reading it when they could, and if they did not see the underlying parody as being themselves, then they were both in denial. For, set in a beanery in Petoskey, a man is courting two women; first one, whom he married, and then another, who is younger and livelier.

At the time of *Porgy and Bess, All God's Chillun, The Emperor Jones,* and the cult of jazz, Hemingway rejected the fashionable assumption that the emotional and sensual life of the Black race was superior to that of the White, an assumption that Anderson, too, had more than just

15. Mellow, *Hemingway: A Life Without Consequences*, 319.
16. John Dos Passos, *The Best Times*, 158.
17. Dos Passos, 177.
18. Dos Passos, 158.

suggested in *Dark Laughter*. Though he had it in mind to differentiate himself from Anderson and Stein and also get out of his contract with Boni & Liveright, breaking with Liveright was not his sole motive in writing the book; for the book has an element of fun as well as malice, and he got pleasure from writing it. But he wanted to follow Fitzgerald to Scribner's and obtain the benefits of a more commercially successful firm, a first-rate editor, and an outlet for his stories in *Scribner's Magazine*. Since the terms of his contract would be broken if Boni & Liveright passed on one of his next three books, and publishing a satire on a best-selling author could be damaging to that author and the firm, Liveright would probably reject his next book and Hemingway could instead sign with Scribner's. Certainly, Maxwell Perkins of Scribner's wanted to publish Hemingway. He had let him know this in a letter full of praise for Ernest's work when he obtained a copy of *in our time*.

Near the end of November, Fitzgerald wrote to Liveright that Hem's new book was "about the best comic book ever written by an American . . . devastating to about seven-eighths of the work of imitation Andersons . . . like a nightmare of literary pretensions behind which a certain hilarious order establishes itself before the end." Fitz even wrote that he hoped Liveright would turn down this "extraordinary and unusual production,"[19] allowing Hemingway to move to Scribner's. Either Ernest put him up to writing this letter or Fitzgerald proposed it, but either way they were in it together. Earlier in the month he had asked Fitzgerald to recommend "Fifty Grand" to *Scribner's Magazine*. Fitzgerald suggested substantial cuts to the story's opening. Hemingway, who had earlier cut the opening pages of "Indian Camp" and the end of "Big Two-Hearted River," recognized his tendency to inflate beginnings and to write past natural conclusions and therefore took Scott's advice and cut the opening two-and-a-half typed pages. Fitzgerald then sent the manuscript on to Perkins recommending it for the magazine. Scott had not only done much to promote Ernest to Perkins at Scribner's, but *The Great Gatsby* had been there when Hemingway needed a model for *The Sun Also Rises*. (There are echoes of *The Great Gatsby* in *The Sun Also Rises*.) It was also

---

19. Reynolds, *Hemingway: The Paris Years*, 337.

Scott, along with Dos Passos, who introduced the Hemingways to a fabulous wealthy couple named Gerald and Sara Murphy, who visited the carpenter's loft in early December to hear him read *Torrents*, and whose enthusiasm for his writing was matched only by their zest for living.

For the Murphys, too, America was rigid and dull, and they had also moved to Paris in 1921 with their three beautiful and well-behaved children, Baoth, Patrick, and Honoria. Avoiding the wealthy American colony of diplomats and businessmen who lived around the Etoile, they first settled into an elegant apartment on the Quai des Grands Augustins and cultivated friendships with artists, musicians, and writers. Sara was the grandniece of William Tecumseh Sherman. Like her famous uncle, she said exactly and forcefully what was on her mind and cared nothing about the pretentions of the high society from which she sprang. The couple had met as children vacationing on neighboring estates in East Hampton, New York. Gerald Murphy's father owned the Mark Cross Company in New York and London, a fine retailer of luxury leather good and fine china and silver, and while Gerald had no interest in business, he had inherited his father's good tastes. Strolling along the Rue de la Beotie one day, Gerald walked into the Rosenberg Gallery and saw paintings by Braque and Picasso and Juan Gris and was astounded. "Something in those paintings . . . was instantly sympathetic and comprehensible and fresh and new. I said to Sara, 'If that's painting, it's what I want to do.'"[20] His career as a painter did not last long, but he did produce eight remarkable canvases, and he and Sara became very good friends with Picasso and Leger. The Murphys gave many parties, once on a houseboat on the Seine for the premiere of Stravinsky's ballet *Les Noces*, and with their taste and style created an ambience of pleasure and good breeding. Sara was a beautiful woman with a lovely figure, and Gerald, with a fine consideration and politeness that moved fast and intuitively, had an extraordinary virtuosity with people.

Dos Passos said of them, "people were always their best selves with the Murphys."[21] Gerald was in his late thirties and Sara was five years older than her husband. They were drawn to Ernest's talent and personality

---

20. Calvin Tomkins, *Living Well is the Best Revenge*, 25.

21. Tomkins, 6.

and began inviting the Hemingways to dinner parties at their apartment. Hadley was happy to go but never felt completely comfortable because she had no fashionable clothes and little sense of style, while everything Sara Murphy touched was exquisite. Ernest admired them both and developed a crush on Sara, who liked him back. Once a friendship was formed with Sara, her loyalties remained forever framed in silver. They were fond of the best of everything. Pauline Pfeiffer, with more money than even the Murphys, cared about the best of everything too. However, celebrity and money meant little to the Hemingways during their marriage. "[We kept] a stiff upper lip about the adulation of the Murphys and this rich, worldly crowd,"[22] remembered Hadley.

Gerald Murphy knew that Hemingway had reservations about him. He did not fit the pattern of Hemingway's male friends; he was not athletic, nor much of a sportsman. Moreover, although Gerald did not court the rich, he felt at home in social situations where wealth was the dominant factor. Like many of Hemingway's male friends, he fell into the habit of giving into or agreeing with Hemingway's opinions and prejudices—something he disliked in himself. Murphy noticed that Hemingway "is never difficult with people he does not like, the people he does not take seriously."[23] He never thought that he had a claim on Ernest's affections, but later in life, remembering his friend, he gave this perception: "Ernest will have given his life one thing, and that is scale. The lives of some of us will seem, I suppose by comparison, piddling. . . . For me, he has the violence and excess of genius."[24]

Hemingway wrote to Ezra, "Feel healthy as hell,"[25] and complained to Ernest Walsh, "We're about broke."[26] He was boxing at a new gym on the Boulevard Raspail with "nice good sized gloves and a hot shower."[27] He also wrote to his father about his book: "It should be on sale in Chicago at various places. The name of the book is In Our Time:" and enclosing

---

22. Mowrer, Sokoloff tapes, Hemingway Collection, JFK Library.
23. Mellow, *Hemingway: A Life Without Consequences*, 297.
24. Mellow, 297.
25. EH to EP, Nov. 8, 1925, *The Letters of Ernest Hemingway, Vol. 2.*
26. EH to Ernest Walsh, Nov. 8, 1925, *The Letters of Ernest Hemingway, Vol. 2.*
27. EH to HL, November, 1925, *The Letters of Ernest Hemingway, Vol. 2.*

some good reviews, added, "There is a long article on me and some dope about Hadley and Bumby with a picture in the NOVEMBER number of Arts and Decoration that might interest you. I wish the book would have a good sale in Chicago and Oak Park as I'd like the people I know to see what the stuff is I'm doing whether they happen to like it or not."[28] Dr. Hemingway bought the book and read the stories with interest, while Grace gathered reviews to forward to Ernest. Around Oak Park his father had had many compliments about his son's achievement, but he could not entirely conceal his belief that the book was lacking in spiritual uplift. "Trust you will see and describe more of humanity of a different character in future volumes,"[29] wrote Clarence.

Hemingway's life was again changing as many of his early friendships in Paris were dropping off or being replaced. He seldom saw Ezra, and Gertrude, already distant, would be even more displeased with his attack on Anderson. McAlmon, once his drinking buddy and publisher, was no longer on speaking terms ("I've defended the little toe nail [*sic*] paring for 3 years," so he wrote to Fitzgerald, "but am through now"[30]). Harold Loeb would soon be alienated by his caricature in *The Sun Also Rises*, and Kitty Cannell, never much of a friend, turned shrill when the novel appeared. Lewis Galantiere lost interest after an unprovoked attack by Hemingway in the *Transatlantic*, and now that the review was dead Ernest saw little of Ford Madox Ford. Only Sylvia Beach remained as strong a friend as she was that first year. But he had many new friends, and their social life was still quite busy. Some, like Dos Passos and Archy MacLeish, were talented hardworking literary men; others like, the Murphys, the Fitzgeralds, and the Pfeiffer sisters, were rich and prominent in their own right.

Pauline Pfeiffer was more and more becoming an emotional fixture in Ernest's life. "She is a swell girl," he wrote Bill Smith in early December. "Her and Hash and I are together all the time. She and I have done some A1 drinking . . . killed on a Sunday two bottles of Beaune, a bottle

---

28. EH to CEH, Nov. 20, 1925, *The Letters of Ernest Hemingway, Vol. 2*.
29. Carlos Baker, *Hemingway: A Life*, 207.
30. EH to F. Scott Fitzgerald, Dec. 24, 1925, *The Letters of Ernest Hemingway, Vol. 2*.

of Chambertin and a bottle of Pommard and with the aid of Dos Passos a q[uart] of Haig in the square bottle, and a quart of hot Kirsch."[31] Gerald and Sara Murphy, too, were becoming good friends. They were renovating a house in Cap d'Antibes on the Riviera Coast called Villa America that would be a magical place inside and out. Even with their wealth and sophistication, they were always kind and generous to their friends. Don Stewart said that any description of Gerald and Sara should begin, "There once was a prince and a princess."[32] They brought verve and imagination to everything, from the clothing they wore, to the way they decorated their house, to the menus for their dinner parties.

Sara Murphy loved Ernest from the outset. Gerald found him charismatic but overwhelming: "He was such an enveloping personality, so physically huge and forceful, and he overstated everything and talked so rapidly and graphically and so well that you just found yourself agreeing with him."[33] Hadley found Sara Murphy "exquisite," and remembered "Sara and Gerald were impressive friends, you know; they were both very good looking, fine featured and blonde. Somehow they matched each other."[34] Sara Murphy remembered Hadley as "a nice, plain girl," and was not impressed; perhaps noting Hadley's meager wardrobe, she thought her "not very bright."[35] Hadley did have difficulty keeping up with the repartee in the conversations of the Murphys and their circle. Dos Passos later remarked, "Conversation in the early twenties had to be one wisecrack after another. Cracks had to fly back and forth continually like birds in badminton."[36] Ernest was funny and could certainly keep up his end, as could Dos Passos, and the Murphys were always quick to respond, but delivering quick, witty remarks was just not part of Hadley's mien.

When *Torrents* returned from the typist early in December, Ernest sent it to Horace Liveright, whom he had actually never met, along with a long, edgy, thoughtful letter. Hemingway must have known that, no

---

31. EH to Bill Smith, Dec. 3, 1925, *The Letters of Ernest Hemingway, Vol. 2*.
32. Mary Dearborn, *Ernest Hemingway*, 199.
33. Dearborn, 200-1.
34. Dearborn, 201.
35. Dearborn, 201.
36. Dos Passos, *The Best Times*, 157.

matter how fine a satire he claimed his book to be, Liveright would never publish a parody of the bestselling book of an esteemed author he had recently signed, but he made a strong pitch anyway. First, he reminded Liveright that "in the golden age of the English novel Fielding wrote his satirical novels as an answer to the novels of Richardson. . . . Now they are both classics," and then, "For a long time I've heard various critics bewailing the lack of an American satirist. Maybe when you read this book you will think they haven't so much bewailing to do now," adding that Louis Bromfield, an author who sometimes pitched books to Harcourt, Brace, "thought it was one of the very funniest books he had ever read and a very perfect American satire."

Ernest, having just written a longer novel closer to his heart, which he knew was very good, and knowing other publishers more preferable than Boni & Liveright were interested in his work, and that if Liveright rejected the book he would be free to break their contract, became bolder and seemingly presumptuous. "The book is the right length for a funny book . . . [but] If you take it you've got to push it," he wrote and scolded about the lack of effort to push *In Our Time*: "I made no kick about . . . the lack of advertising, the massing of all those blurbs on the cover . . . which, grouped together . . . put the reader on the defensive." He then told Horace Liveright, "The only reason I can conceive that you might not want to publish it would be for fear of offending Sherwood . . . In any event it should be to your interest to differentiate between Sherwood and myself in the eyes of the public," and demanded "an advance of $500," but that "I ought to ask for a thousand dollar advance [because] if you get someone like Ralph Barton to illustrate it, and push it as you know how, you can sell 20,000 copies." He signed, "With best regards, yours always, Ernest Hemingway,"[37] and sent the letter and manuscript by ship to New York City.

When Mike Strater learned of the proposition, he had no doubt it was a "cold blooded contract breaker,"[38] but, actually, Ernest had been forthright throughout negotiations with both Liveright and Maxwell Perkins,

---

37. EH to Horace Liveright, Dec. 7, 1925, *The Letters of Ernest Hemingway, Vol. 2*.
38. Baker, *Hemingway: A Life*, 207.

whose initial offer to read his stories had arrived too late. He gave his address at the Hotel Taube in Schruns, Austria, and wrote, "Please cable me there, at once, your decision on *The Torrents of Spring*," adding "in case you do not wish to publish it I have a number of propositions to consider. I want you to publish it, though, because it is a hell of a fine book."[39] Whether *Torrents* was published or not by Boni & Liveright made little difference to Hemingway as he and his family made final preparations for their long-planned, much-anticipated return to the Austrian Alps for another long winter vacation. He probably would have been disappointed if his offer had been accepted because, through the aid of his good friend F. Scott Fitzgerald and the extraordinarily fine stories of *In Our Time*, Maxwell Perkins, an editor Ernest much admired, was even keener that Scribner's publish his next book. On the evening of December 11, the Hemingways gathered their luggage and boarded a train from the Gare de l'Est, traveled through the night, arrived at Schruns late on the following morning to two feet of fresh powdery snow and fine, clear mountain air, and checked into their rooms in the Hotel Taube.

Ernest had a cold and developed laryngitis after reading the whole of *The Torrents of Spring* to their new friends Gerald and Sara Murphy and took to bed with a very sore throat where he began to revise *The Sun Also Rises*; but, with much else on his mind—Pauline Pfeiffer and Horace Liveright—he quickly put the blue notebooks aside to write letters. "Got run down last month in Paris," he wrote his mother. "When I get working so hard that I have no time for exercise I always get run down. Bad cough, lose weight, etc. The mountains will fix all that."[40] Hadley turned Bumby over to Mathilde Braun and recovered her ski legs practicing on the bunny hills. Herr Lent, having already seen a party buried on the slopes, forbade skiing in the high mountains until the snow had time to settle and freeze. They were in the good place again, and everything was going to be fine. Snowy days, frosty nights, good food, and feather beds made them well, and they had the good books they had brought from Paris to last through winter, many checked out from Sylvia's store.

---

39. EH to HL, Dec. 7, 1925, *The Letters of Ernest Hemingway, Vol. 2.*
40. EH to GHH, Dec. 14, 1925, *The Letters of Ernest Hemingway, Vol. 2.*

Ernest first read Turgenev's *Fathers and Sons*, then Thomas Mann's *Buddenbrooks*; he reread Captain Marryat's *Peter Simple*—a book he had read in childhood and found he still loved; and there was *The Moonstone* by Wilkie Collins and nine paperback volumes of Trollope. "Turgenieff to me is the greatest writer there ever was. Didn't write the greatest books, but was the greatest writer," he wrote Archie MacLeish. "War and Peace is the best book I know but imagine what a book it would have been if Turgenieff had written it."[41] He received a letter from his father, who wrote "I bought 'In Our Time' and read it with interest."[42] Ernest replied that "it is nice to have people like it. But it is inside yourself that you have to judge and nothing anybody says outside can help you."[43] As Christmas approached, a second letter came from his father, who had digested his stories, writing, "The brutal you have surely shown the world. Look for the joyous, uplifting and optimistic and spiritual in character. It is present if found. Remember God holds us each responsible to do our best. My thoughts and prayers are for you my dear boy every day."[44]

On a windy day in Paris, Kitty Cannell encountered Pauline Pfeiffer wearing a chic suit and struggling along under a brand-new pair of skis. Pauline explained she was going skiing with the Hemingways in Austria. Kitty was surprised; she did not think they were good enough friends to spend the holidays together. But Pauline had indeed made friends with Hadley and had become more than just friends with Ernest, who had written to his mother that "Pauline Pfeiffer is coming down to spend Christmas."[45] Pauline could be funny and very good company. The poet Elizabeth Bishop said she was the "wittiest person, man or woman, I have ever known." The physical contrast between her and Hadley was striking. "Hadley was a likeable though not alluring girl," remembered Max Eastman, "rather on the square side, and vigorously muscular and independent." Pauline was described by a friend as "trim, neat, kind of birdlike

41. EH to Archibald MacLeish, Dec. 20, 1925, *The Letters of Ernest Hemingway, Vol. 2*.
42. Reynolds, *Hemingway: The Paris Years*, 341.
43. EH to CEH, Dec. 15, 1925, *The Letters of Ernest Hemingway, Vol. 2*.
44. Baker, *Hemingway: A Life*, 207.
45. EH to GHH, Dec. 14, 1925, *The Letters of Ernest Hemingway, Vol. 2*.

with bright eyes and an inquiring look."[46] In addition to her wealth, she wore lovely clothes, and like Hemingway, she was also a writer, having a degree in journalism and working for Main Bocher, the *Vogue* editor. The books Ernest read in Schruns that winter he read with more than normal earnestness, and one of the reasons he did so was to escape the personal dilemma enveloping his life. The love he felt for Pauline growing, he told her that he believed he might take his own life if things weren't settled between him and her and Hadley by the New Year.

For twelve days leading to Christmas, Ernest and Hadley rested and enjoyed life, skiing, eating well, and sleeping soundly. There was a piano in the room for Hadley to play, and in the evenings, they drank and played pool and poker. Hadley beat everyone at pocket billiards and Ernest won enough at poker to buy Bumby a wooden rocking horse to go with the jockey silks, riding cap, and crop sent by the Fitzgeralds for Christmas. "Please thank Scotty [*sic*] for Bumby," he wrote to Scott, mentioning farther down the letter, "Pauline Pfeiffer gets here tomorrow for Xmas and New Years."[47] Warm winds blew and rain fell when Pauline arrived on Christmas day, turning the snow to slush. The Hemingways were now a threesome like it had been before with other women friends like Isabel Simmons in Chamby. Hadley had always enjoyed their companionship, especially when Ernest was working, as he began to work again in the mornings on the draft of *The Sun Also Rises*.

It seemed simple and innocent: the girls dressing alike in sweaters and laughing. Ernest being like a brother, showing Pauline how to bend on her skis and shift her weight, going off some nights on walks alone while Hadley stayed with Bumby. If her husband was infatuated, Hadley was sure it would pass and slipped into passivity. "I do think I have a flaccid nature," she told an interviewer many years later. "I tend to give up before other people do."[48] But this time was different, for Ernest was now in love with two women, and Pauline was hopelessly in love with Ernest and, determined to win him, aggressively insinuated herself in their lives.

---

46. Dearborn, *Ernest Hemingway*, 207.
47. EH to FSF, Dec. 24, 1925, *The Letters of Ernest Hemingway, Vol. 2.*
48. Mowrer, Sokoloff tapes, Hemingway Collection, JFK Library.

Maybe Ernest thought he could follow the Left Bank rules and, like Ezra and Ford, have both mistress and wife, but he had much to learn about Pauline's tenacity and her moral code, and she had much to learn about him—traits that Hadley knew very well. After four years of marriage, she understood his insecurity, and though he wanted to be regarded as a courageous sportsman, she had no illusions about his athletic prowess, having seen him bumbling too many times on the ski slopes and the tennis courts. Though neither knew it at the time, it would be the last Christmas Hadley and Ernest Hemingway would spend together.

The two women presented a striking contrast. Hadley, tall and red-haired, with a full figure that was becoming matronly, was almost alone in the world beyond her small family in Paris. Modest, kind, effacing, and a good sport, she had been married to Ernest for four years, had no reason to suspect his infidelity, and had been secure until his infatuation with Duff. She worried about the lack of money and her dowdy clothes, but she was in love with her husband and absorbed with their two-year-old baby. Pauline, small and dark with a boyish figure, was spoiled, self-assured, ambitious, and, like all the Pfeiffers, used to getting her own way. She wore fashionable clothes and pitied Hadley's humble flat and Spartan existence. With money and no domestic or emotional ties, she was free to do as she wished. Like Duff, she was exciting and flattering. But Duff had been twice divorced, had a child and was poor, irresponsible, and alcoholic, while Pauline was marriageable, stable, and secure. Seeing Hemingway carrying on with Duff, and she must have, would have emboldened Pauline to make the move on Ernest.

On the last day of the year a cable came from Horace Liveright rejecting *The Torrents of Spring*: "It would be in extremely rotten taste," he wrote to Ernest, "to say nothing of being horribly cruel, should we want to publish it."[49] Hemingway immediately wrote Fitzgerald: "I have known all along that they could not and would not be able to publish it as it makes a bum out of their present ace and bestseller Anderson . . . I did not however have that in mind in any way when I wrote it."[50] Critics

---

49. Jeffrey Meyer, *Hemingway: A Biography*, 169.
50. EH to FSF, Dec. 31, 1925, *The Letters of Ernest Hemingway, Vol. 2*.

like Allen Tate would feel that Anderson's feeble fiction provoked and deserved Hemingway's witty and well-executed condemnation. On his part, too, Hemingway would insist that he was attacking the writer for his own good. He maintained that his satire was impersonal and that Anderson's thought and style would be significantly improved by reading the severe strictures of a novice; he wrote Anderson a letter to this effect when *Torrents* was published in May 1926.

Anderson would be hurt by the attack but maintain a façade of friendship, though he would tell Stein, who was very angry when the book appeared, that Hemingway had attacked him because he couldn't "bear the thought of other men as artists,"[51] a pronouncement more out of bitter hurt than truthful observation. And because Liveright wouldn't publish *Torrents*, Hemingway's second book, their option lapsed on his third book. "So I'm loose," he wrote to Scott, further stating in the letter that though he had solid interest from Alfred Harcourt, "I promised Maxwell Perkins that I would give him the first chance at anything if by any chance I should be released from Liveright." Promising to wire Liveright to send the satire to Don Stewart at the Yale Club, from where Stewart could forward it to Scribner's, he asked Scott to write Perkins about the rejection and to tell of his new novel. "I am re-writing The Sun Also Rises and it is damned good." He closed the letter with a postscript asking Fitz, "Do you think I ought to go to N.Y.,"[52] so that he could settle matters quickly.

"Jeest Pauline is a swell girl," Ernest wrote to Bill Smith the day after New Year's. "Anybody who goes big through seven consecutive rainy days when they expected skiing has got something in addition to the usual Christian virtues."[53] The Hearst organization returned "Fifty Grand" unpublished, but Hemingway had an option for the fight story from *Scribner's Magazine* and was not upset. He worked steadily in the mornings on his novel and spent the rest of the day with Pauline and Hadley. Ernest would remember many years later: "When the husband

51. Jeffrey Meyer, *Hemingway: A Biography*, 170.
52. EH to FSF, Dec. 31, 1925, *The Letters of Ernest Hemingway*, Vol. 2.
53. EH to BS, Jan. 2, 1926, *The Letters of Ernest Hemingway*, Vol. 3.

is a writer and doing difficult work and is occupied much of the time and is not a good companion or partner to his wife for a big part of the day, the arrangement has advantages until you know how it works out. The husband has two attractive girls around when he has finished work. One is new and strange and if he has bad luck he gets to love them both."[54] This was a reflection tinted by many, many years, because in Schruns in the winter of 1926, he was so much in love with Pauline that after hearing her talk about her religion he wanted to be Catholic like her. "If I am anything I am a catholic," he wrote to Ernest Walsh. "Had extreme unction administered to me as such in July 1918 and recovered. So guess I'm a super-catholic . . . cannot imagine taking any other religion at all seriously."[55]

It was more than just a convenient declaration of faith due to his intense interest in Pauline, for Hemingway looked back on his Con-gregational training, with his father's unbearable piety and his mother's church politics of who would rule the choirs, as Oak Park hypocrisy and in his heart was never a Protestant. In Italy he had experienced a country where religion was so woven into every facet of the culture that men could joke about it without giving it up, and when he had thought he was dying, the Catholic priest had made a lasting impression upon him. Even before he was involved with Pauline, the ritual and mystery of the Catholic Church was already a strong attraction to someone drawn to all things ancient and medieval. Pauline accelerated his profession of faith, just as she accelerated the dissolution of his marriage, though both would have happened without her.

Bumby remained out and about with his teenaged Austrian nanny, who dressed him in the jockey outfit sent by the Fitzgeralds, too young to understand what was happening to his parents. Though it was a season of avalanches resulting from the spring-like thaw, and in the heart of the mountains a small group of skiers had disappeared, the Hemingway party, leaving their child in Tiddy's care, took the electric train thirteen kilometers up the valley to the Hotel Rossle at Gaschurn for four days of

54. Ernest Hemingway, *A Moveable Feast*, 209-10.
55. EH to EW, Jan. 2, 1926, *The Letters of Ernest Hemingway, Vol. 3.*

glacier skiing. While Hadley and Ernest skied every day, the daily climbs to the slopes leaving them bone tired in the evening, Pauline stayed behind reading. She had brought her skis but "she never got on them," remembered Hadley. "She didn't like the cold."[56] There was a tall green porcelain stove and kirsch to warm them at night. Ernest and Hadley slept beneath down comforters in one room; Pauline slept in a smaller room next door. Ernest included Pauline in their private patois; giving her the nickname Doulbadulla, he was Drum and Hadley was Dulla. Hadley was beginning to really understand that their friendship wasn't so innocent.

He wrote no letters as he continued revising the novel, once shifting the narrative to a detached third-person point of view that did not work, so by mid-January the story was Jake's again, whom the author also made a Catholic, and who, when confronted with his religion in a cathedral, became somewhat mournful for his lack of devotion.

When they returned to Schruns from the high mountains, Pauline returned to Paris. Ernest was excited and a little impatient about his publishing prospects, waiting for Perkins and Liveright to make their next moves. He received his copy of *This Quarter* and wrote Walsh "it is the first exciting magazine I have read since I was 13 and used to wait for the baseball magazines," and vacillated about "The Undefeated," which was printed in the review: "Disliked it when I read the proof. I thought it was a great story when I wrote it . . . Oh Christ I want to write so well and it makes me sore to think that at one time I was writing so well and was evidently in a slump:"[57] an opinion he revised in another letter to Walsh two weeks later: "The Undefeated is a grand story and I'm very proud I wrote it."[58] And as he poured his energy into the ink-filled blue notebooks, struggling along with his manuscript trying to make it jell, he didn't know that his literary future was already being decided.

Horace Liveright, suspicious of Fitzgerald's letters, had written Scott, "we have a contract with Hemingway for three more books and you know

---

56. Mowrer, Sokoloff tapes, Hemingway Collection, JFK Library.
57. EH to EW, Jan. 15, 1926, *The Letters of Ernest Hemingway, Vol. 3.*
58. EH to EW, Feb. 1, 1926.

too that we all, and I, especially, believe in Hemingway. I think he has a big future."[59] Then, on January 8, after receiving Hemingway's letter telling him of Liveright's rejection of *Torrents*, Fitz cabled Perkins: "YOU CAN GET HEMMINGWAYS [*sic*] FINISHED NOVEL PROVIDED YOU PUBLISH UNPROMISING SATIRE."[60] Perkins wired back to Scott: "PUBLISH NOVEL AT FIFTEEN PERCENT AND ADVANCE IF DESIRED ALSO SATIRE."[61] Scott had followed his cable to Perkins with a letter explaining Liveright's refusal and that Hemingway thought it freed him from their contract. He urged Max to write Ernest reassuringly, but "Don't ever tell him I've discussed his Liveright & Harcourt relations with you."[62]

Pauline wrote from Paris almost every day: "I miss you two men. How I miss you two men."[63] She discovered she had left her prized kimono at Gaschurn and asked, "Do you think we drank enough there to get it back?"[64] and offered to run errands by returning their books to Shakespeare and Company. To Hadley she sent woolen socks, a nightgown, a box of pecans, and money to buy gifts for Bumby. Sensing Ernest's deepest commitment, she carefully praised his work in her letters: "The velocity with which The Sun Also Rises is being thrown off staggers me," adding, "My dear Drum . . . wouldn't you consider bringing a small copy of it with you for me to read," and strongly took his side on the negotiations with Liveright. "I think there must be something rotten about a firm that hasn't anyone in it that thinks Torrents of Spring funny . . . I would like to take this up with Liveright. For Liveright's own good. Perhaps if Mr. and Mrs. Hemingway should go to America, or just Mr. Hemingway . . . I might go with them or just him and tell them a few things."[65] Reading her words, Ernest sensed her feelings for him and must have felt very warm about them. He had decided to go to New York and would set sail as soon as his new passport arrived by the end of the month.

59. Reynolds, *Hemingway: The Paris Years*, 347.
60. Reynolds, 347.
61. Reynolds, 347.
62. Reynolds, 348.
63. Reynolds, 348.
64. Reynolds, 348.
65. Diliberto, *Hadley*, 208.

In a carefully wrought letter sent to Horace Liveright on January 19, Hemingway stated that their "contract is quite explicit that your option on further books lapses if you reject my second book," and since Liveright turned *Torrents* down Hemingway therefore regarded himself "free to give The Torrents of Spring and my future books to the publisher who offers me the best terms." He wrote that he knew "publishers are not in the business for their health," but that he was also certain that he would "eventually make a great deal of money for any publisher," and that "you surely do not expect me to have given a right to Boni & Liveright to reject my books as they appear while sitting back and waiting to cash in on the appearance of a best seller: surely not all this for $200." In New York when they met in person, he hoped that his publisher "may have an answer to this letter."[66]

Late in January, Hadley helped her husband pack for New York. They had discussed the possibility of going together and taking their child, at least to Paris, but with their apartment sublet they could not afford it, and so Ernest boarded the train alone while Hadley remained in Schruns with Bumby. Pauline, who had returned their borrowed books to Sylvia Beach and had herself joined the lending library checking out, among other books, Virginia Woolf's *Mrs. Dalloway* and Daniel Defoe's *Moll Flanders*—a picaresque tale of a woman's irregular and highly sexual adventures—wrote to Hadley, "I'm overjoyed that Ernest will soon be here. I feel he should be warned that I'm going to cling to him like a millstone and old moss and winter ivy."[67] In Schruns, the innkeeper's wife, Frau Nels, remembered Hadley in the hotel lounge knitting, very quiet and sad, while Bumby was with Tiddy.

Ernest arrived in Paris on January 28 and took a room at the Venetia Hotel on Montparnasse Boulevard but probably spent most of his nights with Pauline at her apartment on the Right Bank. Her sister, Jinny, was visiting their parents in Arkansas, and so they were alone in a city big enough to hide secret affairs. He was in town for six days, and both were busy during the day. With Parisian fashion houses trotting out their

---

66. EH to HL, Jan. 19, 1926, *The Letters of Ernest Hemingway, Vol. 3.*
67. Reynolds, *Hemingway: The Paris Years*, 349.

spring lines, Pauline worked the shows from early to late, attending at least twenty designer openings and typing out her notes at the end of the day while she could still make sense of them. To Hadley she wrote, "I've seen your husband E. Hemingway several times—sandwiched in like good red meat between thick slices of soggy bread. I think he looks swell, and he has been splendid to me. . . . I had hoped to go with him to Jeu de Palmes [an art center for modern photography in the Tuilleries] this afternoon, but now Doucet has decided to open."[68]

Ernest stopped by Sylvia's to check his mail and buy a copy of *In Our Time* (probably for Perkins) and browse the journals and magazines, finding his name mentioned alongside James Joyce in the *Chicago Tribune's Paris Edition* as writers featured in *This Quarter*. He booked passage to America and made a list of people to see and things to buy in New York City. "I miss Hadley and Bumby terrible," he wrote to Ernest Walsh, probably to assuage his conscience, "and always drink too much when I'm not with them."[69] Arising early Wednesday morning, February 3, he caught the train to Cherbourg, where the *Mauretania* waited for evening tide, carrying in his vest pocket a new gold-tipped fountain pen that was a gift from Pauline, with whom he would rather be in bed, or in bed with Hadley, than on the stormy sea of the North Atlantic enduring another rough passage. The day after he sailed, Pauline wrote Hadley, "Your husband, Ernest, was a delight to me. I tried to see him as much as he would see me and was possible."[70]

After seven days of rough stormy seas, the *Mauretania* docked in New York on February 9, 1926, in the midst of a blizzard dropping foot-deep snow upon the city. Late at night, tired and tight with drink, Ernest checked into a room at the Brevoort Hotel in Greenwich Village, just up Fifth Avenue from Washington Square. Being tight with drink rarely ceased throughout this time he spent in New York, but young Hemingway could hold liquor well as, so he would write to Louis Bromfield, he "Met hell's own amount of people."[71] The day after his arrival, a

---

68. Reynolds, *Hemingway: The Paris Years*, 350.
69. EH to EW, Feb. 1, 1926, *The Letters of Ernest Hemingway, Vol. 3*.
70. Diliberto, *Hadley*, 210.
71. EH to the Bromfields, Mar. 8, 1926, *The Letters of Ernest Hemingway, Vol. 3*.

Wednesday, he met with Horace Liveright at his office in a brownstone front on West 48th Street. The meeting was cordial and friendly, Ernest chatting nicely to everyone and leaving the firm at the end of the meeting no longer under contract. Liveright was not a vindictive man, afterward scribbling, "Hemingway was in and absolutely proved that our contract specified if we rejected his second book we relinquished our option on the third."[72] Ernest worried about his next move: whether to approach Scribner's or try Alfred Harcourt, who was also very interested in his work. Deciding that his promise to Max Perkins took precedence, the next day, sober, he paid his first visit to the Charles Scribner's Sons Building on Fifth Avenue.

Maxwell Perkins was forty-one and wore a fedora indoors and out. He met Hemingway with a firm handshake, and Ernest relaxed. Perkins had read *Torrents* (delivered by Don Stewart, as Hemingway had requested) and found it publishable. In his paper-strewn office on the fifth floor, Max, a tactful man, both warm and aloof, reached a deal with Ernest, offering a fifteen percent royalty starting with the first sale and a fifteen-hundred-dollar advance on the first two books, accepting *The Sun Also Rises* on faith because Ernest had not yet finished the revision and had not brought along a copy. He would have an approved contract drawn up and the advance check written early the next week. It could not have worked out better for Ernest, and until his presence was required to sign the contract, his time was a continual party.

Maybe it was his friend Donald Ogden Stewart who passed him onto the glittering well-supplied-with-liquor-and-gossip literati of New York—some of whom he and Hadley had already met, perhaps even entertained, when they passed through Paris, impressed by him and his reputation as a new kind of writer rising under the tutelage of Pound and Stein—and that he was close friends with F. Scott Fitzgerald and was about to sign a new contract with Scribner's that made his acceptance not only assured but vital to this high colony of theatre and art, many of whom met for lunch in the dining room of the Algonquin Hotel.

---

72. Reynolds, *Hemingway: The Paris Years*, 352.

Although Hemingway was not present at any of "The Vicious Circle" luncheons during the boozy frenetic ten days he spent among them, he was taken up by Robert Benchley and Dorothy Parker, the founders and perhaps most prominent members of the Algonquin Round Table, quickly becoming intimate friends.

Ernest was not famous like many of the people he mixed with in Manhattan during this trip, not yet a star, but, robustly handsome and engaging, he was ready to leave the obscurity of small magazines and presses behind. However, before he downed his first serious shaken martini and rode through town in taxis tight, before he spilled the beans on Paris and informed his famous captive audience of what Ford Madox Ford was really like, he booked passage home on the *Roosevelt*, departing on February 20, and cabled Hadley and Pauline the date of his arrival and news of his new contract with Scribner's. Hadley wanted him back in Schruns and feared, too, him spending time with Pauline on his return through Paris, but, thrilled with the news of the $1500 advance and fifteen percent royalties for his books, she wrote to Isabelle Simmons, now married and living in New York, "Quite a boy, Hemingway. I feel pretty proud."[73]

On the weekend after his meeting with Perkins, Ernest entered the flow of the city with a lot of heavy drinking and a whirlwind of cab rides taking him to private literary corners of the city to parties where men and women authors talked and drank bootleg whiskey, some extolling the writing of Ford Madox Ford. In Greenwich Village one night, carousing with Bobby Rouse, one of the old gang from the Y. K. Smith days in Chicago, they met with John Herrmann, whose novel *What Happens* had been published by McAlmon, and rapped on the window where the novelist Dawn Powell lived with her husband and baby. Powell, small and sassy, pretty and plump, with dark hair cut short like Pauline's, went along to Jack Cowles's house, where Ernest sprawled contentedly on the sofa while Jack, who knew dozens of bootleggers, made drinks. Powell, born in Ohio, would never forget Hemingway: through the course of

---

73. Diliberto, *Hadley*, 210.

their lifelong friendship, he would become the distant character Andy Callingham, the internationally known, publicity seeking, self-involved novelist who makes intermittent appearances in her Manhattan based novels. He received a note from Max to come to the office on Tuesday, February 16, to sign the contract and receive his check and look over the plan for *Torrents*.

When they began their relationship as author and publisher/editor, Perkins would not change nor allow to be changed a word of Hemingway's writing. Hemingway made this a pre-condition of publishing; the only changes allowed were spelling and punctuation corrections. An important aspect of Hemingway's modernism—as of Joyce and others— was an insistence on addressing earthy and unpleasant subjects such as abortion and divorce; the demands of modernity and free speech had to be met. In a short while, Perkins would also send some of his short stories to *Scribner's Magazine,* some of which they would publish; one, "The Killers," they would publish the following year. He signed the contract with his Waterman fountain pen from Pauline and disappeared for the rest of the week into a scotch and martini haze, taking taxis to Broadway shows and more parties. He saw a stage adaptation of *The Great Gatsby* at the Ambassador Theatre and wrote to Louis Bromfield that it was "pretty darn close to the book—is a hit. I had to pay to get in. Would have paid to get out a couple of times but on the whole it is a good play."[74] At a party at the Hotel Merley on the evening of his last full day, he "found everybody cockeyed including myself," he wrote to Isabelle Simmons, and "fell for a girl named Eleanor Wylie. Great love at first sight on both sides."[75] He left the party at nine, rushing back to Brevoort to pack, and missed seeing the *Wisdom Tooth*, a play by Marc Connolly that Marc Connolly himself had wanted him and all the others at the party to see.

The next morning, ferrying across the harbor to Hoboken, New Jersey, to board the *Roosevelt*, falling snow obscured the Statue of Liberty. Unexpectedly, at almost the last moment, Dorothy Parker and Robert Benchley had decided to accompany him, for they wanted to visit Paris.

---

74. EH to the Bromfields, Mar. 8, 1926, *The Letters of Ernest Hemingway, Vol. 3.*
75. EH to Isabelle Simmons, Feb. 25, 1926, *The Letters of Ernest Hemingway, Vol. 3.*

At the pier to see them off was the poet Eleanor Wylie—the girl who Ernest had fallen for at the party. Five days out, Hemingway wrote to Izzy, requesting that to his family she "deny any rumors that I was in N.Y.,"[76] and asking if she would retrieve his gold-tipped pen left behind at the Brevoort. While on board he read the Anita Loos bestseller *Gentlemen Prefer Blondes*, published by Boni & Liveright, and thought it "one of the dullest books I've ever read."[77] When the bock docked in Cherbourg, Ernest may have unhappily taken stock of himself. Though he was succeeding in a difficult profession upon which he had based his life, the long apprenticeship had changed him, and those close to him saw this clearly. Still very sensitive, he had not yet hardened under the pressure, and his moods were deeper and their shifts more sudden. Two women were waiting for him, and he loved them both and wanted them both, and so though he now had some money, he was riding the horns of a terrible dilemma that left him feeling restless and guilty. On reaching Paris he dined with Scott and Zelda, who were about to leave for Nice. They asked him to come to the Riviera; the Murphys had invited him to the Villa America later in the year, and he said he would consider it. The Fitzgeralds must have noticed his preoccupation. His novel was not finished, and he had promised to have it delivered by spring, and there was the new girl waiting for him in her expensive flat on rue Picot.

Pauline, small breasted and slender, was built for the Jazz Age with a pixie hairstyle, thoughtful face, and narrow hips. Her uncle Gus had increased her trust fund, so she had even more money and lived in an opulent Right Bank apartment and worked in a splendid office in a job requiring clothes and flair. It was not for the money that Ernest slept with her but for the excitement she brought to his life. Hadley, tightly corseted at thirty-four, seemed much older than thirty-year-old Pauline, and when the three of them had been together, it was Hadley who seemed out of place. Ernest was beginning to resent her dependence upon him and wished for more intellectual support than she could give him now that she was solely focused on being a mother to Bumby. Their differences

76. EH to IS, Feb. 25, 1926, *The Letters of Ernest Hemingway, Vol. 3.*
77. EH to the Bromfields, Mar. 8, 1926, *The Letters of Ernest Hemingway, Vol. 3.*

would have become stark in the close quarters of Schruns: Hadley was passive, Pauline was active and just as athletic; Hadley was a nominal Protestant, Pauline was a devout Catholic, a mysterious religion with a strong attraction to Hemingway. That winter, the three were poised at a turning point. Hadley was wearying of Ernest's emotional demands and his continuous roving life and was ready for a more regular existence. Pauline not only loved Ernest but recognized his was an enormous talent that needed breathing room and was ready to give up her professional life and her soul to marry him and help forward his career. And Hemingway, having exhausted the literary life of the Latin Quarter, was ready to move up to the next level of intensity, a step for which Pauline was better suited and willing to take with him.

Pauline and Jinny had not really come to Paris looking for husbands, as was said by some people. Jinny preferred women, and Pauline came to Paris to avoid an engagement with her cousin in New York. Raised within the Catholic Church, these two sisters were not dizzy flappers. At thirty, Pauline might have been ready for a husband, but of all the men in Paris, Ernest, a married non-Catholic with a two-and-a-half-year-old son and a doting wife, seemed the least likely prospect. She was rich and he was poor. Though she went to bed with him without remorse, to destroy a marriage and then live in sin with the husband was almost unforgiveable. A priest would not absolve her, and there would also be the confrontation with her mother, Mary Pfeiffer, who would be deeply hurt. Ernest, Left Bank bohemian, badly dressed—his four-year-old tweed suit far too traveled to stand inspection—given to heavy drinking, and with no means of support but his pen, would be hard to present as a suitable husband. But Pauline was deeply in love with Ernest and could not forget the smile and touch of him.

"I should have caught the first train from the Gare de l'Est," Hemingway wrote long afterward, "But the girl I was in love with was in Paris then . . . and where we went and what we did, and the unbelievable wrenching, killing happiness, selfishness and treachery of everything we did gave me such a terrible remorse [that] I did not take the first train or the second or the third." In the first days of March, he finally took the train from Paris to Schruns. Hadley was there with Bumby in lederhosen to meet him.

> When I saw my wife again standing by the tracks as the train came in by the piled logs at the station, I wished I had died before I ever loved anyone but her. She was smiling, the sun on her lovely face tanned by the snow and sun, beautifully built, her hair red gold in the sun, grown out all winter awkwardly and beautifully, and Mr. Bumby standing with her, blonde and chunky and with winter cheeks looking like a good Vorarlberg boy.

He was consumed with guilt, but Hadley, glad to have him back at last, put her suspicions aside. "You made such a fine successful trip. I love you and we've missed you so much," he remembered her as saying. And while they were alone for a while with no visitors, "I loved her and I loved no one else," and though there was not much snow around the village, for February had been like spring, "we had a lovely magic time."[78]

With his buckram notebooks beside his typewriter in an extra room across the hall, he began to revise the novel he promised Max Perkins in time for fall publication. While restarting work, never one to hold back what he truly felt inside, he began a peculiar exercise by writing down ways to kill oneself. The cleanest would be a nighttime plunge from an ocean liner. "There would be only the one moment of taking the jump and it is very easy for me to take almost any sort of jump," and "it would never be definitely known what had happened and there would be no postmortems and no expenses left for anyone to pay."[79] Farther down he wrote that reading about a suicide, and the death of another bullfighter in the ring, made him think about death, for at the age of twenty-six, Ernest Hemingway, a young man on the cusp of success, had no apparent reason to think of suicide. After seven lean, long years with no significant payment for his fiction, he had found a great editor who believed in him and gave him both a wonderful deal for his next two books and a

---

78. Hemingway, *A Moveable Feast*, 210-11.
79. Michael Reynolds, *Hemingway: The Homecoming*, 3.

foothold for his short fiction in *Scribner's Magazine*. There was a terrible emotional dilemma coming to a head: he was in love with two women—the girl in Paris and also his wife with whom he had a child—and maybe this made him think of suicide, but he would not do it then.

The reviews to his collection of short stories, *In Our Time*, were so good he could not believe them. The *New York Times* said he packed "a whole character into a phrase, an entire situation into a sentence or two." In *The Nation*, Allen Tate wrote, "The passionate accuracy of particular observation, the intense monosyllabic diction, the fidelity to the internal demands of the subject—these qualities fuse in the most completely realized naturalistic fiction of the age."[80] He was glad to see the reviews but did not live in the past; and now, back at his desk in the Taube Inn, turning his attention to his novel, he tried a few lines and settings, tried shifting the beginning back to meeting the young matador in Pamplona, but decided for certain that the story had to start in Paris—Pamplona could be introduced later. So, he abandoned his opening chapter and began typing, "This is a novel about a lady,"[81] and for the next fifteen pages filled in the biography and relationships of Duff, Mike, and Jake; not until page sixteen did the words appear: "Robert Cohn was once middle-weight boxing champion of Princeton."[82] He worked hard and made great progress for the first week and a half after his return from New York, then they were joined by friends.

Sara and Gerald Murphy, the new friends they had recently met through John Dos Passos and who were also good friends with the Fitzgeralds, had invited the Hemingways to Antibes in March to sail on the Mediterranean. But Ernest wanted to ski and invited them to Austria instead. On March 11, they arrived in Schruns with John Dos Passos. The next morning, they all bundled into the tiny electric train that ran up the Montafon Valley to Gaschurn to the better snow and steeper slopes and were warmly welcomed at the Hotel Rum Zossle-post, where Ernest and Hadley had stayed in January with Pauline. Their visitors were delighted

80. Reynolds, 4.
81. Ernest Hemingway, Item 200, Hemingway Collection, JFK Library.
82. Ernest Hemingway, *The Sun Also Rises*, 3.

with the setting. "Everything was fantastically cheap," remembered Dos Passos. "We stayed at a lovely old inn with porcelain stoves," and "We ate forellen im blau [trout] and drank hot kirsch . . . It was like living in an old fashioned Christmas Card."[83]

Ernest gave them ski lessons and then took Dos and Gerald up to Madlener Haus to ski down the glacier. There were no tow ropes or lift. They put seal skins under their heavy wooden skies and climbed the slopes to the top. When they went down the slope, Dos went easy, sitting down whenever he saw a tree, but Gerald, who was older, struggled with determination. "Ernest would stop every twenty yards or so to make sure we were all right," remembered Gerald, "and when we got to the bottom, about a half hour later, he asked me if I had been scared. I said, yes, I guess I had. He said then that he knew what courage was, it was grace under pressure. It was childish of me, but I felt absolutely elated."[84] Hadley remembered that Gerald, who was twelve years older, was amused by Ernest's take-charge attitude and started calling him "Papa." She thought "it was a name that suited him very well. He wanted people to look up to him. He wanted to be something important in everybody's life."[85]

At the end of a strenuous day of skiing they warmed themselves at the Rossle bar drinking kirsch and listening to each other's stories. While they sat there warm and pleased, Dos's new play, *The Moon is a Gong*, was opening in Greenwich Village, and they all drank a toast to its first performance. Dos also talked about his recent trip to Marrakesh and Tangiers where he said he had met some interesting if elderly whores but had lived the life of a fifty-five-year-old virgin from Massachusetts. Amidst the camaraderie and good liquor, Ernest, after some urging, did something he rarely did and that was to read the revised typescript of his novel aloud. He read the part about fishing in Burguette and then put down his manuscript and told stories about the Festival of San Fermin.

The Murphys lavishly praised his novel and said they wanted to join the Hemingways in Pamplona in July to see the wild bulls and experience

---

83. Dos Passos, *The Best Times*, 158.
84. Mellow, *Hemingway: A Life Without Consequences*, 327.
85. Mowrer, Sokoloff tapes, Hemingway Collection, JFK Library.

the wild nights described by Ernest. The Hemingways found the Murphys generous and understanding; they were able "to give each day the quality of a festival"[86]; but Hadley sat silent as they spoke about Pamplona. She remembered the last fiesta when all the men had been fools around Duff, who didn't pay her hotel bill, and this year Pauline would be coming, too, and unlike Duff, she was neither engaged nor a drunk. Dos remembered these days in the Vorarlberg as "the last unalloyed good time" they all had together. They laughed so hard at meals it was an effort to stop long enough to eat, and at night they drank plenty of hot kirsch and slept "like dormice" under great featherbeds. "We were like brothers and sisters," he wrote. "It was a real shock to hear a few months later that Ernest was walking out on Hadley."[87]

When their visitors left, Ernest settled back into his writing, worked long hours every day, and relaxed in conversations. The closing weeks of March were still a time of avalanches, and Hemingway discussed death on the slopes with Herr Lent's young assistant, Fraulein Glaser, who shared a macabre tale about uncovering a man killed in powder snow: he was found still standing, waving his hand and smiling back at a friend. "We became great students of Avalanches," Ernest remembered. "Most of the writing I did that year was in avalanche time."[88] He wrote in his journal that he must finish *The Sun Also Rises* and then write short stories for four or five months. As he revised the last five chapters of his novel, beating them out on the noisy old Corona, having decided to retain the first-person narrative, the work went smoothly. He lavished all his descriptive powers on the climactic bullfight scenes of Pedro Romero and the departure of the revelers from Spain. Upon completing the revision of *The Sun Also Rises*, they were ready to return to Paris. He had a completed typescript of a ninety-thousand-word novel—and waiting for him in Paris, too, was Pauline.

The city was gray and wet when they returned on Tuesday of Holy Week and stayed at the Hotel Venetia until their apartment sublet ended

---

86. Baker, *Hemingway: A Life*, 214.
87. Dos Passos, *The Best Times*, 177-78.
88. Hemingway, *A Moveable Feast*, 204.

on Good Friday, April 2. On the first evening, to make their return official, they sat in the Closerie des Lilas; the next day it was duly noted in "Latin Quarter Notes" that Hemingway was back. Max had sent the proofs of *Torrents,* and Hemingway, politely acquiescing to changing the name of a real person, quickly made corrections, and just as quickly sent *The Sun* to a typist to clean up his 330-page manuscript. It had taken Ernest Hemingway five years to learn to write a short story the way he needed to write one, but he had his first novel written and revised from scratch in eight months. He had read *The Great Gatsby* and though discouraged at first, for who could ever write so well as Fitzgerald, it inspired him, too. Hemingway's story about the war generation and Fitzgerald's eulogy for the Jazz Age were written in different keys but played the same theme: the post-war world was sick at heart, its values defunct, and its over-age children at a loss of purpose. Both men, writing better than they knew, had created the classics of their age. Ernest was a young man among many, writing as best as he could. He was not thinking about classics, and reading over his novel, making small changes for the typist, he clearly saw the awkward scaffolding written to support the story's structure to get him going, and knowing now where it wasn't necessary, took it out in large chunks. It was a new kind of writing that broke new ground on telling a long tale. Ezra and Gertrude, and Hadley, too, had pointed him toward Henry James, the grand master of the American novel who specialized in building his story around special exquisite moments, but Ernest was never converted: James was dead, and as far as Hemingway was concerned, so were his notions of writing.

The galley proofs of *Torrents* were read by him and Hadley during the slow periods of the six-day bike races held in the Velodome D'Hiver on the second week of their return. They sat in the stands with blankets, a picnic hamper, and red wine, dropping in and out of the dimly lit arena as teams of racers pushed toward the finish. Ernest admired the bikers and the brotherhood they shared with its code of ethics; he studied them intensely and imitated their dress, sometimes wearing a jersey. When the French team won with a tremendous burst in the final hours, Ernest was on his feet cheering with all the hardcore fans. Life was good in Paris that spring. He had one book finished and a second one at the typist. The Curtis Brown literary agency, responsible for foreign rights for Boni & Liveright, had sold *In Our Time*, which had already been translated into Italian and Russian, to Jonathon Cape in London, who paid Ernest $125 against the royalties. Everything he had worked so long and hard for was coming true. The only dark part was returning to Hadley after meeting with Pauline. He would disappear to secretly see Pauline, his guilt giving way to the excitement of the affair that he somehow felt justified pursuing as long as Hadley didn't know. But there was a problem keeping Pauline as a mistress: she did not want to be a mistress; she wanted to be a wife.

When the rains returned in the middle of April and the days became chilled and gray, in the dampness of their coal-heated apartment, Hadley's sniffles turned into flu and Bumby started coughing and would not stop. The Latin Quarter was changing, too, putting on stagey affairs to invite and trap tourists at places like the Dingo, the Jockey, and the Gypsy Bar as more and more Americans gawked around Montparnasse with their pockets full of cheap francs crowding the old haunts. Then Chink Dorman-Smith came to town, and he and Ernest, and Hadley, too, stayed up late drinking and reminiscing about the good old times. Together at the Olympic Stadium they watched the Royal Military Academy at Sandhurst, Chink's alma mater, defeat France's national military academy in Rugby, and then on April 20 Ernest took Chink to the opening of the Walt Whitman exhibit at Shakespeare and Company where Sylvia made a fuss over Chink, asking him to sign the guestbook on the same page with the signatures of James Joyce, T. S. Eliot, Paul Valery, and Jules Romain. Later that night when they returned to the carpenter's loft, Hadley, leaving Bumby in their care, left and attended the opening, too. Scott Fitzgerald wrote from Antibes that the fifteen-thousand dollars he received for the movie rights of *The Great Gatsby* would barely see him and Zelda through the year. Ernest had little sympathy and jokingly replied, "Am recommending to Mr. Walsh that he give you *This Quarter's* $2000 bucks [a phantom award promised by Walsh to several writers—Hemingway included—that would never materialize] and have just called my attorney to make you my heir."[89] Then, on the last Saturday of the month, Ernest mailed the freshly typed manuscript of his novel to Max Perkins.

The Sun Also Rises was received in New York the first week of May, the only novel that Perkins had ever contracted completely unseen. *Torrents* had been a slight coterie book, clever to the New York critics but inaccessible to the general reader. To get back the advance given Hemingway, *The Sun* would have to sell out its first edition and few new writers ever attracted that much attention. Max carefully read the manuscript. Nothing happened in the first few pages except talk about a woman named Brett Ashley and gossip concerning the Latin Quarter, but Max read on. Quite abruptly, a Jew named Robert Cohn appeared with only two friends, the narrator Jake being one of them. Still, the novel did not seem to be going anywhere. Then, quietly, it began to happen as the narrator, less self-conscious, began to let the action flow: quick studies of the streets of Paris that were tight and perfect—the sidewalk tables, the prostitutes and taxi cabs. There would be some editing to make the book work, but Perkins could do it. He had to get it through the board, headed by seventy-two-year-old Charles Scribner, who was formidable on obscenity and was not going to publish what he considered a "dirty book." Perkins argued for Hemingway as strongly as he had for Fitzgerald's *This Side of Paradise* seven years before. Young writers, he told the men, were the future of the firm, and if Hemingway were turned down, they would avoid Scribner's for its conservative position. When the meeting was over, the board, with serious reservations, accepted the book.

---

89. EH to FSF, April 16, 1926, *The Letters of Ernest Hemingway, Vol. 3.*

Dorothy Parker

Fraulein Glaser, Hemingway, Dos Passos, and Gerald Murphy on the slopes above Schruns

198

Hemingways in Schruns

Horace Liveright

Hadley and Pauline at Schruns

In Our Time

This Quarter

Robert Benchley

Elinor Wylie

Sara Murphy with children

Scribner's building, New York City

The Murphys

A LONG, LONELY SEASON SHROUDED BY FAIRY DUST

ERNEST MADE plans for their annual tour of the bullfight season and also a trip to Antibes where the Murphys had offered the Hemingways the guesthouse at the Villa America. But little that spring and summer would go as planned. At the end of April, Pauline and Jinny Pfeiffer invited Hadley to tour the chateaux in the Loire Valley. Hadley remembered being "foolishly flattered that they'd invited me to go along with them," but realized in retrospect, "they'd invited me along to reveal the truth to me about Ernest and Pauline." Hadley had long been eager to tour the valley, but it did not interest Ernest and so they had never gone. Jinny drove a rented car and the trip started very well. The Loire River ran full and fast, and the trees were turning green. "We had lots of fun together, stopped at good places and ate deliciously, and of course the old castles were a delight." Then the trip took a dark emotional turn. Pauline became strange, lapsing into long silences and getting angry when Hadley asked questions. "[She] would get very moody and quite often snap at me and I felt most uncomfortable." Hadley intuitively asked Jinny if Ernest was somehow involved in her sister's moods. When Jinny replied, "I think they are very fond of each other," their affair suddenly became clear. Falling in love with Ernest had been for Hadley a great "explosion into life." He had rescued her from a tormented past and given her a fulfilling happiness. Now he was in love with someone else, someone who she had thought was her friend, someone she had unknowingly encouraged to befriend her husband. Hadley's pleasure in the castle country drained away, and she was the one who became quiet and bad tempered. "I imagine I was a little stiff and cold, aloof, really quite horrid."[1]

Alone again with Ernest in their apartment in Paris, Hadley could hardly keep from crying as she confronted Ernest about his love for Pauline. Ernest, his logic twisted by guilt and selfishness, flushed red. He angrily rebuked her for bringing it out into the open and stalked downstairs to walk the rainy streets. "What he seemed to be saying to me," Hadley recalled, "was that it was my fault for forcing the issue. Now that I had broken the spell our love was no longer safe."[2] Doors were slammed and for days and nights they argued bitterly. He seemed to imagine that they could go on as before: Hadley still a loving and devoted wife even as he had Pauline for a mistress. But that was something she couldn't do. And now that the affair was out in the open, Pauline stopped being coy and tried to meet with Hadley to convince her to give up her husband. "Through Ernest I got a message that Pauline wanted to talk to me," remembered Hadley, who still wanted to save her marriage. "I refused because I thought she would best me in any off-hand conversation . . . she was very quick, very smart. I wished I was that smart."[3] Anxiety and remorse would never leave them. Encountering Kitty Cannell on the street, Kitty innocently asked how Pauline had enjoyed her mountain vacation. "Well, you know what's happening," Hadley replied coldly. "She's taking my husband."[4] How were they going to face the summer with Pauline planning to join them at the Murphys' villa in Antibes and go along with them to Pamplona?

The turbulence of his crumbling marriage brought a well of creativity to the surface as Hemingway began working on fiction to take his mind off the pain. The first story he wrote was inspired by one of Fraulein Glaser's macabre tales and became a reflection of his callous treatment of Hadley: "An Alpine Idyll" is about a peasant who uses the open mouth of

1. Hadley Mowrer, Alice Sokoloff tapes, Hemingway Collection, JFK Library.
2. Jeffrey Meyer, *Hemingway*, 175.
3. Mowrer, Sokoloff tapes, Hemingway Collection, JFK Library.
4. Bertram Sarason, *Hemingway and the Sun Set*, 146.

his frozen dead wife to hang his lantern in the woodshed. Back in reality, as the Hemingways continued to quarrel, Bumby was sick in his bedroom with whooping cough, Pauline was in Italy visiting her aunt and uncle, and all of Ernest's friends were out of town. He wrote to Fitzgerald, "I've not had one man to talk to or bullshit with for months."[5] Full of self-pity, Ernest was determined to leave for Madrid by the middle of May, where he planned to work and write short stories in the morning and attend bullfights in the afternoon. He would go by himself if the baby had not recovered, and Hadley could join him later. He packed his bag, and on May 13, took the night train to Madrid to find it "fine and cold and dry with a very high sky and lots of dust blowing up my nose."[6] The veterinarians called off the corrida on Saturday, May 15, because the bulls were small and sick. Ernest stayed in his room at the Pension Aguilar and wrote as a man seeking penitence.

That morning he worked on a tale called "Today is Friday," about the Crucifixion, with Roman soldiers rehashing the day in a wine shop as if it were a sporting event. After lunch, he reworked a story begun the previous fall about Nick Adams encountering mobsters in a small diner in upper Michigan, lopping off the first two pages of the old draft and picking up the story at "The door of Henry's lunch room opened and two men came in."[7] He was cutting the beginnings of stories to start at a dramatic moment. The two men wait for a man who never comes; they were going to kill him, and then they leave. He left it with the cook and owner of the restaurant full of fear. Full of juice, he "got dressed and walked to Fornos, the old bullfighter's café, and drank coffee and then came back"[8] to his room where he began revising the story about Nick and the young Indian girl. The young Indian girl is Nick's sweetheart, and he learns from his father on a summer night that she had been with another guy: Nick cries and his father tries to comfort him unsuccessfully. The story, "Ten Indians," was a story of loneliness and betrayal that Hemingway finally understood alone in his cold Madrid hotel bed. Everything he

---

5. EH to F. Scott Fitzgerald, May 4, 1926, *The Letters of Ernest Hemingway, Vol. 3.*
6. EH to FSF, May 15, 1926, *The Letters of Ernest Hemingway, Vol. 3.*
7. Hemingway, *Short Stories – The Killers*, 215.
8. Reynolds, *Hemingway: The Homecoming*, 28.

wrote in Madrid was about lonely or betrayed men. He learned about it one way from Joyce, who wrote about betrayal so lovingly, and he learned about it from looking in the mirror.

Ernest did not speak Spanish well enough to converse with others and have meaningful conversations, but during the day, watching Niño de la Palma perform unspectacularly in the San Ysidro bullfights, or walking to the Prado to see the new Goyas and afterward sip brandy on a sidewalk café, his loneliness was not dispelled but he felt okay. He wrote to Pauline and Hadley, and they wrote back, but he had to lie to each woman, even if only by omission, and this did not cheer him. Hadley knew about Pauline's affections now, but he could not tell her how desperately in love he had become with "Fife," as they both called her. He tried not to think about it, but alone at night in the dark, the old terrors of being blown up in the war returned. He wished that Hadley were with him, but she had taken the train south to the Riviera with Bumby and his nurse, Marie Rohrbach, to join the Murphys at Antibes. When Hadley arrived at Villa America, a doctor determined Bumby had whooping cough, and Sara, who had a horror of germs infecting her children, even washing coins they brought into the house, sent Hadley and Bumby to a hotel where they did not stay long because the Fitzgeralds had rented a nearby house, the Villa Paquita, which they did not like, moved to another, and offered the Villa Paquita to Hadley. She and Bumby and the nurse moved in.

"You've never seen anything as lovely as Antibes and the Murphys' place is divine,"[9] wrote Hadley to Ernest. Once a sleepy coastal village on the Cote d'Azur between Cannes and Nice, Antibes had become a watering hole for the rich, due in part to the affluence and style and tastes of the Murphys. That summer Rebecca West, Charles MacArthur, Isadora Duncan, and several other noteworthies were staying in hotels that had sprung up along the shore. The Fitzgeralds and MacLeishes rented villas nearby. It was a summer of ribald frivolity and recklessness for the village's rich visitors. There were nude swimming parties, of which Hadley did not partake, and wild, extravagant engagements. One night,

---

9. Gloria Diliberto, *Hadley*, 218.

Scott Fitzgerald and the boisterous Charles MacArthur herded a band of musicians into one of the villas and locked them in to play for the evening's party.

For the Hemingways and their social circle, the center of life at Antibes was the lavish Villa America, which was a beige stucco house with fourteen rooms on seven acres of flower and herb gardens on a hillside looking out onto the blue Mediterranean Sea; inside was a shiny black tile floor, white walls, and a fireplace framed with mirrored glass, chairs and sofas upholstered in black satin. Though not so nice and big, the Villa Paquita was quite nice too. "It's adorable here," Hadley wrote. "There is . . . a fenced in yard with poppies and orange trees so Bumby can play without anybody and Marie is being grand (awfully impressed of course, too, with everybody's flow of gold)."[10] Gerald wrote Ernest that Bumby was improving under the doctor's care and, though quarantined, they were not ignored, as the Murphys, the Fitzgeralds, and the MacLeishes visited every night outside the gates with cocktail shakers.

Ernest wrote to Maxwell Perkins from Madrid on May 20, "I've heard nothing from you as yet about receiving The Sun A.R. mss. nor about the story ["Alpine Idyll"] I sent."[11] He also enclosed a letter to forward to Sherwood Anderson, his earliest literary benefactor and role model, whom he relentlessly satirized in *Torrents of Spring*. Hadley and Dos Passos had warned him that he would appear unkind, and Anderson would be deeply hurt. He had not listened then, but now with the parody about to be published, Hemingway belatedly admitted that it probably would hurt Sherwood's feelings, and in a rather confused and almost insidious manner, he tried to explain himself in the letter. "It is a joke and it isn't meant to be mean," he wrote to his old friend. "If when a man like yourself who can write very great things writes something that seems to me, (who have never written anything great but am anyway a fellow craftsman) rotten, I ought to tell you so . . . if we have to pull our punches and if somebody starts to slop they just go on slopping from then on with nothing but encouragement from their contemporaries."

---

10. Diliberto, *Hadley*, 220.
11. EH to Maxwell Perkins, May 20, 1926, *The Letters of Ernest Hemingway, Vol. 3*.

He added, "because you had always been swell to me and helped like the devil on the In Our Time I felt an irresistible urge to push you in the face with true writer's gratitude." His words kept getting more twisted: "it may not hurt you at all," and "I think you'll think the book is funny," and signed "Best always to you and your wife from Hadley and me."[12] Anderson later said it was possibly the most patronizing letter written from one writer to another and that Ernest's "absorption in his ideas may have affected his capacity for friendship."[13]

The letter that Max Perkins carefully composed to Hemingway on May 18 was more than enthusiastic about *The Sun Also Rises*: "a most extraordinary performance," he called it. "No one could conceive of a book with more life in it." He was especially impressed with the bullfight scenes and Jake and Bill's fishing expedition on the Irati River: "they . . . are of such a quality as to be like actual experience,"[14] adding, "the humor in the book and the satire . . . are marvelous, and not in the least of a literary sort."[15] What he didn't say was that the opening Paris part of the manuscript was not as well written as the part set in Spain, nor did he mention that the mindless drinking, sexual permissiveness, and random profanity disturbed Mr. Scribner. However, he did raise the matter of the tale of Henry James and his bicycle that Jake and Bill joked about in Burguete.

Henry James was a Scribner's author, and though recently dead, was the patriarch of American letters. Ford Madox Ford, who had known James, told a story about him injuring himself on a bicycle that rendered him impotent. "There is one hard point," Perkins wrote Hemingway, "a hard one to raise too, because the passage comes in so aptly and rightly. I mean the speech about Henry James . . . I do not see how that can be printed . . . There are also one or two other things that I shall bring up in connection with the proof, but there is no need to speak of them here."[16] If the Henry James remark was negotiable, then other points would

12. EH to Sherwood Anderson, May 21, 1926, *The Letters of Ernest Hemingway, Vol. 3*.
13. Charles Fenton, *The Apprenticeship of Ernest Hemingway*, 105.
14. Carlos Baker, *Hemingway: A Life*, 220-21.
15. James R. Mellow, *Hemingway: A Life Without Consequences*, 328.
16. Reynolds, *Hemingway: The Homecoming*, 25.

follow easily enough. Max ended the letter calling the book "astonishing and more so because it involves such an extraordinary range of experience and emotion all brought together in the most skillful manner."[17]

The novel had been the subject of a lot of debate at Scribner's. The James story and its analogue in Jake Barnes's emasculating war wound and his impotence were matters of concern among the editors. But two of the old-timers on the board, William Brownell and John Wheelock, both very conservative—Brownell had vetoed Fitzgerald's first book—argued for its acceptance. "The tragedy is real and impressive as an incident of war that must often happen and that few have ever thought of as one of war's inevitable horrors,"[18] wrote Brownell; and Wheelock, to Perkins's amazement, felt there was no question that the book should be published by Scribner's. And so, several days after his letter to Hemingway, Perkins was able to write to Charles Scribner: "You wanted to know the decisions on Hemingway: We took it with misgivings." Among young writers the firm had a reputation of being ultra-conservative, and had they declined *The Sun Also Rises* it would have confirmed that reputation and the word would have gotten around. "That view of the matter influenced our decision largely," Perkins reported. "I simply thought in the end that the balance was slightly in favor of acceptance."[19] On the following day, May 28, *The Torrents of Spring* was published and most of the reviews were fairly good. The *New York Times* thought it "a specialized satire . . . which would appeal mainly to Mr. Hemingway's fellow craftsmen." The *Evening Post* called it "delicious fun."[20] But Harry Hansen in the *New York World* was not impressed: "Parody is a gift of the gods. Few are blessed with it. It missed Hemingway," adding "when Hemingway published 'In Our Time' it was Sherwood Anderson who turned handsprings and welcomes this new comer [*sic*] to the ranks of America's great men . . . and now Hemingway pays him back."[21]

---

17. Mellow, *Hemingway: A Life Without Consequences*, 328-9.
18. Mellow, 329.
19. Mellow, 328.
20. Reynolds, *Hemingway: The Homecoming*, 43.
21. *New York World*, May 30, 1926, p. 4M.

The Hemingways' original plan for the spring and summer had been to leave Bumby at Antibes with the Murphys, go to Madrid for the San Ysidro bull fights, and then return to Antibes until it was time to leave for Pamplona in July. But their plans had changed, and Hadley felt estranged and isolated in Antibes because of the quarantine imposed upon Bumby. While their well-dressed friends sat on straw mats on a private beach, chatting and watching their children frolic in the water, Hadley passed the time indoors, rubbing liniment oil on Bumby and cajoling him into taking medicine.

Sara Murphy did what she could to help, paying the doctor bills and sending her chauffer with groceries, but her generosity hid a slight coldness. Sara knew about Ernest's affair with Pauline, and though sympathetic to Hadley, she preferred Pauline's company. Hadley was aware of Sara's feelings. "I had a terrible time because I was so unhappy," she remembered. "Nobody liked me. My hair misbehaved, and my clothes misbehaved. Actually, I didn't have any clothes to speak of."[22] She received letters from Ernest complaining how lonely he was, and she wrote back to him almost every day. Ernest implored Hadley to join him, even sending along their joint passport so she could cross the border into Spain. She returned the passport before the end of May so that he could join her on the Riviera where Pauline would also be waiting. Ernest had also been writing to Pauline, asking about the Catholic Church, which she was encouraging him to know more about.

Pauline was writing to Hadley, too, asking if she could join her. She said she wanted to keep her company and help her take care of Bumby. She wasn't afraid of the whooping cough, she wrote, because she'd had it as a child. Hadley did not want to see her but agreed to let her join them. "There's room for Fife," she wrote to Ernest, "if she wants to stop here and have the whooping cough with us."[23] Hadley had been afraid that if she told her not to come then Ernest would stay away, too, or that maybe they would go off together. "I should have said to her, 'No,

22. Mowrer, Sokoloff tapes, Hemingway Collection, JFK Library.
23. Diliberto, *Hadley*, 223.

you can't have my husband.' But I didn't."[24] She was growing tired of the awkward, painful situation. When Ernest wrote to Scott that he was having a lousy time in Madrid while Hadley luxuriated on the Riviera, her feelings boiled over: "I'm living here the cheapest possible . . . I've got a headache & a heartache and I work for the common good and am sorrier than I can say that I havn't [sic] been able to expend myself more on you." She also told him that Pauline would be glad to come to Madrid and, that if he thought it "wisest" not to use the passport, Pauline would "make Madrid a place of pleasure instead of the awful strain of a place it's been to you alone."[25] Pauline cabled a few days later that she would be coming to Antibes. She would arrive before Ernest. As Pauline grew bolder, Hadley slipped further into passivity; she wanted to save her marriage, but she didn't know how to fight for Ernest.

Ernest finally left Madrid, changing trains three times, spending a night in Pamplona, and arrived in Juan-les-Pins on May 29. To meet him at the station were Hadley, the Murphys, and Pauline. That night, Sara and Gerald hosted a small party at a nightclub celebrating Ernest's arrival with champagne and caviar. Though tired and tightly wound, Ernest was the center of attention with Pauline on one arm and Hadley on the other. Ada and Archie MacLeish were there and so were the Fitzgeralds. Among these beautiful people there was tension in the beautiful air as Pauline and Hadley sat with a forced, tight-lip levity that Ernest tried to dispel with humor as each was beginning to understand the high stakes of the game they were playing. Ernest sensed Hadley's hurt and anger but did not fully realize the burden she had had with Bumby's illness, nor was he comfortable staying in the Villa Paquita, which placed him in Fitzgerald's debt. But these were slight compared to the behavior of Scott Fitzgerald, who ruined the celebration.

As Sara and Gerald lavished on Ernest more adulation than Scott was capable of gracefully observing, he began an irritating repertoire of drunken attention-grabbing tricks. First, he insulted Gerald, loudly saying that champagne and caviar were an out-of-date affectation, and

---

24. Mowrer, Sokoloff tapes, Hemingway Collection, JFK Library.
25. Reynolds, *Hemingway: The Homecoming*, 35.

then he turned and stared at a pretty woman so long and rudely that people complained. He then began to throw ashtrays. Zelda, with a fuchsia peony in her dark-blonde hair, sat staring strangely and saying nothing throughout the disastrous episode. Gerald Murphy, a man of self-possession and talent, finally lost his temper and walked out of the party. The Fitzgeralds, Gerald would later say, "didn't want entertainment, or exotic food; they seemed to be looking forward to something fantastic . . . something had to happen, something extravagant."[26]

Ernest was disgusted, too, but appeared the next morning at Fitzgerald's villa and gave him a copy of *The Sun Also Rises* to read and critique. As bad as he had been on the night of the party, Scott rose to the occasion and read the manuscript carefully over the next few days, for he had made large promises about Hemingway to Max Perkins. Though not a theorist like Hemingway, Fitzgerald understood his friend's approach to fiction and knew how stories worked and why (and Ernest knew Scott knew this), and he gave to Hemingway in a carefully delineating letter the finest editing advice the author could possibly receive. Hemingway read, listened, and understood and made the recommended changes that made the story more whole and fitting and helped it become a true literary classic. When reviewing *In Our Time*, Fitzgerald had marveled at the lack of exposition in the stories. But in writing this novel, Hemingway was letting expository prose take the place of dramatized action, and Fitzgerald was struck by the emptiness of the first fifteen pages that presented biographical data of Lady Brett Ashley and Mike Campbell, and an abrupt intervention of Jake Barnes telling about himself as narrator, which could easily and more effectively be incorporated into the movement of the story, and calling it "sloppy, careless, and ineffectual,"[27] he took the overwritten introduction apart.

Scott moved cautiously in expressing his objections to this beginning. He warned Ernest that he had certain comments to make. Then, wanting him to revise the first part of his manuscript, but not lose their friendship, he wrote the ten-page handwritten letter that alternated between severe

---

26. Nancy Mitford, *Zelda*, 120-1.
27. Reynolds, *Hemingway: The Homecoming*, 40.

and quite possibly hurtful criticism with apologies and reassurances to soften the blows. *I've listened to others with profit*—he was saying between the lines, reminding Ernest that he had received excellent advice from Edmund Wilson—*now you should listen to me*. In addition to criticism, he also praised Hemingway, wanting him to remember that writing a novel was "a new departure for you, and I think your stuff is great. You were the first American I wanted to meet in Europe—and the last."[28] The first chapter, Scott wrote, gave an impression of "condescending casuallness" and that "there are about 24 sneers, superiorities and nose-thumbings-at-nothing that mar the whole narrative" which made for an "elephantine facetiousness."[29] He thought the tone of the beginning was all wrong and did not match that of the more maturely ironic Jake who told the rest of the story as narrator. It was his judgment that the book didn't get going until the start of Chapter III (in the published novel) when Jake picks up Georgette and takes her dinner and to the Bal Musette where Brett appears. But Fitzgerald did not suggest a wholesale amputation of the beginning; he recommended paring it down by eliminating the worst parts. The rest of the book was "damn good,"[30] though he did advise against using the real names of Aleister Crowley and Harold Stearns and to cut a long anecdote centering on Ford Madox Ford.

Fitzgerald either walked the letter over to the Villa Paquita, where the Hemingways were still staying, or Ernest came to the Villa St. Louis to call for it. Reading it over must have been painful, but Hemingway was too intelligent a craftsman to dismiss Fitzgerald's suggestions out of pique. He took them to heart, talked them over with Fitzgerald, and settled upon a more drastic remedy. Instead of paring down the beginning or removing the worst scenes, he decided to entirely cut the first fifteen pages and start the book with "Robert Cohn was once middleweight boxing champion of Princeton. Do not think that I am very much impressed by that as a boxing title, but it meant a lot to Cohn,"[31] and communicating his decision in a letter to Max Perkins that he wrote on June 5: "I was very

---

28. Kenneth Lynn, *Hemingway*, 346.
29. Reynolds, *Hemingway: The Homecoming*, 40-1.
30. Reynolds, 42.
31. Ernest Hemingway, *The Sun Also Rises*, 3.

glad to get your letter and hear that you liked The Sun a. r. Scott claims to too." Then, after giving his address, he wrote, "I believe that . . . I will start the book at what is now page 16. There is nothing in those first sixteen pages that does not come out, or is explained, or re-stated in the rest of the book . . . I think it will move much faster from the start that way." And then as if the idea was his and not Fitzgerald's, "Scott agrees with me. He suggested various things in it to cut out . . . which I have never liked—but I think it better just to lop that off."[32]

Perkins agreed to the change with some reluctance, "but you write like yourself only, and I shall not attempt criticism," believing readers not used to Hemingway's style might find biographical information helpful. However, leaving it out reinforced Ernest's iceberg theory of omission that had been so successfully used in "Big Two-Hearted River," and also saved him the trouble of a further revision, which he did not feel like doing. What worried Perkins more than the cuts were Hemingway's references to real people: "I know who Roger Prescott [Glenway Prescott] is quite well. . . . Why not call him Prentiss. You don't want to harm him." The matter with Henry James was settled by dropping the last name and using only Henry. There were too many people still around who knew the great author well—"four right in this office who were his friends,"[33] wrote Perkins. One criticism of Scott's did stand apart: he thought that Jake was more like a man in a moral chastity belt than one left sexually maimed by a war wound, but it was too late for Hemingway to make such a change. Max also wrote that Robert Bridges, the editor of *Scribner's Magazine*, had declined to publish "An Alpine Idyll" because the story was "too terrible, like certain stories by Chekhov and Gorky"[34] and dealt with a stark reality that most people wanted to keep covered up, and tactfully brought up the lesser issue of using certain words and phrases like "bitch" and "bulls have no balls"[35] in the novel. Hemingway did not completely agree with him: "I think that words—and I will cut anything I can—that are used in conversation in The Sun etc. are justified

32. EH to MP, June 5, 1926, *The Letters of Ernest Hemingway, Vol. 3.*
33. Mellow, *Hemingway: A Life Without Consequences*, 332.
34. Baker, *Hemingway: A Life*, 221.
35. Hemingway, *The Sun Also Rises*, 142.

by the tragedy of the story."[36] He would wait for the galleys to arrive later in the summer to be ready for fall publication. Meanwhile, there was life on the Riviera.

During the summers in the twenties on the Riviera, the Murphys with their gorgeous Villa America hosted many of the most beautiful and accomplished figures of the twentieth century. It was a way station for writers and artists who Sara and Gerald attracted with their impeccable tastes. Their airy house opened onto Arabian maples, desert holly, persimmons, palms, and cedars of Lebanon, terraced and cared for by three gardeners. On the far side, adjoining an old French farmhouse-turned-guest-cottage, were the vegetable garden and an orchard of orange, lemon, tangerine, olive, and nut trees. At the bottom of the hill was a renovated donkey stable, La Ferme des Oranges, where the Murphys housed their overflow of summer guests. Archy MacLeish remembered, "one of the best luncheons I ever ate in my life was eaten under a linden tree outside their little villa on d'Antibes. It was served on a blue china dish on which were some perfectly boiled new potatoes and butter."[37] Life around the Murphys floated on an air of wonder and the possibility of the unexpected or the unlikely. They often sailed along the coast from the port where they kept a yacht. Beyond his Mark Cross, Boston money, Gerald had many talents to sustain him. He had collaborated with Cole Porter on a satirical ballet that was produced at the Theatre des Champs-Elysees in Paris, and he was a first-rate painter who studied with Fernand Leger and exhibited in Paris salons. He always tried hard to meet the expectations of others. This trait was particularly obvious in his relationship with Ernest Hemingway, whom he came close to worshipping.

In the summer of 1926, with their friends gathered around them, laughter came easy and often to everyone but Zelda Fitzgerald, who seemed to live within her own strange world. She "was aloof and remote," said Ada MacLeish. "It was not that she did not pay attention to what one was saying, but a strange little smile would suddenly, inexplicably cross her face. She answered questions if they were put to her, but otherwise she

36. EH to MP, July 24, 1926, *The Letters of Ernest Hemingway, Vol. 3.*
37. Reynolds, *Hemingway: The Homecoming*, 44.

remained distant."[38] Her beauty was hardening into something remote and scary, as were her thoughts. "Gerald," she said once without provocation, "Don't you think Al Jolson is just like Christ."[39] Again, too, she made it clear that summer that she had little respect for Hemingway. Maybe she resented her husband's adulation of the younger writer; maybe she was too much like Ernest in her self-centered hardness. It made for some unpleasant moments in all that sunlight. When asked what Ernest's new novel was about, she replied, "Bull fighting, bull slinging, and bullshit."[40] Scott would defend his friend, but Zelda would not change. No one, she was certain, could be as masculine as Ernest projected himself to be. She continued to needle the Hemingways with acute remarks, which Ernest did not like but Hadley knew were perceptive.

What Hadley did not say was that, in that summer at Juan-les-Pins, her complacency had reached its limits as a backdrop of misery played out against the good fortune of her husband's career. Outside the sun was shining on a curving, white beach that cupped the Golfe de Juan where sea-blown pine trees grew down almost to the curl of the blue water. Up the coast, on the headland jutting out into the Mediterranean, the town of Antibes glittered atop its white seawall. In the markets were fresh fish and vegetables, tart goat's cheese, dry white wines, good olive oil, and crusty bread. "There we were a trois,"[41] Hadley remembered in reference to Pauline's presence. The days were a blur, time suspended for three weeks. Pauline may even have gotten into bed with them one morning. Inside the Villa Paquita, Hemingway smelled the sweet smell of eucalyptus from his son's sick room. When the lease expired, Ernest and his family, along with Pauline, moved into the conveniently close Hotel de la Pineda where their rooms had their own little garden.

"Here it was that the three breakfast trays, three wet bathing suits on the line, three bicycles were to be found," remembered Hadley many years later. "We spent all morning on the beach sunning or swimming, lunched in our little garden. After siesta time there were long bicycle

38. Reynolds, 46.
39. Mitford, *Zelda*, 123.
40. Reynolds, *Hemingway: The Homecoming*, 46.
41. Mowrer, Sokoloff tapes, Hemingway Collection, JFK Library.

rides along the Golfe de Juan."[42] One day, the Murphys took everyone out on their yacht and docked in Monte Carlo for lunch and a little gaming. Their outdoor activity left them all looking terrific. The three were living in closed quarters and half-dressed most of the time, but Hadley was probably not yet aware that Ernest and Pauline were intimate; certainly there would not have been a *ménage à trois* sexual arrangement among them—something neither woman nor even Ernest would have liked. Hadley accepted their humiliating domestic *ménage à trois*, hiding her pain and unhappiness. She had hoped that his passion for Pauline would subside as it had with Duff, but a realization was setting in: "things got very [close] between her and Ernest," said Hadley. "They were very much in love, and they were hooked on the path of getting themselves together."[43]

Gerald Murphy had an endearing habit of calling younger women "daughter," using it more on the diminutive Pauline than he did on Hadley. Ernest started using the nickname, too, and Pauline fell further into the spirit by using the name "Papa," first for Gerald and then for Ernest. It caught on like wildfire when she called Ernest "Papa." Ernest seemed pleased, but often his mood turned black. Archie MacLeish remembered that he could be stricken with "the horrors" at any time, even on a sunny beach surrounded by friends. Archie knew that Ernest was filled with remorse for the coming storm of an increasingly inevitable divorce. "I never saw a man go through the floor of despair as he did,"[44] observed MacLeish. However, as Hemingway wrote to the critic and poet Isidor Schneider, nothing could keep him from certain pleasure: "Bycycle [*sic*] riding is very exciting to me. The roads are fine here, very smooth, and run alongside the sea and we ride 50 and sixty miles a day and stop at little towns for lunch and swim on the beaches when it is hot . . . I have never been so healthy. Hadley is as thin and as fine as before we were ever married and had children . . . But it will be very exciting to go back into Spain again where no one takes any exercise and where everyone stays up all night."[45]

42. Mary Dearborn, *Ernest Hemingway*, 222.
43. Mowrer, Sokoloff tapes, Hemingway Collection, JFK Library.
44. Dearborn, *Ernest Hemingway*, 223.
45. EH to Isidor Schneider, June 29, 1926, *The Letters of Ernest Hemingway, Vol. 3*.

By July, Bumby had fully recovered from the whooping cough and was sent with Marie Rohrbach to spend another summer with her family in Brittany. The Hemingways, Pauline, and the Murphys took the train to Pamplona for the Fiesta de San Fermin, and soon they were all sitting on the square under the arcade of the Café Iruna, sipping Fundador brandy with soda, eating grilled prawns, and observing the bootblacks swiping shoes with their rags. "My God, you could not get in all the bootblacks," wrote Hemingway in *Death in the Afternoon*, "or all the fine girls passing; or the whores; or all of ourselves as we were then."[46] He had brought them into Pamplona a week early to acclimatize them and gradually bring them up to drinking speed. They stayed in rooms in the Quintana. Later in the week, Villalta and Niño de la Palma, two of the matadors, moved in across the hall. The Murphys were impressed that Ernest knew the matadors well enough for introductions.

During the leisurely days preceding the fiesta there were walks along the river below the walls of the old French fort, where village women pounded their sheets clean in the water and boys skipped stones from the banks. Everything they saw brought back to Ernest and Hadley earlier summers, especially their first one in 1923, when they were by themselves and very happy together. Now, Pauline came into all these places with her brilliance and witty tongue too witty for Hadley to keep up with. Sara and Gerald made little of the tensions for always there was something to drink, something new to see and strange to buy (Gerald bought a guitar for his oldest son). Ernest delighted in being their guide, navigating them through the week of the feria, which began as always on July 6 with the cannon fire, explosion of the fife and drum corps, the bands and the Moorish giants of papier-mâché. The Murphys afterward said the two weeks in Pamplona had been the most intense moments of their lives.

In the plaza one evening, Ernest led an excited crowd cheering for the Murphys to dance the Charleston. The Murphys obliged the revelers with a polished and spirited rendition in the floodlights to a jazz band. They had barrera seats for every corrida that put them as close to the ring as possible where they watched the action closely. Gerald said the

---

46. Ernest Hemingway, *Death in the Afternoon*, 273.

bullfighters lived "in a region all their own . . . and . . . make you feel that you are as you find most other people—half-alive." The first time Sara saw blue intestines come leaking out of the picador's gored horse she left the ring in disgust, only to return later to yell as loud as anyone else. "I shall never forget it," she told Ernest, "and no one has anything on me about liking bullfights—even if I don't like seeing bowels."[47] Gerald wanted to join the young men racing before the bulls in the morning streets, but his better judgment kept him from it. Eager to prove himself to Hemingway, he had done well enough during a morning amateur, armed with his raincoat against a charging bull, where taking his place in the ring among hundreds of other young men, and holding his raincoat in front, Ernest yelled, "Hold it to the side." So, he moved it just in time to let the bull pass "and Ernest said something about a veronica."[48] At night, the fireworks lit up the sky and dazzled the eye. There was fife and drum music and everyone drinking.

On the morning after the fiesta ended, the party of five from Antibes, subdued in post-fiesta shock, boarded the train to San Sebastián. Six weeks of Pauline Pfieffer had pushed Hadley to the limit of her grace, and all she could do was try to be polite. The Murphys and Pauline continued on to Bayonne, where Pauline entrained north to Paris and the Murphys returned to the Villa America. The Hemingways remained in San Sebastián. Their public faces were still in place, but neither knew how long they could keep up the charade of their marriage. Hadley now knew she had been wrong to ignore the affair and was angry and hurt and a little scared. They received a letter from Gerald thanking them for Pamplona. "It's the finest thing we've ever experienced," he wrote, and added, "As for you two children: You grace the earth. You're so right: because you're close to what's elemental. Your values are hitched up to the universe. We're proud to know you. Yours are the things that count. They're a gift to those who know them too."[49] Gerald knew their marriage was on the rocks, and even though he and Sara had invited Pauline to Antibes and had taken her along to the fiesta, and would take her

47. Reynolds, *Hemingway: The Homecoming*, 48.
48. Calvin Tomkins, *Living Well is the Best Revenge*, 99.
49. Gerald Murphy to EH/HH, July 14, 1926, Hemingway Collection, JFK Library.

side as the marriage ended, he was still trying to make them feel better. Pauline wrote them letters too.

The Hemingways moved south to Madrid for more bullfights and then on to the coastal port of Valencia for an eight-day feria, but they were no longer a compatible couple. There were arguments and bitter words followed by long silences. They drank and could not sleep. At the Aguilar Pension in Madrid, one of Pauline's letters followed them: chanting in the phrases of the dissatisfied wife in Hemingway's "Cat in the Rain," she wrote, "I'm going to get a bicycle and ride in the bois. I am going to get a saddle too. I am going to get everything I want. Please write to me. This means YOU Hadley."[50] Hadley was galled by her rival's continuing pretense of friendship. She refused to write back and spoke sharp words to Ernest that she later regretted. Ernest never mentioned "the other woman" in the letters he wrote from Spain. "Hadley sends you and mother and all the kids her best,"[51] he wrote to his father from Valencia on July 24. And then to Mike Strater, "I am terribly sorry about your mother's death. So is Hadley. She sends her love and her sympathy to you both," but further down he let it slip, "Everything is all shot to hell in every direction."[52]

Their marriage was over, and they both knew it. Early in August, returning to Paris, they stopped at the Villa America and told the Murphys of their intention to separate. Don Stewart was at Antibes honeymooning with his bride and had difficulty accepting the news; to him, the Hemingways had seemed such a perfect couple. The Murphys understood. Gerald offered Hemingway the Left Bank studio he leased for his painting on the rue Froidevaux as long as he might need it. In something of a daze, not yet fully believing in the end of his marriage to a woman he still loved, he immediately accepted the offer. Gerald would also discreetly put $400 into Ernest's bank account in Paris acting on the hunch "that when life gets bumpy, you get through to the truth sooner if you are not hand-tied by the lack of a little money."[53]

50. Pauline Pfeiffer to EH, July 15, 1926, Hemingway Collection, JFK Library.
51. EH to CEH, July 24, 1926, *The Letters of Ernest Hemingway, Vol. 3.*
52. EH to Henry Strater, July 24, 1926, *The Letters of Ernest Hemingway, Vol. 3.*
53. Mellow, *Hemingway: A Life Without Consequences*, 334.

Beach party by Antibes

Cote d'Azur Eden Rock

Juan-les-Pins

Murphys and Pauline with Hemingways at Pamplona

Scott and Zelda on the Beach

Villa America

GENTLE INTO THE
NIGHT AND THE BREAK
OF DAWN

LATE IN June, Max Perkins had written to Ernest on the matter of the use of words in *The Sun Also Rises*: "I think some words should be avoided so that we shall not divert people's attention from the qualities of this book to the discussion of an utterly impertinent and extrinsic matter."[1] He singled out "a particular adjunct of the bulls" mentioned by Mike Campbell "a number of times"[2] and suggested replacing the words with blanks to avoid charges of indecency. Ernest took his time and near the end of July finally replied from Valencia, Spain. "I never use a word without first considering if it is replaceable," he wrote, acquiescing to some recommendations: "where Mike when drunk and wanting to insult the bull fighter keeps saying—tell him bulls have no balls. That can be changed." But on other words he disagreed: "in the matter of the use of the word Bitch by Brett—I have never once used this word ornamentally nor except when it was absolutely necessary and I believe the few places where it is used must stand:" and explained his thoughts further: "The whole problem is, it seems, that one should never use words which shock altogether out of their own value or connotation . . . I think that words—and I will cut anything I can—that are used in conversation in The Sun etc. are justified by the tragedy of the story." He promised to go over the proof "very carefully" and gave hint to his

---

1. Scott Berg, *Max Perkins: Editor of Genius*, 97.
2. Max Perkins to EH, July 1926, Hemingway Collection, JFK Library.

editor of his wrenching marital situation: "As for our returning in the fall—the financial situation is so rotten—it being very tenuous and easily affected by . . . one thing or another—that I see no prospect of it . . . In several ways I have been long enough in Europe."[3]

The galleys for the novel had been waiting on him in Antibes along with a long letter from Max. Hemingway did not understand how nervous New York publishers were in the face of the conservative keepers of public morals and Max warned him, "It would be a pretty thing if the very significance of so original a book should be disregarded because of the howls of a lot of cheap, prurient moronic yappers. You probably don't appreciate this disgusting possibility because you've been too long abroad, and out of that atmosphere."[4] Hemingway had read quickly through the galleys on the train from Antibes, and as soon as he settled into Gerald's studio, with the light coming in through the French windows, he sat down to his task. The work took his mind off the enormity of his separation with Hadley. He changed the names of real people: Glenway Wescott to Roger Prentiss, made the Henry James bicycle story into Henry's bicycle, and confirmed he was cutting the first fourteen pages to begin the novel with "Robert Cohn was once middleweight boxing champion of Princeton."[5] He worked steadily, even through the arguments with Hadley and meetings with Pauline, and finished the revisions on August 26 and mailed them to New York on the following day with the dedication "THIS BOOK IS FOR HADLEY AND FOR JOHN HADLEY NICANOR,"[6] which he thought was the least he could do for the woman he had loved for six years. He also sent along the completed version of "The Killers," typed up on his five-year-old Corona, though he had no hopes for a quick sale because if "Fifty Grand," which was only about a fixed prize fight, was too tough to sell then a story about hired killers and a crooked fighter would be even harder.

Paris was hot and sweaty and always filled with tourists. Earlier in the month, on August 12, two young Americans arrived unnoticed among

---

3. EH to MP, July 24, 1926, *The Letters of Ernest Hemingway, Vol. 3*.
4. Berg, *Max Perkins: Editor of Genius*, 97-8.
5. Ernest Hemingway, *The Sun Also Rises*, 3.
6. Hemingway, dedication page.

the throng in the Gare de Lyon. Trying to be civil to each other, but mostly silent and in a kind of stupor from the alcohol they had drunk on the train, once outside the station they went separate ways. Hadley couldn't face living in their old apartment with all its memories and so took rooms at the Hotel Beauvoir on the Avenue de l'Observatoire, across from the Closerie des Lilas and just down the street from the sawmill, and Ernest moved into Murphy's studio at the end of a block of studios on a gravel courtyard across the lane from the Montparnasse Cemetery. The studio was a large, high-ceilinged room with a cement floor and a skylight. "There was a gas stove in one corner to cook on and in the other corner a stairway went up to a little platform built across one end of the studio where his bed and washstand were . . . a curtain separated the platform from the rest of the studio."[7] On another side were a window and a washstand. The walls were whitewashed and hung with Gerald's "synthetic cubism"[8] art, in which he presented the reality of everyday objects; razors, a wasp, a cigar box, a watch; in precise detail in an abstract manner admired by many people (a harbinger to Andy Warhol). At first it was exciting and romantic to live in monastic austerity and sometimes have Pauline in his hard narrow bed at night.

Alone in the heat, his possessions minimal and his time his own, he worked on the galleys, and, trying not to think about the separation from Hadley, wrote a story about a couple's return from Antibes. "A Canary for One" was about the emptiness of their separation. He knew how the story would end and wanted to get the reader to the end able to catch it fresh. He did not directly show the emptiness of a marriage that had fallen apart; it was more like something small flitting past the periphery of one's vision. By the final draft he did not need to say anything so obvious; the flat tone of his narrator and the wordy American lady missing the point were enough. There were dim echoes of Henry James, famous for stories that were indirect, but Ernest was doing one better. Using images of wreckage stored in his memory and fresh from newspapers—a farmhouse burning in a field, the husband silent and deliberately unengaged—all

---

7. Michael Reynolds, *Hemingway: The Homecoming*, 54.
8. Kenneth Lynn, *Hemingway*, 350.

added up without him saying anything until the end. It was a piece of himself on the page, using part of his grief over Hadley, leaving out the tears and arguments and pain, revising the story until he had it exactly right. It took two months, and his pain helped him transform himself into his art.

Though they were separated, the Hemingways still loved each other and cared about the other's well-being. "Ernest felt very sorry that he was doing this to me," remembered Hadley. "He had dreadful remorse. It made me suffer to see the way he suffered . . . but I tried to make him feel it was all right."[9] Still, the times they saw each other during the first weeks did not go well. She lashed out one night when they were drinking, and feeling remorseful the next morning, wrote him a note: "Such is alcohol . . . My mind, as I recall things I said in that damn taxi, was positively senile . . . you were really sweet and held yourself in noble."[10] When Don Stewart took Hadley home from a party, she cried all the way back to the hotel. She was not yet ready to take the final step. After the trauma of her youth, her father's suicide and her mother's insistence that she could not lead a normal life due to a back injury, and living in shadows as a young adult, she had met a man who showed her the world. After the birth of their son, she had driven herself to the edge of exhaustion in the effort to be his ever-ready companion. But facing the future without this difficult but unforgettable man was a prospect for which she could see no compensation.

She knew he hated to be alone and in a last effort to save her marriage, at a dinner at the Lilas with Paul and Winifred Mowrer, she told Ernest that if he and Pauline agreed not to see or communicate with each other for one hundred days and were still in love at the end of that time, then she would agree to a divorce if he still wanted one. What she hoped was that in the course of this time he would find out how much he missed her and Bumby and come back to them. She wrote the agreement on a slip of paper, signed her name, and handed it to Ernest. She also added that she and Ernest should see as little of each other as possible, "When we

---

9. Hadley Mowrer, Alice Sokoloff tapes, Hemingway Collection, JFK Library.
10. Hadley to EH, Aug. 20, 1926, Hemingway Collection, JFK Library.

are lonely we must take care of ourselves by seeing other people."[11] The separation seemed unnecessary to Pauline and Ernest, but together at last without fear of onlookers, they agreed to Hadley's "one hundred days"[12] because they wanted the divorce. However, neither felt capable of staying away from the other if both were in Paris and so Pauline took leave from *Vogue* and booked passage for America on a Red Star Line ship sailing from Boulogne late in September. When the boat docked in New York City, she went to the Scribner's office, wrote Ernest that *The Sun Also Rises* would come out late in October, spent time with the Murphys, who were also in New York, and John Dos Passos, who, though disappointed with his separation from Hadley, wrote Ernest that Pauline was a very nice girl. From New York, she took the train to Piggott, Arkansas, to be with her parents.

Hadley moved into an apartment close to Gertrude Stein on rue des Fleurus where she and Bumby lived comfortably. She requested that Ernest bring her items from their abandoned flat on Notre-Dame-des-Champs, listing them in letters: "I want my . . . Dresden teapot and about 8 Dresden cups and saucers . . . all the old French blue plates . . . For furniture—Chinese table, double decker mahogany bureau—Breton folding table . . . Mummy's baby portrait."[13] Every time he went back, piling the residue of their lives into a cranky wheelbarrow to push through the public streets like a junk man, he felt absurd and like he was doing penance, announcing to the Latin Quarter that he and his wife were separated. At the end, Hadley recalled, "he was weeping down the street and I know he was very sorry for himself."[14] She felt sorry for him, too, and told him "I want you to take the Massons and Miro when you move the big things out."[15] He centered Miro's *The Farm* on the 30-foot wall of the studio to keep company with Gerald's cubism. The huge painting needed a wall to let it breathe; it had always been cramped when it hung above their bed on Notre-Dame-des-Champs.

---

11. Hadley to EH, Oct. 16, 1926.
12. Hadley to EH, Sept. 13, 1926.
13. Reynolds, *Hemingway: The Homecoming*, 54.
14. Alice Sokoloff, *Hadley: The First Mrs. Hemingway*, 91.
15. Hugh Eakin, "The Old Man and the Farm," *Vanity Fair*, Oct. 2018.

October was a bad time for Ernest. He felt lousy and in an emotional half-world kind of place. Wandering from Murphy's cold studio, trying to avoid his old haunts, he would cut through Montparnasse Cemetery, thinking on the dead and those yet to die, and walk past the graves of Guy de Maupassant and Charles Baudelaire, syphilitics whose brilliance had burned out early. Eating in cheap cafes unfrequented by the Montparnasse crowd, he found solitude oppressive and was in no mood to make new friends. When he and Hadley sometimes met on the streets he looked as forlorn as she had hoped he would be. "Your little face had a harrowed expression," she wrote to him. "If it's loneliness and worriedness about Pauline remember that it's only three months and that those three months will make her happier ever after . . . it's sad that we have found out I can't make the grade."[16] He would come to take Bumby for a visit. When he brought Bumby back, Archie MacLeish would often come along too. "Our life has all gone to hell which seems to be the one thing you can count on a good life to do," Ernest wrote to Fitzgerald. "Needless to say Hadley has been grand and everything has been completely my fault in every way."[17]

Despite the one-hundred days written agreement, Pauline wrote many letters to Ernest from Piggott using her sister as their intermediary: "By writing you everything I can keep you very close to me and very much in my life until I see you again."[18] When she told her mother about him her mother became very upset and asked about Hadley; and Pauline, too, began to feel terrible remorse over Hadley and wrote Ernest that she thought they hadn't given her a chance. Pauline took her Catholicism seriously and felt that some suffering on her part was warranted. She even wrote Hadley a contrite letter; "You not only couldn't do a low thing, you didn't even think one;"[19] offering to extend their separation beyond three months. But Gerald Murphy, whose money Ernest now lived on, thought otherwise: "Hadley's tempo is a slower and less initiative one than yours," he wrote to Ernest, "and that you may accept it out of deference

16. Reynolds, *Hemingway: The Homecoming*, 65.
17. EH to F. Scott Fitzgerald, September 1926, *The Letters of Ernest Hemingway, Vol. 3*.
18. Pauline Pfeiffer to EH, Sept. 24, 1926, Hemingway Collection, JFK Library.
19. Mary Dearborn, *Ernest Hemingway*, 227.

to her . . . I would consider it a dangerous betrayal of your nature."[20] He was also concerned for Ernest's art: "We believe in what you're doing, in the way you're doing it. Anything we've got is yours."[21] And though Hemingway felt lonely, especially when more than one day passed without a letter from Pauline (he was like his father, who had expected Grace to write daily letters when they were separated), he used his isolation to write, and his writing was going well. He began to write something about the war in Italy: "Toward evening it was not so hot but it was still dusty and the dust settled on the road:" but it wasn't quite right so he tried it again: "When it was dark the dew came and settled the dust on the road that we marched on:"[22] but that wasn't right for him either, so he put the fragments away to begin again on the Italian war another day.

In the early mornings he would escape into his fiction, living between and under the lines, knowing how his characters felt in the country he had created. After finishing the galleys of *The Sun Also Rises*, he wrote several excellent stories. To his surprise, Max cabled that Robert Bridges accepted "The Killers" for publication in *Scribner's Magazine* and would pay $200; his first significant remuneration for a single story. He also wrote a story set in Milan that began: "In the fall the war was always there but we did not go to it anymore."[23] It was about a hospital ward where recovered but not yet rehabilitated soldiers went each day for physical therapy; he would call it "In Another Country," and it would be accepted by *Scribner's Magazine* too. Hemingway's art came from his pain, and his art was changing forever the American short story. An English publisher was bringing out *In Our Time*, and Edward O'Brien wanted "The Undefeated" for *The Best Short Stories of 1926*. *The Atlantic Monthly* would accept "Fifty Grand," and while he wasn't yet collecting the great fees that his friend Fitzgerald was paid for his stories, he was heading in that direction as he and Max Perkins would soon begin to discuss assembling a new short story collection.

20. Reynolds, *Hemingway: The Homecoming*, 59.
21. Reynolds, 58.
22. Reynolds, 67.
23. Ernest Hemingway, *The Complete Short Stories*, "In Another Country", 206.

Ernest was working hard and hardly sleeping at night. He suffered without Pauline and tried to adjust to the awkward new role he played in the lives of Hadley and their son in her absence. It was hard to give up Hadley's many attentions, their pet names, and her flattering dependency. During this time, he became close friends with Archie MacLeish. He often biked across the river to the Avenue du Bois de Boulogne, where the MacLeishes were house-sitting a large luxurious apartment with maids and butlers (belonging to Pierpont Morgan Hamilton, whom Archie may have known at Harvard), to have dinner and take a shower. When Dorothy Parker, the sharp-witted writer for *The New Yorker* who was devoted to Ernest, passed through Paris on her way back to New York and her dying mother, Ernest was in attendance, sharing lunches and sending her off with some books from his personal library. She wrote him a genuine thanks—"I was touched with your sweetness and sympathy"[24]—not knowing, because he had been so nice with his public face, how deeply she had offended him by constantly referring to her half-Jewish background, her abortion, her suicide attempts, and her dislike for Spain. And when she was out of Paris, he composed a wicked poem about her called "Tragic Poetress," about her abortions, slit wrists, and overdoses of veronal. One night at the MacLeishes with Don Stewart present, he read the poem as a comic interlude, but no one laughed. Don was appalled. Archie and Ada were both offended for, unlike his satiric attacks on Sherwood, Ford, and T. S. Eliot, this one was purely personal. Hurt by his friends' response, he sent it to Pauline, and even she didn't like it, calling it "shrill."[25]

On the night of October 11, Hemingway and MacLeish caught an overnight train to Spain and arrived the next afternoon in the ancient town of Zaragoza for the bullfights and the feria of El Pilar that celebrated the appearance of Virgin Mary to St. James. They were lone Americans among the tens of thousands packed into the narrow streets for the religious procession led by a carriage-borne lantern. Like many of Ernest's Paris friends, MacLeish was older and better educated, a Harvard

24. Reynolds, *Hemingway: The Homecoming*, 81.
25. Reynolds, 82.

graduate with a Yale law degree, but he accepted the younger high school graduate from Oak Park on equal terms, and though he had four volumes of poetry and a verse play in print, MacLeish recognized in Hemingway's fiction and in his person something that others were beginning to call "genius." In the afternoons they watched bullfights in the Plaza de Toros and at night, over late dinners in their hotel, they talked about love and marriage and art.

Under the pressure of being separated from Pauline and with the impending divorce from Hadley, Ernest's dark side was exposed one evening when Archie said that James Joyce, like Picasso in painting, was changing the form of literature. Hemingway, who admired Joyce and had learned a lot from the Irishman's short stories, vehemently replied that *Ulysses* was not as great as some claimed, and then when MacLeish suggested that Ernest "should relax a little bit and give Joyce credit [for] there were some aspects of Joyce's work that Ernest should think about,"[26] Ernest exploded with an intense, unwarranted anger that brought their evening to an awkward silence. His terrible mood disappeared over the course of the following day, and he went on with their holiday as if nothing had happened. Upon their return to Paris there were letters waiting from Pauline and Hadley.

Pauline was struggling too. Isolated in northeast Arkansas in the rich Mississippi River bottomland owned by her father, she was buried in the heart of despair and took long bike rides to build up her stamina and forget her pain. She tried to keep busy in Piggott, a small town of about two thousand, but would often be overcome with fits of depression. Her mother's attitude made Pauline doubt herself and think more about what she and Ernest were doing. "We must be good to each other and to other people," she wrote, "because we have been very, very cruel to the people we love most." And she believed that Hadley had been "very wise to want to wait three months for all of us to think things over."[27] Tormented and doubtful that she would hold together under the pressure of her mother's disapproval and the guilt she felt over Hadley, Ernest tried desperately to

26. Reynolds, 70.
27. Dearborn, *Ernest Hemingway*, 229.

buck her up. "The worry is like a band of some sort across the inside of the top of my head," he wrote in November. "All I can think is that you are all that I have and that I love more than all that is and have given up everything for . . . as long as I had you I could stand anything and get through anything . . . all I want is you Pfife and oh dear god I want you so . . . I pray for you hours every night and every morning when I wake up."[28] By Hadley's terms, their three-month separation included no corresponding and when Hadley found out they were writing and telegraphing each other she was surprised and disappointed.

The Sun Also Rises appeared in bookstores on October 22, 1926, in a dust jacket that was printed in gold, black, and tan, with a gold apple on either side of the title and beneath it the figure of a drowsing woman clothed in the style of Greek antiquity. Pan's pipe lay near her sandaled foot and another gold apple rested in the palm of her left hand. At the bottom, printed in bold black letters, was the name "ERNEST HEMINGWAY: author of 'IN OUR TIME' and 'THE TORRENTS OF SPRING.'" It was the first truly Modern Novel put before the public by a major publisher and the first reviews were marvelous. *The New York Times* called it "a truly gripping story, told in a lean, hard athletic prose that puts more literary English to shame."[29] In the *New York Herald Tribune* Conrad Aiken wrote, "The dialogue is brilliant. If there is better dialogue being written today I do not know where to find it. It is alive with the rhythms and idioms, the pauses and suspensions and innuendos and short-hands, of living speech."[30] Burton Rascoe, writing for the *New York Sun*, said, "Every sentence that [Hemingway] writes is fresh and alive."[31] Even the negative reviews, the most common complaint being that the characters were degenerate and immoral, helped sell more books. Grace Hemingway cut the review from the *Chicago Tribune* and mailed it to her son: "*The Sun Also Rises* is the kind of book that makes this reviewer at least almost plain angry, not for the obvious reason that it is about utterly degraded people, but for the reason that it shows an

28. EH to PP, Nov. 12, 1926, *The Letters of Ernest Hemingway, Vol. 3.*
29. *New York Times Book Review*, Oct. 31, 1926.
30. Conrad Aiken, *New York Herald*, Oct. 31, 1926.
31. Burton Rascoe, *New York Sun*, Nov. 6, 1926.

immense skill . . . Ernest Hemingway can be a distinguished writer if he wishes to be. He is, even in this book, but it is a distinction hidden under a bushel of sensationalism and triviality."[32]

Although they had agreed to stay apart, Ernest brought a copy to Hadley's apartment on a Thursday evening. She wrote him the next morning, "I am bowled over by [the book] and true to form am fondest of all of the dedication. . . . I'm awfully proud and grateful."[33] In America his book was selling very well, and in Paris it was the talk of the literary community of which he had been a fixture for years. The gossip column in the Paris *Herald* stated, "It contains a great deal of the Left Bank, a dash of the Grand Boulevards, and the great open spaces of the sanded arenas."[34] The *Tribune* reported, "young Mr. Hemingway, who is apparently arriving . . . is doing the really remarkable feat of making a reputation among his own countrymen out of his own country," and a few weeks later, as the book continued selling, the same columnist congratulated himself by writing, "We said . . . that a Hemingway cult was in a fair way to being founded."[35]

Hemingway responded to the reviews, even those that were negative, with a healthy skepticism. Writing to Maxwell Perkins he found the critical reception "pretty interesting and there seems to be a difference of opinion about it—I've always heard that was good." If he seemed to want to argue with some of the reviewers—"It's funny to write a book that seems as tragic as that and have them take it for a jazz superficial story"[36]—more than anything else, the reviews made him pause and reconsider what he had achieved, especially when he heard that Edmund Wilson had written to the poet John Bishop Peale that he thought *The Sun Also Rises* the "best novel by any one of my generation."[37] He was, however, too, still anxious about Pauline and tried alleviate his loneliness with work and drink.

---

32. *Chicago Daily Tribune*, Nov. 27, 1926.
33. Gloria Diliberto, *Hadley*, 239.
34. Reynolds, *Hemingway: The Homecoming*, 73.
35. Reynolds, 74.
36. EH to MP, Nov. 18, 1926, *The Letters of Ernest Hemingway, Vol. 3*.
37. EH to MP, Dec. 21, 1926.

Hadley knew Pauline and Ernest were suffering, and feeling anxiety herself, she began to reconsider the situation. Early in November, she asked Ernest to take care of Bumby for a week while she took a trip to Chartres with Winifred Mowrer for rest and relaxation. Ernest stayed in her apartment with Bumby. Away from Paris, a change of mood came over Hadley. Despite her heartache, she enjoyed the quiet days at Chartres and, no longer tied to Ernest's roller coaster of emotions, discovered a new wholesomeness to herself. Until they separated, she had been determined to save her marriage, but in this ancient pilgrimage site she began to think of life without Ernest. Her highs wouldn't reach the peaks she had had with him, but her lows would not be so low either—and some of Ernest's lows were almost suicidal. During Mass in the cathedral on Armistice Day a peace came over her, and on Sunday Winifred's husband Paul, who the Hemingways had known and liked since coming to Paris, arrived and gave her his advice on the end of a long romance. Now knowing her marriage was over, she sent Ernest a letter that began not with a pet name, but simply, "My dear Ernest," and wrote, "I can see with my simple judgment, I am free to seek a divorce. I took you originally for better or worse (and meant it!), but in the case of your marrying someone else, I can stand by my vow only as an outside friend. That's quite all I want to say . . . You mustn't really mind or be hurt later if this is so . . . the three months separation is officially off," and ended it without a pet name too: "Much Love, Hadley."[38]

When she returned to Paris, Ernest had not yet received her letter and they got into another fight. "I am terribly sorry that I did not get your letter until after I had seen you," he wrote on the day after he finally got her letter, "because I did not know what decisions you had made . . . [and] hurt you again and again." Their years together were much on his mind as his feelings toward Hadley became tender. "Your letter like everything that you have ever done is very brave and altogether unselfish and generous." He said he would begin "finding out the details and about lawyers" for their divorce and encouraged her "to go to America"

---

38. Hadley to EH, Nov. 16, 1926, Hemingway Collection, JFK Library.

if that was what she wished to do. "No matter what you do," he wrote, "I am writing to Scribners that all the royalties from The Sun Also Rises should be paid to you . . . it is the only thing that I who have done so many things to hurt you can do to help you—and you must let me do it," and assured her that he would not be lacking, for "I could accept money from Pauline whose Uncle Gus seems always wanting to give it to her." At the end of the long letter, loving her again, he wrote, "I think perhaps the luckiest thing Bumby will ever have is to have you for a mother. And I won't tell you how I admire your straight thinking, your head, your heart and your very lovely hands and I pray God always that he will make up to you the very great hurt that I have done you—who are the best and truest and loveliest person that I have ever known."[39]

In mid-November, Ernest warmed himself by the stove in Sylvia's bookstore and browsed through her magazines and newspapers to read the reviews of The Sun Also Rises that were appearing. Conrad Aiken in the Herald Tribune saw the influences of Anderson, Stein, and Fitzgerald's Gatsby but called Hemingway "the most exciting of contemporary American writers of fictions." The book's characters were unattractive, but "if their story is sordid, it is also, by virtue of the author's dignity and detachment in the telling, intensely tragic."[40] In the Atlantic Bruce Barton wrote that Hemingway "writes as if he had never read anybody's writing, as if he had fashioned the art of writing himself." Hemingway's people were immoral, drank too much, had no religion or ideals (a critical demurrer in many of the reviews), but, he asserted "they have courage and friendship, and mental honestness. And they are alive. Amazingly real and alive."[41] Ernest Boyd in the Independent wrote that when the reader was not swept along by the astonishing dialogue—"subtle, obvious, profound, and commonplace—but always alive"—there was the careful enumeration of little facts "whose cumulative effect is to give them the importance of remarkable incidents."[42]

---

39. EH to Hadley, Nov. 18, 1926, The Letters of Ernest Hemingway, Vol. 3.
40. Reynolds, Hemingway: The Homecoming, 81.
41. James R. Mellow, Hemingway: A Life Without Consequences, 334-5.
42. Mellow, 345.

Even adverse criticism about the immoral characters and the sparse new modern writing gave Hemingway's book the status of importance and seriousness. The book was changing the landscape of English prose and literature itself. Dorothy Parker said, "There was a time when you could go nowhere without hearing of *The Sun Also Rises*."[43] The critic Richard Barrett said that the youth of America "learned [*The Sun Also Rises*] by heart, deserting their families and running away from college, and immediately took ship to Paris to be the disciples of the new faith under the awnings of the Dome and the Rotonde."[44] The first edition of five thousand was sold out by mid-December, as had a second printing of two thousand copies. "The Sun has risen . . . and is rising steadily,"[45] remarked Max Perkins, who, expecting the book to do well into the spring, ordered a third printing.

Hadley's trust funds were still ample enough to support her comfortably in Paris, and the royalties from *The Sun* would prove to be a boon. Once the divorce proceedings were under way, she felt much better. There would still be moments of gloom and bad days when she couldn't stop crying, but on the whole, she was strong and able to cope. In some ways she was even relieved, for she could never have continued to keep up with Ernest's energetic and demanding life. "In the very, very long run," she remembered many years later, "I think it was for the best. You know, Paul [Mowrer—whom she would later marry] always said he thought I would have died if I'd stayed with Ernest."[46] She carefully explained to Bumby that Hemingway and Pfeiffer were much in love, and she never criticized Hemingway nor expressed bitterness about him. Hadley had gained greatly from her marriage and was more self-assured and independent at the end of it. He had rescued her from an oppressive sister, convinced her she was not an invalid, taught her sporting skills (which she was quite good at), brought her to Paris, traveled with her in Europe, and introduced her to some of the leading artists and writers

---

43. Dorothy Parker, *New Yorker*, Oct. 29,1927, 92.
44. Dearborn, *Ernest Hemingway*, 235.
45. Kenneth Lynn, *Hemingway*, 360.
46. Mowrer, Sokoloff tapes, Hemingway Collection, JFK Library.

of the time. She had known and loved and lived with Hemingway as a remarkable and fine young man.

While reviewers were extolling *The Sun Also Rises*—the vigor of the prose and the vivid dialogue, the sustained tension of action and Hemingway's ability to state and develop a theme at novel length—his public and private life began a gradual transformation. People he did not know in places where he had never been began to talk about him. Some that he once knew well began to resent his success; others he knew only in passing began to speak of him most familiarly. So long as he had published with small literary magazines like *This Quarter* and *Transatlantic Review* or with Left Bank publishers of limited editions like Robert McAlmon, Hemingway was one of a crowd, a piece of the Montparnasse firmament. Of the Paris writers he had first known, only Ford Madox Ford published books on more than a coterie basis. Ezra Pound, for all his stature, did not yet have a commercial publisher for his poetry. Gertrude Stein, the doyen and arbiter of rue de Fleurus, published with obscure presses at her own expense. The peerless James Joyce made more money from the charity of rich women than for Sylvia Beach's publication of *Ulysses*. Hemingway's move to Boni & Liveright with *In Our Time* raised him only slightly among his peers, but when he signed the contract with Charles Scribner's Sons he moved into the major leagues and his first long novel was soon considered a milestone in the evolution of the twentieth-century American novel. That this shift took place at the same time he was moving to a more sophisticated woman seems to have been coincidental, but it was all of a piece within his life.

Gossip on the Left Bank was that Hemingway had written a vicious satire and exposé about Montparnasse and its most treasured inhabitants. Kitty Cannell saw at once that Ernest had listened carefully to her conversation style and had projected it upon the character and experience of the Jewish secretary, Francis Clyne, and despite saying "I'm really tougher than the big he man and I can stick up for myself,"[47] she was very upset. She was even more upset that the schlemiel character Robert Cohn was

---

47. Dearborn, *Ernest Hemingway*, 236.

based up her lover Harold Loeb, who was sick by the caricature of himself in the novel and would bemoan Hemingway's treachery for the rest of his life: Had he not bought Ernest oyster and bottles of Pouilly-Fuisse and helped get him published? Duff Twysden was reportedly furious at first but then relented, jokingly remarking to Ernest at the Dingo one night that she had, in fact, not slept with the bullfighter. *The Herald* gossip columnist said, "One of the protagonists (and what a savage portrait), is easily recognized as one of Hemingway's literary pals. Several well known habitués of the Carrefour Vavin are mercilessly dragged through the pages . . . Hemingway is noted for being an observant journalist and for not respecting the feelings of friends."[48]

The day after Ernest received Hadley's letter, Jinny Pfeiffer cabled her sister that their separation was terminated at Hadley's request and suggested Pauline return to Paris. Their mother, Mary Pfeiffer, had started accepting the idea that her daughter loved Ernest above everything else, and Pauline was feeling more confident. When with friends, Ernest was unsparing on himself about the divorce. Having a drink with Bill Bird in the Caves Mura, when he blurted out the news and Bill asked why, he answered flatly: "Because I am a son of a bitch."[49] But he was healthy, his head was in good shape, and he was going well, despite being depressed at times. In December, while talking to lawyers about divorce proceedings, he would write anguished letters to Pauline about "being just horribly cock-eyed lonesome" and having "the horrors at night and a black depression,"[50] and "what I miss worse is not having any intimacy with you," but that would change when they were together again as he wrote, "I know it will be swell."[51]

Pauline wrote him reassuringly that she was sailing back to Europe on December 30. When her boat docked in Cherbourg on January 8, Hemingway was there to meet her. They took the train to Austria to join her sister and the MacLeishes for an extended skiing vacation at the luxurious Hotel Rossli in Gstaad, where they soon learned that Hadley

48. Reynolds, *Hemingway: The Homecoming*, 73-4.
49. Carlos Baker, *Hemingway: A Life*, 229.
50. EH to PP, Dec. 2, 1926, *The Letters of Ernest Hemingway, Vol. 3*.
51. EH to PP, Dec. 3, 1926.

had been granted a divorce. In the spring when they married in Paris, the new Mrs. Hemingway, with the support of her parents and her uncle Gus Pfeiffer, was a very wealthy woman. For the rest of his life, even after his divorce from Pauline many years later, Ernest would always have more than enough money to do whatever he wanted to do. But he had never lacked for anything he had ever really wanted anyway, for his true wealth had always been within the creativity of his soul, and this was a fact that he knew well.

In early November, when Pound asked for something from Ernest for his new review, Hemingway wrote a two-line poem: "The Lord is my shepherd, I shall not want him for long."[52] It was a strange little verse for a neophyte Catholic to be writing, especially one who needed the church's historic bosom upon which to rest his remarriage case. But when he and Hadley were happiest married, he had written stories of marriage gone wrong. His deep love for his father did not prevent him from using the Doctor in his fiction. There was no choice between life and writing: his fiction came first. That winter in Murphy's studio he wrote stories with the precise clarity of a master engraver, and not everything he wrote would he read before others or even have in print for others to read.

He had not written to Gertrude in a while and broke with her completely that fall, apparently even without seeing her, by writing satirically about her prose in a near exact imitation. He wrote it out in a prose poem, parodying her style to explain what had happened. At Sylvia's bookstore he had checked out her *Composition as Explanation*, an attempt by Miss Stein to justify her method and herself. Her remarks as always were enigmatic. Hemingway read the book as closely as he could, but Gertrude was no longer the writer he had so admired on first coming to Paris. She was godmother to his son, and having praised her in print, defended her in the cafes and to all his friends, it was not easy to call it quits. After eating her food, taking her advice, drinking her wine and liqueurs, and learning her deep lessons, now it came down to "a very great writer who had stopped writing because she was too lazy to write for other

---

52. Reynolds, *Hemingway: The Homecoming*, 83.

people because writing for other people is very hard because other people know when things do not come out right and are failures."[53] Writing this informal treatise (and then putting it away) he let the associations leap along, sometimes connecting with an idea, sometimes with a word. "Gertrude was never crazy / Gertrude was very lazy."[54] By putting it on paper he made it final, and then he put the paper away for the rest of his life to let scholars at last find it after his death. The many bonds of his early years of writing in Paris were done: Hadley, Gertrude, Sherwood, the little magazines and the coterie publishers. They were all behind him now, yet with the publication of his first novel he had carried them all forward into the future by putting their ideas into the mainstream of culture.

It has been said that for a time everyone wrote like Ernest Hemingway, and that means that they wrote like Gertrude Stein and Ezra Pound, too, for they were deeply embedded within his prose. With the publication of *In Our Time* and the huge success of *The Sun Also Rises*, Modern Literature arose from the esoteric culture that had nourished it and blossomed and never stopped blooming.

---

53. Reynolds, *Hemingway: The Homecoming*, 84.
54. Reynolds, 85.

Cocktail by Gerald Murphy

The Sun Also Rises

Ernest and Pauline at San Sebastián

de Maupassant - Cimitiere Montparnasse

SELECTED BIBLIOGRAPHY

Ackroyd, Peter, *Ezra Pound and His World*, New York, Charles Scribner's Sons, 1980.

Anderson, Sherwood, *Winesburg, Ohio*, New York, Huebsch, 1919.

————, *Triumph of the Egg*, New York, Huebsch, 1921.

————, *A Story Teller's Story*, New York, Huebsch, 1924.

————, *Death in the Woods & Other Stories*, New York, W.W. Norton & Co., 1933.

Baker, Carlos, *Ernest Hemingway: A Life Story*, New York, Charles Scribner's Sons, 1969.

Beach, Sylvia, Shakespeare and Company, Lincoln, Nebraska, University of Nebraska Press, 1956.

Berg, A. Scott, MAX PERKINS, Editor of Genius, New York, NY, Riverhead Books, 1978.

Bloom, Harold, *Bloom's BioCritiques: Ernest Hemingway*, Philadelphia: Chelsea House Publishers, 2002.

————, editor, *Modern Critical Interpretations: Ernest Hemingway's THE SUN ALSO RISES*, Philadelphia, Penn, Chelsea House Publishers, 1987 (twelve essays by named scholars).

Blume, Leslie M. M., *EVERYBODY BEHAVES BADLY: The True Story Behind Hemingway's Masterpiece THE SUN ALSO RISES*, New York, Houghton Mifflin Harcourt Publishing, 2016.

Burrill, William, *HEMINGWAY: The Toronto Years*, Toronto, Ontario, Doubleday Canada Ltd., 1994.

Cowley, Malcolm, EXILE'S RETURN: A Literary Odyssey of the 1920s, New York, NY, Penguin Books, 1994.

Curnutt, Kirk, *Ernest Hemingway and the Expatriate Modernist Movement*, Farmington Hills, Michigan, The Gale Group, 2000.

Dearborn, Mary V., *Ernest Hemingway*, New York, Alfred A. Knopf, 2017.

"The Death of Love in *The Sun Also Rises*" by Mark Spilka from *Twelve Original Essays on Great American Novels*, edited by Charles Shapiro, © 1958 by Wayne State University Press.

Defazio, Albert, Sandra Spanier, and Robert W. Trogdon, The Letters of Ernest Hemingway, Vol 2, 1923–1925, New York, Cambridge University Press, 2013.

Dell, Floyd, *Moon-Calf*, New York, NY, Alfred A. Knopf, 1921.

Diliberto, Gioia, *Hadley, a Life of Hadley Richardson Hemingway*, London: Bloomsbury Publishing, 1992.

Donaldson, Scott, *Hemingway vs. Fitzgerald*, Woodstock, New York, The Overlook Press, 1999.

———, *Fool for Love: F. Scott Fitzgerald*, University of Minnesota Press, 2012.

Dos Passos, John Roderigo, *The Best Times: An Informal Mem*oir, Harper Collins, 1968.

Duffey, Bernard, *The Chicago Renaissance in American Letters*, The Michigan State University Press, 1956.

"*The End of The Sun Also Rises:* A New Beginning" by Carole Gottlieb Vopat from *The Fitzgerald/Hemingway Annual*, 1972, edited by Matthew J. Bruccoli and C. E. Frazer Clark, Jr., © 1973 by the National Cash Register Company, Dayton, Ohio.

"Ernest Hemingway and the Rhetoric of Escape" by Robert O. Stephens from *The Twenties, Poetry and Prose: Twenty Critical Essays*, edited by Richard E. Langford and William E. Taylor, © 1966 by Everett Edwards Press, Inc.

"False Dawn: *The Sun Also Rises* Manuscript" by Michael S. Reynolds from *A Fair Day in the Affections: Literary Essays in Honor of Robert B. White, Jr.*, edited by Jack D. Durant and M. Thomas Hester, © 1980 by Jack D. Durant and M. Thomas Hester.

Fenton, Charles A., *Apprenticeship of Ernest Hemingway*, New York: The Viking Press, 1954.

Fitzgerald, F. Scott, *The Jazz Age*, New York, NY, New Directions Publishing, 1996.

———, *The Stories of F. Scott Fitzgerald*, New York, NY, Charles Scribner's Sons, 1951.

———, *A Life in Letters*, New York, NY, Charles Scribner's Sons, 1995.

Griffin, Peter, *Along With Youth: Hemingway, The Early Years*, New York: Oxford University Press, 1985.

Hemingway, Ernest, *The Complete Short Stories of Ernest Hemingway*, New York, N.Y, Scribner Paperback Fiction, Simon & Schuster, 1987.

———, *A Moveable Feast*, New York, NY, Charles Scribner's Sons, 1964.

———, *The Torrents of Spring*, New York, NY, Charles Scribner's Sons, 1926.

———, *The Sun Also Rises*, New York, NY, Charles Scribner's Sons, 1926.

———, *A Farewell to Arms*, New York, NY, Charles Scribner's Sons, 1929.

———, *Death in the Afternoon*, New York, NY, Charles Scribner's Son, 1932.

———, *The Green Hills of Africa*, New York, NY, Charles Scribner's Sons, 1935.

———, *Dateline: Toronto*, New York, NY, Charles Scribner's Sons, 1985.

———, *The Nick Adams Stories*, New York, NY, Charles Scribner's Son, 1972.

Hemingway, Leicester, My Brother, Ernest Hemingway, Fawcett Publications, 1963.

"Hemingway's Morality of Compensation" by Scott Donaldson from American Literature 43, no. 3 (November 1971), © 1971 by Duke University Press.

"Implications of Form in *The Sun Also Rises*" by William L. Vance from *The Twenties, Poetry and Prose: Twenty Critical Essays*, edited by Richard E. Langford and William E. Taylor, © 1966 by Everett Edwards Press, Inc.

Jackson, Bryer, Margolies, Prigozy, *F. Scott Fitzgerald: New Perspectives,* Athens, Georgia, University of Georgia Press, 2000.

Joyce, James, *Dubliners,* New York, NY, The Viking Press, 1968.

Kennedy, J. Gerald Kennedy, and Jackson R. Bryer, editors, FRENCH CONNEC-
TIONS: Fitzgerald and Hemingway Abroad, New York, NY, Harper & Row, 1998.

Lardner, Ring, Jr., *The Lardners*, New York NY, Harper & Row, 1976.

"Living Well is the Best Revenge" by Calvin Tompkins from *The New Yorker*, July 20,
1962.

Lurie, Mark, *Galantiere, The Lost Generation's Forgotten Man*, West Palm Beach, Florida,
Overlook Press, Inc., 2017.

Lynn, Kenneth S., *Hemingway*, New York: Simon and Schuster, Inc., 1987.

McAlmon, Robert, Being Genuises Together 1920–1930, San Francisco, North Point
Press, 1984.

Mellow, James R., *Hemingway, A Life Without Consequences*, Reading, Massachusetts,
Addison-Wesley Publishing, 1992.

——, *Charmed Circle: Gertrude Stein & Company*, New York, NY, Praeger Publishing, 1974.

Mellow, James R., *Invented Lives: F. Scott and Zelda Fitzgerald*, New York, Houghton
Mifflin, 1984.

Meyer, Jeffrey, *Hemingway, A Biography*, New York, Harper & Row, 1985.

"Meyer Wolfsheim and Robert Cohn: A study of Jewish Type and Stereotype" by Jose-
phine Z. Knopf from Tradition: *A journal of Orthodox Jewish Thought* 10, no. 3
(Spring 1969, © 1969 by the Rabbinical Council of America).

Milford, Nancy, *Zelda, A Biography*, New York, NY, Harper & Row, 1970.

Miller, Madelaine Hemingway, *Ernie: Hemingway's Sister "Sunny" Remembers*, New
York, NY, Crown Publishers, 1975.

Mowrer, Hadley Richardson Hemingway, interview with Alice Sokoloff, 1972,
Hemingway Collection, JFK Library, Boston, Massachusetts.

——, letters to Ernest Hemingway 1920-21, Hemingway Collection, JFK Library,
Boston, Massachusetts.

"A Natalie Barney Garland" by George Wickes from *The Paris Review/letters and essays*.
Issue 61, Spring, 1975.

"The Old Man and *The Farm*: The Long, Tumultuous Saga of Ernest Hemingway's
Prized Miro Masterpiece," Hugh Eakin, *Vanity Fair*, October 2018.

Putnam, Samuel, *Paris was our Mistress*, Carbondale, Illinois, Southern Illinois University Press, 1970.

Rena Sanderson, Sandra Spanier, & Robert W. Trogdon, editors, THE LETTERS OF
Ernest Hemingway, Volumes 1, 2, & 3, New York, NY, Cambridge University
Press, 2015.

Reynolds, Michael, *The Young Hemingway*, New York, NY, W. W. Norton and Company, 1986.

——, *The Paris Years*, New York, NY, W. W. Norton and Company, 1989.

Reynolds, Michael, *The Homecoming*, New York, NY, W. W. Norton and Company,
1992.

Rideout, Walter B., *Sherwood Anderson, A Writer in America*, Madison: The University
of Wisconsin Press, 2006.

Rodriguez, Suzanne, *Wild Heart: A Life: Natalie Clifford Barney*, New York, HarperCollins Publishers, Inc., 2002.

Sarason, Bertram D., *Hemingway and The Sun Set*, Washington, DC, NCR/Microcard Editions, 1972.

Sanford, Marcelline Hemingway, *At the Hemingways*, London, Putnam, 1963.

Sokoloff, Alice Hunt, *Hadley, The First Mrs. Hemingway*, New York, NY, Dodd Mead and Company, 1973.

Sokoloff, Alice Hunt, edited tapes of conversations with Hadley Mowrer, 1972.

Spanier, Sandra, and Robert W. Trogdon, The Letters of Ernest Hemingway, Vol 1, 1907–1922, New York, Cambridge University Press, 2011.

Sanderson, Rena, Sandra Spanier, and Robert W. Trogdon, The Letters of Ernest Hemingway, Vol 3, 1926–1929, New York, Cambridge University Press, 2015.

Stein, Gertrude, *The Autobiography of Alice B. Toklas*, New York, Harcourt, 1933.

—, Three Lives, New York, The Grafton Press, 1909.

"*The Sun Also Rises*: One Debt to Imagism" by Linda W. Wagner from The Journal of Narrative Technique 2, no. 2 (May 1972), © 1972 by Eastern Michigan University Press.

Tompkins, Calvin, *Living Well is the Best Revenge*, London, Andre Deutsch, 1972.

"*Toreo*: The Moral Axis of *The Sun Also Rises*" by Allen Josephs from *The Hemingway Review* 6, no. 1 (Fall 1986), © by Ohio Northern University.

Townsend, Kim, *Sherwood Anderson*, Boston: Houghton Mifflin Company, 1987.

Tytell, John, *Ezra Pound: The Solitary Volcano*, Chicago, Ivan R. Dee, 1987.

"The Wastelanders" by Carlos Baker from Hemingway: The Writer as Artist by Carlos Baker, © 1956, 1963, 1972, 1980 by Carlos Baker. Princeton University Press.

West, James L. W. III, F. Scott Fitzgerald: A Short Biography, New York, NY, Scribner's, 2011.

"What's Funny in *The Sun Also Rises*" by James Hinkle from *The Hemingway Review* 4, no. 2 (Spring 1985), © 1985 by Ohio Northern University.

White, Ray Lewis, *Sherwood Anderson's Memoirs*, Chapel Hill: The University of North Carolina Press, 1969.

Wineapple, Brenda, *Sister Brother: Gertrude and Leo Stein*, New York, G. P. Putnam and Sons, 1996.

Wilhelm, J. J., *Ezra Pound in London and Paris: 1908–1925*, The Pennsylvania State University Press, 1990.

Williams, William Carlos, *The Autobiography of William Carlos Williams*, New York, New Directions, 1967.

Wilson, Edmund, *Letters on Literature and Politics*, New York, NY, Farrah, Straus & Young, 1977.

———, *The Shores of Light: A Literary Chronicle of the Twenties and Thirties*, New York, NY, Farrah, Straus & Young, 1952.

———, *The Twenties*, New York, NY, Farrah, Straus & Young, 1975.

INDEX

ABOUT THE AUTHOR

WYLIE MCLALLEN grew up in Memphis, Tennessee where his family has deep historical roots. At the University of Tennessee, while obtaining a degree in History and English, he studied Fiction and Composition under a distinguished man of Southern Letters, Professor Robert Drake. Dr. Drake was a close friend of author Flannery O'Conner and was able to personally introduce his students to the poet and novelist James Dickey.

Wylie worked as a programmer analyst at Malone & Hyde Inc., a wholesale grocery distributor in Memphis, and later owned a small business services center. He currently resides with his wife, Nickey Bayne, in Vancouver, British Columbia, where they have raised two grown children. He continues to write both history and fiction and is the author of *Tigers by the River*, a true story about the early years of pro football in American published by the Sunbury Press, and just released by the Sunbury Press, a two volume history of the early years of Modern Literature, *Hemingway and the Rise of Modern Literature*.